JOKERS WILD

JOKERS WILD

Legalized Gambling in the Twenty-first Century

Thomas Barker and Marjie Britz

PRAEGER

Westport, Connecticut
London

Library of Congress Cataloging-in-Publication Data

Barker, Thomas.
    Jokers wild : legalized gambling in the twenty-first century / Thomas Barker and
Marjie Britz.
        p.   cm.
    Includes bibliographical references and index.
    ISBN 0–275–96587–2 (alk. paper)
        1. Gambling—United States.   I. Britz, Marjie.   II. Title.
HV6715.B37   2000
795'.0973—dc21   99–059852

British Library Cataloguing in Publication Data is available.

Library of Congress Catalog Card Number: 99–059852
ISBN: 0–275–96587–2

First published in 2000

Praeger Publishers, 88 Post Road West, Westport, CT 06881
An imprint of Greenwood Publishing Group, Inc.
www.praeger.com

Printed in the United States of America

The paper used in this book complies with the
Permanent Paper Standard issued by the National
Information Standards Organization (Z39.48–1984).

10 9 8 7 6 5 4 3

Contents

Chapter 1

Introduction

In recent years the studies of gambling and tobacco use have become social experiments in the process of how laws are made and changed in defining deviant behavior. Deviant behavior "is behavior subject to legal procedures aimed at curtailing the behavior" (McCaghy, Capron, and Jamieson, 2000, 106). The behaviors for legal purposes can be divided into Mala in se and Mala Prohibita acts. According to *Black's Law Dictionary*, Mala in se acts are those which are wrong in themselves, inherently evil acts such as murder, stealing, rape, perjury, and robbery (*Black's*, 1991, 659). There is little, if any, debate that these behaviors should be crimes. Mala Prohibita behaviors, on the other hand, are those "Acts or omissions which are made criminal by statute but which, of themselves, are not criminal" (*Black's*, 1991, 659). Mala Prohibita crimes transgress the accepted moral code and include abortion, homosexuality, pornography, drug offenses, gambling, and tobacco use. Whether or not Mala Prohibita behaviors such as gambling and tobacco use become labeled legal or illegal behaviors depends on who wins the conflict that takes place between competing interest groups.

Mala Prohibita laws tend to become interest group specific because moral standards are not homogeneous across social classes, ethnic groups, the sexes, or generations. However, the process of legislation allows interest groups to impose their moral standards, or publicly stated moral standards, on other less powerful, less vocal, or less united groups. American society is, and always has been, characterized by conflicts of interests. This conflict between interest groups is, and always has been, at the center of the debate over gambling. The ebb and flow of legalized gambling must be viewed in the context of time, place, and changing attitudes on the part of those who attach the labels to the behavior.

We see the resolution of this conflict between gambling interest groups as a high-stakes poker game with Jokers—the extra playing card able to make the hand different from what it seems to be—as the wild cards. The stakes, real or imagined, include industry profits, jobs, economic development, community revitalization, and tax revenues on one side and crime, community disorganization, and the social effects of problem and pathological gambling (e.g., bankruptcies, family breakups, suicide, and youth gambling) on the other. The legislators who define gambling as legal or illegal respond to those who play the most Jokers in the form of campaign funds, votes, prestige, and pressure. In this high-stakes game the players do not follow the rules according to Hoyle; the outcome is determined by the power, organization, and sophistication of those playing. Deception is permissible and expected. Hyperbole often rules. The players (anti- and pro-gambling groups) are performing for the audiences (legislator or voters), not each other. As in most poker games, some players have more skill and more at stake than the other players. Nevertheless, there are winners in this contest between interest groups. Unfortunately, there are also losers.

Twenty-five years ago, legal gambling, particularly casino gambling, was a pariah Las Vegas industry considered to be dominated by organized crime. A deviant activity being conducted in Sin City and run by criminals. The tobacco industry, now a pariah industry, was considered to be a respectable form of business. Smoking and the use of tobacco products are now outlawed in public places in most states and on federal properties. On the other hand, legalized gambling is in an unprecedented growth period in the United States and worldwide (Eadington and Cornelius, 1997). Legalized gambling, like kudzu, has spread throughout the United States. As of this writing, there are only three states—Utah, Hawaii, and Tennessee—with no forms of legal gambling.

The legalization of gambling is not a new phenomenon in our nation's history. According to Rose (1986), there have been three waves of legalized gambling to sweep the nation. The first wave lasted from colonial times to the decades before the Civil War and was characterized by public and state-sponsored lotteries. The second wave began after the Civil War when many state governments turned to lotteries to relieve the financial hardships created by the war. A series of scandals, particularly the Louisiana Lottery scandal of the 1890s, brought the second wave to an inglorious halt, leading many states to incorporate gambling prohibitions in their state constitutions. Rose marks the beginning of the third wave of legalized gambling with the legalization of the New Hampshire

Lottery (sweepstakes) in 1964. The United States is currently riding the crest of this third wave.

Even though legalized gambling has spread throughout the United States, any discussion of gambling brings into play heated debate about basic values and issues. John Zipperer, writing from a Christian perspective, says that "gambling is the last agreed-upon sin for many Christians" (Zipperer, 1998, 22). He states that denominations that disagree on abortion, female pastors, and capital punishment all agree that gambling is a sin. On the other hand, the American Gaming Association (AGA)—the national lobbying association for the commercial hotel casino–entertainment industry takes the position that gambling, particularly casino "gaming," is entertainment, implying enjoyment and relaxation (American Gaming Association, 1998, 1–1). The debate involves matters of personal freedom and responsibility or protecting people from themselves. Anti- and pro-gambling forces, as we shall see, often engage in the liberal use of hyperbole and misinformation in support of their positions. Nevertheless, there is support for both the pro- and anti-gambling arguments.

An objective and unbiased examination of the legalized gambling issue and its effects on individuals, groups, and communities is needed. Guiding our examination will be the questions, Has the third wave of legalized gambling peaked? Is the gambling market saturated? Will we see a return to prohibition for some forms of gambling? This analysis is timely as we move into the twenty-first century with gambling, an anonymous cash-based industry, as the United States' fastest-growing industry.

We begin with the premise that legal gambling is, at best, problematic behavior with good and bad consequences. Therefore, we must address the following. What is the nature and extent of legalized gambling? What is the history of legalized gambling in the United States? Should some forms of gambling be prohibited and all forms regulated by some government entity (state, tribal, or federal government)? State-sponsored gambling—lotteries and Indian gambling—may be the economic salvation for revenue-starved states; however, does it call into question the proper role of the state or tribal nation in promoting a potential harm on its citizens? Is gambling in some forms entertainment (enjoyment and relaxation) for some people, possibly the majority? For others, possibly a minority, is it a social and individual problem, a disease? Does legalized gambling have differential impacts on certain special populations (youths, athletes, senior citizens, and women)? Has legalized gambling revitalized deteriorating or deteriorated communities? Would this be true for all communities? Our inquiry will begin with an examination of the nature and extent of legal gambling.

REFERENCES

American Gaming Association. (1998). *Responsible Gaming Resource Guide.* 2nd ed. Washington, D.C.: American Gaming Association.

Eadington, William R., and Judy Cornelius, eds. (1997). *Gambling: Public Policies and the Social Sciences.* Reno: Institute for the Study of Gambling and Commercial Gaming, University of Nevada, Reno.

McCaghy, Charles H., Timothy A. Capron, and J. D. Jamieson. (2000). *Deviant Behavior: Crime, Conflict, and Interest Groups.* 5th ed. Boston: Allyn and Bacon.

Rose, I. Nelson. (1986). *Gambling and the Law.* Hollywood, Calif.: Gambling Times Inc.

Zipperer, John. (1998). "Christians Agree that Gambling Is a Sin." In Rod Evans and Mark Hance, eds., *Legalized Gambling: For and Against.* Chicago: Open Court.

Chapter 2

Where Are We Now?
Gambling Today

EXTENT AND NATURE OF LEGAL GAMBLING

Monies Gambled

Our academic and work experiences, along with our previous writings and research on crime and criminal justice issues, lead us to believe that the amount of monies illegally gambled in this country is huge. The estimates for illegal sports betting alone vary from $30 to $100 billion annually. Illegal gambling may be larger in terms of people involved and money gambled if we take into account full-time bookies, numbers runners, illegal slot machines, and part-time operators who run sports, cards, poker, and crap games. Illegal gambling also takes place in sports pools, poker games, and "gray" machines (designated for amusement only but pay off) in fraternal, veterans, and social clubs. We simply don't know the extent and monies bet. No one does. Those who do venture a money figure for illegal gambling are engaging in unscientific guesstimates. Furthermore, this illegal gambling is unlicensed, unregulated, and untaxed. However, there are very accurate figures on the monies legally gambled. Several gambling industry accounting terms must be understood before one can grasp the true nature of monies spent on gambling:

Handle: The gross amount wagered on any form of gambling. *Gross wagering, betting, gross betting* or *gross amount bet, money staked, turnover,* and *lottery sales* are in various systems of accounting synonyms for *handle*. (The handle is the total amount bet, not lost.)

Drop: In casino revenue accounting, cash and cash equivalents (traveler's checks, certified checks, cashier's checks, money orders) exchanged for chips and (if played) risked against the casino; player's bankroll.

Drop and *handle* are often confused, but there is a distinction between the two. Handle is the total amount wagered, or bet: A chip may be wagered (bet) many times before the game goes to a decision and the chip is won or lost.

Casinos report *handle* for slot operations because the revenue accounting of win to handle is accurately known. The machines are set to report the coins/cash going in and the coins or payouts going out. However, the handle for table games is calculated differently. There is no accounting of how much each player bets on each turn of the cards, roll of the dice, or spin of the wheel. Therefore, the system of accounting begins with the *drop*, the amount of money used at the table to buy chips. The amount of cash and credit collected at each table is compared with the amount of chips remaining at the table when the final count is done. However, the amount a player wagers is not always equal to the amount of cash exchanged for chips, a point well understood by money launderers. A player could exchange $1,000 in cash for chips at a table, lose $100, and then cash in $900 at the cage. Nine hundred dollars would be successfully laundered. Casinos, or at least many, constantly monitor for this practice, but it does occur. Nevertheless, the *drop* and the *handle* are the starting point for the calculation of the win.

Gross Gambling Revenue: Handle less payouts or prizes or winnings returned to the players. Gross gambling revenue is the source of gambling industries' revenues and gambling tax receipts (*IGWB*, 1998, 5).

The win does not represent profit because operating costs, loan interest or amortization, depreciation, and taxes have not been taken out yet. It is similar to a nongambling business's net sales revenue.

The failure to understand these terms, or misusing these terms, can lead to serious misunderstandings. For example, suppose a slot player began with a bankroll of $100 and played a three-coin quarter machine with an average 93.27 percent payoff. He would begin with the $100 and get back $93.27 (theoretically) the first time he ran his money through the machine. If he continued to play until his $100 bankroll was gone, he would have put his money through the machine 71 times for a total of 1,967 plays on the machine. The player's total wager (handle) would be $1,475; however, the win (gambling revenue) for the casino would be $100, the player's original bankroll (Raley, 1999, 1). The *International Gaming and Wagering Business* (*IGWB*, 1998, 5) reports that a player could statistically generate a handle of $10,000 at a table game with a casino advantage of 1 percent before losing a bankroll of $100.

The 1997 handle (amount bet) for the gambling industry was $638.6 billion, an 8.7 percent increase from 1996. The gross gambling revenue (amount won) was a record $50.899 billion, a 6.2 percent increase. Nevada and New Jersey casino table games and slots accounted for the largest share of the handle: $324.5 billion. However, lotteries accounted for the largest share of the gross revenues: $15.5 billion. The gambling industry pays a substantial sum in federal, state and local taxes. The *IGWB* estimated that gambling privilege taxes for 1997 were $18.5 billion. This figure does not include normal taxes gambling businesses pay, for example, corporate income and real estate taxes (*IGWB*, 1998).

Nature of the Industry

Gambling Defined

The legal gambling industry is composed of numerous types of activities/games, taking place in varied settings run by private and public (government) entities. However, the elements of chance, consideration (something of value), and prize/reward define gambling, no matter what the setting, activity, or public/private proprietorship. Thompson (1997, 3) defines gambling as "an activity in which a person subjects something of value—usually money—to a risk involving a large amount of chance in hopes of winning something of greater value, which is usually money."

The activities, or gambling forms, vary by the element of chance present. Some forms of gambling, such as bingo, slot machines, keno, lotteries, craps, and roulette, are pure chance events with no skill that can affect the outcome. The player, no matter what he or she thinks, cannot affect the outcome of independent, random events. Begging or cajoling the dice will not influence the results. Slot machines, where outcomes are determined by random-number generators, are not influenced by the superstitions or antics of the player. Anyone visiting a casino and watching crap shooters or slot players will see this fact is either unknown or ignored by the players. Skill can reduce, but never eliminate, the odds against the player in some games, such as blackjack, poker, and sporting and racing events. One could argue, and some do, that the stock market and other financial markets are gambling with a large amount of skill involved. The National Council on Problem Gambling includes the stock market in their list of forms of gambling. In fact, commodities trading is an example of gambling by any definition.

Arthur Reber (1996) divides gambling into two types of games—Type L (lose) and Type W (win) games. Type L games, such as casino table games of roulette, baccarat, craps, keno, slot machines, and lotteries, are "games in which the house [or the state in lotteries] has the advantage,

Table 2.1
House Win per $100 in Nevada, July 1, 1996–June 30, 1997

Game	House Win
Wheel of Fortune	$45.00
Red Dog	32.00
Keno	26.93
Let It Ride	23.98
Caribbean Stud Poker	23.90
Roulette	23.17
Pai Gow Poker	21.24
Bacarrat	15.45
Twenty-One (Blackjack)	14.10
Craps	14.06

Source: Adapted from *American Casino Guide*, 1998, 11.

where the expected value of your wages is some number below zero, and if you play long enough, you will eventually go broke" (43). Type W games, such as blackjack, poker, video poker, thoroughbred racing, dog racing, and sports betting, are games in which "winners and losers sort themselves out on the basis of each game and how to play it" (120).

The authors do not imply that all who play Type L games will lose every time or that those who play Type W games will win every time they play. Even Type W games are a mixture of chance and skill. Skill is never enough to totally eliminate the house's edge. The house edge is the casino's inherent mathematical advantage, based on the laws of probability, over the player. Depending on the game and the bet, the advantage can vary from a low of 1.06 percent betting with the house in bacarrat to a high of 30 percent in keno. The house edge for slot machines is often as high as 20 percent. The state edge for lotteries is 45 to 50 percent; for every $1 bet, the state keeps $0.45 to $0.50. The theoretical house advantage is not as important to the player as understanding the practical matter of how much the house receives from the money the player bets. For example, for every $100 bet in a Nevada casino, the house wins $45 in the Wheel of Fortune game and $14.06 in craps (*American Casino Guide*, 1998). The house win for other Nevada games is shown in Table 2.1.

For some casino games (video poker and blackjack), it is possible to reduce and even gain an advantage over the casino through skillful play. Skillful blackjack players, using what is known as "The Basic Strategy" and employing card-counting strategies, can, "if they play their cards right and have a bankroll large enough to absorb a string of sizable losses . . . take a casino for hundreds of thousands of dollars in a single sitting" (O'Brien, 1998, 63). The casinos moved from one- and two-deck games to six to eight decks dealt from a shoe (receptacle for holding cards) to defeat card counters. In addition, suspected card counters are ejected from Nevada casinos. Atlantic City casinos shuffle the decks frequently when card counters are at the table. Certain variations of video poker games pay off better than others, and it is possible to skillfully play them for a return rate of over 100 percent; in effect, the machine will pay back more than the player puts in (Scott, 1998). The casinos know this and are constantly changing the games and payback schedules to frustrate the "professional" video poker players. A large industry of "how-to" books, journals, computer software, and newsletters has grown up to tell players how to beat the casino games. The how-to books and tapes offer contradictory advice, but they sell. A recent search of Amazon.com revealed that 172 how-to books had been printed since 1990. The magazine *Strictly Slots: The Magazine for Slot & Video Poker Players* has recently (December 1998) begun publication. According to the editor, the new magazines is

[a] magazine you [slot players] could trust and rely upon to help you make smarter gambling choices. But most of all, we wanted it to be a magazine that was fun—written by people who know that the slots aren't there just to take your money, or to entice you with big jackpots, but to offer a unique form of entertainment unlike any other. In short, a magazine that celebrates the slot experience. (Fine, 1998, 6)

Unfortunately, beating the casino is not as easy as the how-to industry would have the reader believe. Perceived skill and the possession of a "winning strategy" to beat the house or the bangtails (horses) have carried many players down the road to ruin and despair. Chance and luck— good or bad—can never be eliminated from gambling. Knowledgeable gamblers know that Lady Luck is a fickle mistress. Gambling in any form, even if you own the casino or invest in the gambling industry, is still a gamble. Several casinos and casino operators, including Donald Trump, have gone bankrupt. The Sands Casino in Atlantic City is currently going through bankruptcy. The Harrah's Jazz in New Orleans and the Treasure Bay in Biloxi, Mississippi, have just come out of bankruptcy. Three Reno, Nevada, closed in 1997. Bob Stupak's misadventure with Las Vegas's Stratosphere Tower is a classic story in casino bankruptcies and proof of the real estate maxim: There are only three things important in real estate—location, location, location (Smith, 1997). Investors, socially sanctioned gamblers, in gambling stocks can attest to the volatility of the market.

Casino Gaming and Gambling Machines

Dropping the *bl* from *gambling* leaves *gaming*, the term preferred by the casino industry. *Gaming* sounds more official, professional, and clinical than *gambling*. Faragher (1995) says that "gaming" is the more polite term. However, a rose is a rose is a rose, and no matter what it's called, gambling is gambling is gambling. Casino industry spokesmen argue that they are in the entertainment business, not the gambling business. The only time the term *gambling* is used is when they are addressing the problems (e.g., underage and problem gambling) associated with the industry. The recurrent theme in the gaming literature is that a visit to the casino is an entire entertainment experience, involving staying in a class hotel, seeing shows, eating at fine restaurants, and visiting shops. However, all U.S. casinos do not resemble the glitzy "entertainment centers" of Las Vegas. Many casinos are little more than gambling dens—grind joints—providing no amenities or entertainment other than gambling. Dan Bosey, the Massachusetts House Chair of the Joint Committee of Government Regulations, which oversees gambling, in testimony before the National Gambling Impact Study Commission referred to the lottery as gaming "which is much less harmful sounding than gambling."

I. Nelson Rose, a noted gambling expert, writes that *gaming* "is more properly limited to actual games requiring the player to put up some stake and to participate in the play of a game against other players or the house" (Rose, 1986, 76). This would apply to casino table games but not slot machines—the producers of 65 percent of the casino industry's revenue. Although table games (roulette, craps, blackjack, Let It Ride, Caribbean stud, Pai Gow poker, Red Dog, Sic Bo) fit Rose's definition, these games are played by a minority of casino visitors. As stated, these games require knowledge of the game and betting strategy. For example, craps—one of the most exciting casino games—has 24 different possible bets (for or against the shooter) on every roll of the dice. The average craps shooter usually has from 5 to 15 bets riding on every roll of the dice. Craps is no game for the neophyte or the faint of heart; learning the game in a casino setting can be costly and embarrassing. The game requires four dealers and a boxman to keep up with the bets and payoffs. The intricacy of most table games makes gambling machines popular to the majority of casino visitors.

Gambling machines include slot machines, video gambling machines, and video lottery terminals (VLTs). The video machines—a product of the computer age—are run by computer logic boards. Slot machines have independent spinning reels that run electronically by inner circuits and transistors. Payoffs for slot machines are determined by random-number generators. Numbers are assigned to the symbols and the blanks on each reel. Manufacturers determine the payoff percentages of slot machines by assigning more numbers to the blanks than the jackpot symbols; however, the numbers are still picked randomly. The manufacturers make machines available to the casinos with several different payoff percentages. The casinos, in effect, order the various machines with the payoff configurations they desire.

It may sound like the manufacturer, and even the casino, could "cheat" the slot player by setting the win percentages really low. Nothing could be further from the truth. No manufacturer or casino would risk their license to "gaff" a machine, especially when there is no need to: They have the edge. Furthermore, every state, except South Carolina, that allows gambling machines sets a minimum-win percentage rate; for example, in Mississippi, no machine can be set for less than an 80 percent payout. In New Jersey, the minimum payout requirement per machine is 83 percent. Nevada's minimum-win percentage per machine is 75 percent. At this time, South Carolina does not set a minimum payout requirement on poker machines. The August 1998 win percentage for quarter machines in Atlantic City ranged from a low of 89.2 percent at the Resorts to a high of 91.5 percent at Harrah's and the Tropicana (Fine, 1998, 82). The September 1999 win percentage for quarter slot machines in Atlantic City ranged from a low of 89.6 percent at the Resorts to a high of 91.6 at Harrah's ("Slot Report Percentages," 1999, 78). Some players won big, others lost big, and some broke even. Nevertheless, slot machines can be beaten. The slot editor for *Casino Player* states:

Can Slot Machines Be Beaten?

Of course! If you buy the right hammer and plant one or two whacks firmly on the belly glass, you should be able to get right to the money. A good drill would help as well. This is a great strategy for people who can't wait to go to jail. (Scoblete, 1998, 52)

The modern gambling machines are sophisticated technological innovations (mechanical "one-armed bandits" have not been manufactured since 1979). They have touchtone screens or panel command buttons, 3-D graphics, bill validators, player-selectable games, multiline pays and bonus screens, multicolored displays, adjustable pay tables, digital sound effects, live-action video, and magnetic card readers for slot club members. New games carry names like Piggy Bankin', Reel 'em In, Sphinx, Volcano Island, Wheel of Fortune, Treasure Wheel, Odyssey, Empire, Jeopardy, Roaring 20s, and Filthy Rich. The new Elvis slot machine (International Game Technology) comes complete with 14 Elvis hits and live video footage. The Elvis machine is also an example of the "Megajackpot" wide-area progressive machine linked to similar machines in a number of casinos. The progressive jackpots begin at $100,000. International Game Technology, one of the largest manufacturers of gambling machines in the world, sold 77,000 machines in 1998 ("Report to Stockholders," 1998).

Gambling machines known as VLTs are gambling machines operated and regulated by a state's lottery commission. In spite of what the states that allow them say, legal definition, regulation by the state's lottery commission, and central linkage to the lottery network are the only factors that make these gambling machines different from those found in privately owned casinos. VLTs are computer processors executing state-approved games such as blackjack, keno, several versions of poker, and spinning reel slot machines. The prize money is often awarded with tickets rather than an actual coin drop (Thompson, 1997, 164).

Gambling machines appear to be especially appealing to those unfamiliar and/or threatened by table games and those who have grown up in the computer game age (Aronovitz, 1997). Video gambling machines, which make use of games such as poker, blackjack, craps, hi-lo, and roulette, require some minimum knowledge. Slot machines, on the other hand, only require money and the ability to press the button or pull the lever. Gambling machines of all types can be played with a significantly lower bankroll. Slots allow the player to play at any level he or she wishes, from pennies to hundred-dollar tokens. A slot player can play a nickel, dime, or quarter machine for some time with a $100 bankroll; that would be impossible at a $5 minimum craps, blackjack, or roulette table.

Casinos, Gambling Machines, and Cruises to Nowhere

Our literature review revealed that as of December 1998, 34 states had casino gambling (land-based, riverboat/dockside, Indian, and offshore cruises commonly known as cruises to nowhere) or gambling machines (see Appendix A). Casinos accounted for 51.6 cents of every U.S. dollar gambled in 1997 (IGWB, 1988, 9).

Gambling-Lotteries

Thirty-eight states, including the nation's capital, have gambling-lotteries. Their sales gross revenue—less prizes, operating expenses, and government revenue (GT-Revenue) for 1997 are shown in Table 2.2. Although we will discuss lotteries more fully later, we should point out that lotteries are the only forms of gambling that are state monopolies. They also offer the worst odds, rank first in gross revenues, have the highest profit rating of any form of gambling, and are the largest source of government gambling revenues.

Table 2.2
Lottery Revenues

State	Sales	Gross Revenue	Expenses	GT-Revenue
Arizona	$244,803,109	$119,663,947	$40,005,498	$84,517,508
California	2,063,134,691	1,032,599,209	320,697,872	727,626,107
Colorado	360,887,813	145,776,084	53,045,017	94,590,410
Connecticut	769,789,676	319,111,507	66,534,437	253,511,489
Delaware	103,263,422	49,511,139	15,360,223	34,477,667
D.C.	202,889,000	101,250,000	34,540,000	69,327,000
Florida	2,070,058,000	1,042,551,000	240,188,000	817,537,000
Georgia	1,720,241,000	793,687,000	235,158,000	568,223,000
Idaho	86,983,000	33,661,177	15,914,000	18,408,443
Illinois	1,569,442,000	742,029,385	170,850,059	587,169,055
Indiana	587,931,009	256,052,024	84,075,562	176,319,107
Iowa	173,655,030	76,757,910	34,236,575	43,437,676
Kansas	185,356,681	87,042,076	31,113,101	56,843,270
Kentucky	569,055,000	339,868,000	229,187,000	153,729,000
Louisiana	280,653,849	140,880,580	42,465,984	101,640,742
Maine	146,255,002	64,092,781	24,055,161	41,786,124
Maryland	1,043,583,184	491,876,318	99,609,411	392,266,907
Massachusetts	3,189,013,000	952,173,000	256,170,000	721,246,000
Michigan	1,599,322,000	732,864,000	169,482,000	595,108,000
Minnesota	368,516,685	144,068,756	59,929,615	81,447,949
Missouri	439,592,300	197,728,976	66,402,577	132,663,927
Montana	28,197,360	13,864,781	7,563,015	6,603,260
Nebraska	76,619,725	36,224,658	16,750,546	20,591,499
New Hampshire	176,655,620	76,505,913	25,248,830	54,206,785
New Jersey	1,556,078,320	743,352,016	130,985,029	647,576,604
New Mexico	82,084,000	40,713,000	20,233,000	20,273,000
New York	3,992,314,000	2,026,162,000	435,558,000	1,542,757,000
Ohio	2,299,998,441	1,312,220,322	987,778,119	751,985,240
Oregon	333,070,313	125,453,541	52,655,562	76,730,028
Pennsylvania	1,710,013,923	852,813,307	161,806,033	700,244,666
Rhode Island	142,607,334	63,311,741	21,089,000	45,056,532
South Dakota	28,033,945	12,584,607	6,687,084	6,370,162
Texas	3,745,469,123	1,593,732,120	432,649,897	1,179,798,481
Vermont	77,323,313	31,729,419	8,145,521	23,706,054
Virginia	920,830,808	445,455,024	114,364,718	324,470,069
Washington	408,201,390	149,906,355	55,676,812	94,573,878
West Virginia	162,782,552	69,958,980	26,054,350	45,347,966
Wisconsin	431,091,169	187,070,916	54,474,787	137,721,084
Total	$33,941,808,612	$15,149,197,727	$3,944,294,926	$11,447,888,689

Source: McQueen, 1988a, 43.

Parimutuel Wagering

Parimutuel wagering—a system where winnings are based on a common pool made up of the players' bets—on horses, dogs, and jai alai is present in 45 states (see Table 2.3). The bettors, in effect, wager among themselves with the track operating, for a fee, as the middle, facilitating the wagering.

In 1997, the total gross wagering (handle) for parimutuel betting was $17.9 billion. This is a 23 percent increase since 1982 and a 1.6 percent increase from 1996 to 1997 (*IGWB*, 1998). The on-track handles for horses, greyhounds, and jai alai have dropped dramatically during these same periods (1982–1997: horses, 65.28 percent; greyhounds, 40.78 percent; jai alai, 64.7 percent). The dramatic increases for horse and greyhound ITW (inter-track wagering) and OTB (offtrack betting) have been responsible for the handle increases. However, as stated above, many racetracks have installed VLTs and video poker machines to draw in players and increase revenues. Some racetracks faced with a dwindling handle are adding card rooms. In fact, the Alabama legislature is now considering legalizing video poker machines at the state's greyhound dog tracks. The first effort, requiring only legislative approval, failed. The new attempt, if approved, would require a referendum in the counties of three of the tracks and the city (Birmingham) in one of the dog tracks.

Gambling machines at racetracks are very profitable. "So video card games are not a license to print money, but in some cases, slot machines come close, as demonstrated in Rhode Island and West Virginia" (McQueen, 1998b, 60). In 1997, the slot machines at Rhode Island's Lincoln Park racetrack generated $96.9 million in gross revenue from 1,202 machines. The track's gross revenue for parimutuel betting was $13.1 million. West Virginia's Mountaineer Park has 1,000 VLTs (McQueen, 1998b). The addition of card rooms, VLTs, and slot machines causes many racetracks to resemble casinos without table games.

Eight states—Connecticut, Kentucky, Maryland, Nevada, New York, Pennsylvania, Oregon, and Nebraska—allow telephone wagering on horse races. This "in home" betting has implications for Internet gambling.

Sports Betting

Sports betting, probably the most prevalent (friends, office pools, bookies) form of gambling and reportedly the largest source of revenue for organized crime, is only legal in Nevada and Oregon (state lottery based on National Football League games). However, the points spread on major sports events is carried in newspapers, radio, television, and numbers online services. Nevada sports books are forbidden by law from accepting bets on Nevada teams. Technically, sports betting is legal in

Table 2.3
Parimutuel Wagering

State	Horses	Dogs	Jai Alai
Alabama	Yes	Yes	
Arizona	Yes	Yes	
Arkansas	Yes	Yes	
California	Yes		
Colorado	Yes	Yes	
Connecticut		Yes	Yes
Delaware	Yes		
Florida	Yes	Yes	Yes
Idaho	Yes	Yes	
Illinois	Yes		
Indiana	Yes		
Iowa	Yes	Yes	
Kansas	Yes	Yes	
Kentucky	Yes		
Louisiana	Yes		
Maine	Yes		
Maryland	Yes		
Massachusetts	Yes	Yes	
Michigan	Yes		
Minnesota	Yes		
Missouri	Yes		
Montana	Yes		
Nebraska	Yes		
Nevada	Yes	Yes	Yes
New Hampshire	Yes	Yes	
New Jersey	Yes		
New Mexico	Yes		
New York	Yes		
North Dakota	Yes		
Ohio	Yes		
Oklahoma	Yes		
Oregon	Yes	Yes	
Pennsylvania	Yes		
Rhode Island		Yes	Yes
South Dakota	Yes	Yes	
Vermont	Yes	Yes	
Virginia	Yes		
Washington	Yes		
West Virginia	Yes	Yes	
Wisconsin	Yes		
Wyoming	Yes		

Source: Thompson, 1997, 166.

Delaware and Montana, but they are not operating. Nevada's 137 sports books handled $2.6 billion in 1997 (*IGWB*, 1998). College and professional football account for the largest share of sports betting, followed by basketball.

Other Forms of Gambling

Seven states (California, Florida, Maryland, Montana, North Dakota, Oregon, and Washington) allow limited-stakes card rooms. The handle for these five states was $10.4 billion (*IGWB*, 1998). California, with the largest number of card rooms, had a handle of $9.5 billion. The California poker parlors are established by local option and regulated by the state.

Bingo, the most common form of legalized gambling, has always been perceived as recreation rather than gambling. It is a way to spend time, not win money. High-stakes Indian bingo parlors may change this perception. Bingo traditionally has had a higher public approval than any other form of gambling. The typical bingo operation is for charitable purposes; sometimes the games are operated by private firms. Excluding Indian facilities, there are 37,000 charitable bingo halls in 46 states (*IGWB*, 1998). The 1997 handle for these bingo halls was $3.9 billion. In addition, other charitable games (pull-tabs, punchboards, raffles, "Las Vegas" nights) allowed in 41 states had a 1997 handle of $6 billion.

Cockfighting, a centuries-old form of "entertainment" and gambling, is legal in Louisiana, Oklahoma, and New Mexico (*National Gaming Summary*, 1998b). Jacksonville State University (Jacksonville, Alabama) is nicknamed the Gamecocks, and cockfighting, although illegal, takes place regularly in the rural areas around the university. The raising of fighting gamecocks is also a major industry in the area. Dogfighting, also illegal, takes place in many rural areas of Alabama. Barker is aware of one veterinarian who bred and raised dogs for fighting. The same veterinarian cared for the injured dogs. All forms of animal fighting were banned in November 1998 in Missouri.

Indian Gambling

Indian gambling is 10 years old. The *IGWB* in its "The United States Gross Annual Wager Report—1997" (1998) states that 148 tribes in 24 states had a handle of $80.1 billion. Even though the Mashantucket Pequot Foxwood's Casino in Connecticut is the largest and most profitable casino in the world, most of the 276 Indian gambling facilities are small.

CONCLUSION

We began our inquiry into legalized gambling in the United States with the question, Where are we now? The answer is that legal gambling is the norm in the United States. Sixteen North American surveys conducted from 1989 to 1997 reveal that 80 to 92 percent of the respondents say they have gambled in their lifetime (Minnesota State Lottery, 1998). The gambling industry is big business and growing. The U.S. casino industry alone employed an estimated 337,000 people in 1995 (Bybee and Mayer, 1998, 15). The international investment bank Bear Stearns & Co. has a banking and research division serving the gambling industry and includes "gaming" as a leisure industry along with lodging, cruise lines, skiing, golf, fitness, timeshares, bowling, ice skating, theme parks, film exhibitions, live entertainment, and themed restaurants. Anyone who desires to play the lottery or a gambling machine (slot, video, or VLT), visit a casino, or engage in some other form of gambling can easily do so and legally. Before 1988, the visit to Atlantic City or Las Vegas required a plane trip and time, not to mention money. Now, a visit to a casino—land-based, riverboat, Indian, or day cruise—is within driving distance for most Americans. The lotteries in the 37 states and the District of Columbia are aggressively advertising and introducing new games. Multimillion-dollar lottery jackpots are hot topics on national and local news, stimulating feverish buying among in-state and out-of-state buyers. We will now examine how we arrived at the present nature of gambling in the United States: Legalized gambling is the norm in the United States.

REFERENCES

American Casino Guide. (1998). Dania, Fla.: Casino Vacations.
Aronovitz, Cory. (1997). "To Start, Press the Flashing Button: The Legalization of Video Gambling Devices." In William R. Eadington and Judy Cornelius, eds., *Gambling: Public Policies and the Social Sciences.* Reno: Institute for the Study of Gambling and Commercial Gaming, University of Nevada, Reno.
Bybee, Shannon, and Karl Mayer. (1998). "Gaming and the Economy." *IGWB* 19(12): 15, 24–27.
Eadington, William R., and Judy Cornelius, eds. (1997). *Gambling: Public Policies and the Social Sciences.* Reno: Institute for the Study of Gambling and Commercial Gaming, University of Nevada, Reno.
Faragher, Scott. (1995). *The Complete Guide to Riverboat Gambling.* New York: Citadel Press.
Fine, Adam. (1998). "Welcome Aboard!" *Strictly Slots: The Magazine for Slot and Video Poker Players* (December): 6.
"Gambling in Maryland a Private Matter between Player and Charity." (1994). *The Grand Rapids Press,* December 24.
International Gaming & Wagering Business (IGWB). (1998). "The United States Gross Annual Wager—1997" (August). Special supplement.
McQueen, Patricia A. (1998a). "The Quest for Efficiency." *IGWB* 19(4): 43–48.
McQueen, Patricia A. (1998b). "Reeling Them In." *IGWB* 19(5): 56–70.
Minnesota State Lottery. (1998). *Gambling in Minnesota: Gambling Participation Rates of Minnesota Adults.* Report 1997-1.

National Gaming Summary. (1998a). July 26.

National Gaming Summary. (1998b). November 9.

O'Brien, Timothy L. (1998). *Bad Bet: The Inside Story of the Glamour, Glitz, and Danger of America's Gambling Industry.* New York: Random House.

Plume, Janet. (1999). "Bayou State Bonfire." *Casino Journal* (January): 70–74.

Raley, Tom. (1999). "Slot Play." *Play the Odds* (January): 1.

Reber, Arthur S. (1996). *The New Gambler's Bible.* New York: Crown Trade Paperbacks.

"Report to Stockholders." (1998). International Game Technology.

Rose, I. Nelson. (1986). *Gambling and the Law.* Hollywood, Calif.: Gambling Times Inc.

Scoblete, Frank. (1998). "Gaming's 50 Most Frequently Asked Questions." *Casino Player* (December): 50–60.

Scott, Jean. (1998). *The Frugal Gambler.* Las Vegas: Huntington Press.

"Slot Report Percentages." (1999). *Strictly Slots* (December): 78–84.

Smith, John L. (1997). *No Limit: The Rise and Fall of Bob Stupak and Las Vegas' Stratosphere Tower.* Las Vegas: Huntington Press.

Thompson, William N. (1997). *Legalized Gambling: A Reference Handbook.* 2nd ed. Santa Barbara, Calif.: ABC-CLIO.

Chapter 3

New Wine in Old Bottles

America's current fascination with gambling is not a new phenomenon; it is New Wine in Old Bottles. When Columbus and his crew introduced playing cards into the New World, they found the natives gambling on games, tests of skill, and footraces. The Native Americans often lost all of their possessions. On occasion they lost their freedom, gambling themselves into periods of slavery (Chafetz, 1960). Two thousand-year-old archeological discoveries in Clark County, Nevada (home of Las Vegas), reveals that gambling contests were a part of Native American rituals (Martin, 1996). Psychiatrist Edmund Burke (1958, 10) argued that gambling is part of our culture: "Every person in our culture is a potential gambler, either of the harmless or dangerous variety." Whether or not one agrees with Burke, gambling as a social issue and social problem is a part of American history. The United States had a love-hate relationship with gambling—intermittently prohibiting, then regulating gambling.

THE COLONISTS

Not all of the early American settlers were Puritans seeking religious freedoms. Some had been gamblers in England—where cards, dice, betting on horse races, cockfights, and lotteries flourished. They came to the New World to redeem themselves after gambling away their fortunes and lands through gambling. The 1710 Statute of Anne—"An Act for the better preventing of excessive and deceitful Gaming"—was eventually passed to protect the landed aristocracy and restrict the collection of gambling debts. The Statute of Anne was incorporated into the laws of

South Carolina, Tennessee, Georgia, and Virginia. (Note: The Statute of
Anne incorporation will again come under legal scrutiny in South Carolina where several class action lawsuits have been filed to recoup gambling losses.)

The Massachusetts Bay Colony quickly outlawed the possession of
dice, cards, and gambling tables. Gambling, although considered by the
Puritans to be evil, was not prohibited because it was against the teach-
ings of God. Gambling, along with dancing and singing, was prohibited
because it promoted idleness (Blakey, 1976). Gambling was a challenge
to the Puritan work ethic. The harsh nature of the Puritans' existence—
threats of starvation, disease, and Indian attack—did not allow for idleness. Professional gambling, or gambling as a way of life, was dangerous
for the burgeoning community's survival.

Other colonists not imbued with the Puritan ethic saw gambling in
moderation as recreation. Whatever view prevailed, it wasn't long before
the colonists, without an organized taxing system and no revenues,
turned to the English tradition of using lotteries as revenue-raising devices to finance public works. Discussions of sin gave way to visions of
economic salvation for the colonists.

Lotteries

The early Americans were familiar with the frequent English lotteries.
The first recorded state-sponsored English lottery was conducted in 1569
to repair and maintain the country's harbors (Blakey, 1976). Lotteries
were often used to finance public projects. In fact, the Virginia Company
of London financed the 1612–1615 Jamestown settlement through English
lotteries (Rosecrance, 1988). In spite of arguments that lotteries unfairly
impacted the poor, all 13 colonies raised funds through lotteries for
roads, bridges, jails, churches, libraries, hospitals, and colleges. Commercial banking systems, taxation, or other financing systems had not
been developed at this time. Prior to 1790, there were only three incorporated banks in America. The colonies were forced to use lotteries to
finance public works (Brenner and Brenner, 1990). The colonists, as well
as present-day Americans, resisted increased taxes. Lotteries supported
the construction of Yale, William and Mary, Union, Columbia, Dart-
mouth, University of North Carolina, Harvard, Brown, Princeton, and
Pennsylvania (Chafetz, 1960; Rosecrance, 1988).

The Continental Congress, without the power to tax, instituted a national lottery to raise $10 million to fight England. The lottery was a
failure and disbanded before the war ended. Nevertheless, by 1750 most
of the original states had begun to authorize and regulate existing lotteries. By 1795, about 2,000 authorized lotteries operated (Rosecrance,
1988). The lotteries' and the winners' names appeared in New York

newspapers. (The *Columbian Centinel* of June 5, 1790, reported, "Two apprentices belonging to Mr. Bemis, Paper-Maker, in Watertown drew the 1000 dollar prize in the Williamstown Lottery" (Chafetz, 1960, 40).

Card Playing

Card playing existed in public and private settings and among the elites and the working classes. Local inns, roadhouses, and taverns were the sites of card and dice games and pitching the large copper pennies. Card playing was so prevalent among the Revolutionary troops that George Washington, a gambler himself, had to forbid the "playing at cards, or other games of chance" (Chafetz, 1960). Thomas Jefferson kept a journal of his wins/losses at backgammon, cross, pyle (card game), and lotto during the three-week period he drafted the Declaration of Independence. According to his journal, Mrs. Jefferson lost at cards during this period. Benjamin Franklin, an avid gambler, manufactured playing cards and sold them at his post office.

Horse Racing

The first known written report on horse racing in England is dated 1174 (McDonald, 1967). And it wasn't long before racing horses appeared in the colonies. The first shipment of racehorses arrived in Jamestown in 1610. Racing began in earnest in 1620 (Rosecrance, 1988, 15). The early colonists established a uniquely American style of racing—quarter horse racing. Quarter-of-a-mile long, all-out sprint races took place on straight roads or on level land cleared of trees.

The first American racetrack was built in Salisbury Plains (now Garden City, Long Island, New York) in 1666 (Chafetz, 1960). The track was the scene of horse races conducted by and for New York's aristocratic upper class. The lower classes were excluded from attending or betting on horse races. In 1767, a York County, Virginia, judge imposed a fine on a tailor stating, "it being contrary to Law for a Labourer to make a race, being only a sport for Gentlemen" (Chafetz, 1960, 16). These early horse races involved wagers among the participants and spectators. The first professional bookmakers and a parimutuel system of betting did not appear at tracks until the end of the nineteenth century.

NINETEENTH-CENTURY GAMBLING

Gambling in all its forms continued in America following the Revolutionary War and the growth of the new nation. In the early nineteenth century new gambling forms appeared among the wealthy and merchant classes—stockjobbers (stockbrokers) and land speculators. The poor continued to play the lotto and cards, pitch pennies, and fight cocks. Horse racing spread throughout the young nation.

Gambling became further divided along class lines. Stock and land speculation along with horse racing, taking place at tracks constructed for that purpose, and private card playing in clubs and residences were prevalent among the wealthy and social elite. Public gambling in inns and taverns, racing and cockfighting in hastily constructed/cleared settings, and the lottery prevailed among the lower classes. There was anti-gambling sentiment during this period of our nation's history. However, the gambling laws passed were directed at public gambling or lotteries—the gambling of the lower classes—and gambling as an occupation or primary source of livelihood.

The working classes often resented the paternalistic protection of self-righteous reformers who would save them from the evils of the lottery and its disparate impact on them. The lottery represented a cheap ticket for a dream life not available through hard work and thrift. Chafetz (1960) reports that some Southern slaves bought their freedom with lottery winnings. Denmark Vesley became the most famous lottery winner of the period, when the slave used his $1,500 winnings to buy his freedom (Fenich, 1996). The publication of the names of lottery winners in the existing print media often stimulated feverish lottery sales, somewhat analogous to today's Powerball Mania.

A series of lottery frauds, scandals, and evangelical Christian opposition, fueled by the moral reform of Jacksonian Democracy, led to prohibition of state and private lotteries by 1840. Many states passed constitutional provisions prohibiting state-sponsored lotteries, requiring constitutional amendments in the 1980s when these states enacted lotteries as revenue-generating sources.

Gambling as a Way of Life

In the early 1800s, professional gamblers began to appear in the inns, taverns along the Mississippi River, and the rivers of the expanding frontier. The flatboat traffic at the time brought gamblers, merchants, settlers, and other travelers down a river. The cardsharps, making use of marked decks and sleight of hand, plied their nefarious trade in the gambling dens that opened along the Mississippi River. The river traffic stopped at the gambling capital of the United States—New Orleans. Hell holes like "Pinch Gut" in Memphis, the "Landing" in Vicksburg, the "Swamp" in New Orleans, and Natchez-under-the-Hill became infamous (Chafetz, 1960).

Gambling was becoming a commercialized business. Banked games, where the players bet against the house and not each other, became the rule in these river gambling dens. Through the use of free whisky, willing women, rigged games, and robbing (often murdering) the unlucky winners, these gambling dens took advantage of cash-laden travelers and merchants.

The emerging middle class in the river towns began to believe that wide-open gambling was damaging their city's reputations and commercial growth. In 1835, enraged citizens' actions, including wholesale whippings and lynchings starting with the "Landing" in Vicksburg, brought the river gambling dens to a violent close. Notices from vigilante groups were posted all along the river, warning gamblers to leave town. This was the first, but not the last, vigilante action against professional gamblers in our nation's history.

The outcast inhabitants of the river gambling dens moved onto the riverboats. The steamships traveling the Mississippi and Ohio Rivers expanded gambling throughout the South and into the Midwest. Cincinnati became well known as a wide-open gambling town. At one time, vigilante action was threatened against the Cincinnati gamblers. The mayor's intervention stopped the potential violence.

The splendor and romantic image of the shallow-bottomed paddle wheelers, spewing smoke from the stacks as they gracefully traveled the Mississippi, was not always accurate. The riverboats, not only the scene of gambling, became the instruments of gambling. Huge sums of money were won and lost on riverboat races. The most famous riverboat race took place in 1870 between the steamships the *Natchez* and the *Robert E. Lee* (Chafetz, 1960). The race stimulated large-scale betting throughout the United States and Europe. Unfortunately, many riverboats exploded from overheated boilers during the races, often with large losses of life (Chafetz, 1960).

The period from 1840 to 1860 is considered the glory days of the flamboyant riverboat gambler. The swaggering professional gamblers, decked out in their undertaker black or gray coats, white ruffled shirts, diamond or pearl stickpins, and gold chains, holding immense pocket watches, were Kings of the River.

The professional gamblers plied their trade at poker and three-card monte on the riverboats, victimizing the unsuspecting travelers, until the arrival of the trains and the expansion of the West. The cardsharps moved bag and baggage, marked cards included, onto the trains. Some moved into the cites growing up in the Midwest—Chicago, Cleveland, St. Louis, and Cincinnati. Others flocked to the gold and silver mining towns of the West where liquor, gambling, and willing women were all found under the same roof. The professional gamblers went, as they always have and always will, wherever the money and the suckers came together. However, the gambler's life was not as romantic as movie and TV portrayals of the Maverick brothers. Their motto appeared to be, Live fast, die broke. Most did, often violently. Few died of old age attended to by their children and grandchildren.

Gambling in California

Following the gold rush, San Francisco replaced New Orleans as the nation's gambling capital. Throughout California, gambling became a major source of entertainment for the miners and prospectors. By 1850, the State of California and many of its cities granted licenses to gambling dens to raise revenues (Dunstan, 1997). However, municipal corruption and a depression blamed on gamblers led to lynchings of professional gamblers in San Francisco in 1856. In a reaction against commercial gambling, all banked games were declared illegal in 1860 (Dunstan, 1997, II-6). Prohibition did not stop gambling in California. Public gambling and banked games became illegal but tolerated. San Francisco's Barbary Coast was packed with gambling halls into the 1870s (Chafetz, 1960). The slot machine was also invented and first used in San Francisco in 1895. However, by this time most of the professional gamblers had moved to Nevada's silver mining towns and the western cow towns.

Gambling Western Style

From the time of the early trappers and mountain men, gambling was often the only entertainment in the open spaces of the West (Chafetz, 1960). The stories of their riotous "rendevous" are legendary. However, western gambling reached its zenith with the cowboys and gunmen-gamblers like Luke Short, Wild Bill Hickock, Doc Holliday, Bat Masterson, and the Earps. Hickock dealt poker at several saloons—one too many as it turned out. Doc Holliday and Wyatt Earp ran a card club in Tombstone. The gunmen gamblers were skilled masters at five-card draw poker. Card playing, particularly draw poker, was the primary game in the western casinos and saloons. Stud, roulette, dice, and faro were also played. However, lotteries were never very popular in the wide-open spaces of the Western Territories and their sparsely populated cities. In addition, these areas were largely settled after the anti-lottery sentiment of the 1840s.

In the late nineteenth century (1865 to mid-1880s), the cowboys from Arizona, Colorado, the Dakotas, Kansas, Nebraska, New Mexico, Montana, Texas, and Wyoming, after long and lonely drives on the cattle trails to the railheads of Abilene, Dodge City, Ellsworth, Hays, and Wichita, were only interested in three things: whoring, drinking, and gambling. They were joined in these wide-open cities by buffalo hunters, railroad workers, and soldiers. The gamblers, women, and saloon owners eagerly waited in the CBSs—combined casinos, bordellos, and saloons.

When the cattle drives began fading, gold was discovered in the Black Hills of Dakota Territory. The gamblers, women, and saloons moved to towns like Deadwood Gulch. On August 2, 1876, Wild Bill Hickock was shot in the back of the head in Deadwood while playing poker. The hand he was holding at the time of his death—two pairs, aces and eights— has been known since as "the dead man's hand." Reform movements led by farmers with families interested in statehood combined with changing times soon spread to Deadwood, the West's last wide-open town. Commercial gambling was largely confined to the mining towns in Nevada.

Death of the Lottery

The use of lotteries as state-supported revenue-generating devices had a brief resurgence after the Civil War. In 1869, in an attempt to recover from the disastrous effects of the Civil War, the Louisiana legislature licensed and chartered the Louisiana Lottery Company. The lottery known as "The Serpent" was entitled to operate for 25 years. The Serpent payed the state $40,000 a year toward the maintenance of Charity Hospital in New Orleans (Chafetz, 1960). At first the tickets were only sold in Louisiana. However, by 1877 tickets were being sold in every state and territory in the Union. The 1890 handle for The Serpent was reported to be $1.25 million. The sale of Louisiana lottery tickets in states that prohibited lotteries increased opposition to The Serpent.

A series of scandals involving fraud, skimming of profits, and public corruption, at one time implicating 23 pro-lottery Louisiana senators, led to a governor's veto of a bill extending the lottery's charter. Because of the national scandal involved, President Benjamin Harrison urged Congress to pass legislation prohibiting the use of the U.S. Postal Service by lotteries. In September 1890, Congress prohibited the use of the mails by lotteries and excluded newspapers carrying lottery advertisements from using the mails. This law is still in effect. The lottery was dead for 70 years, until the 1964 New Hampshire Lottery.

Nevada Gambling

The 1859 Comstock Load gold discovery near the California border brought the veterans of the California gold rush and their gambling behaviors into Nevada (Martin, 1996). Towns like Gold Hill, Virginia City, and Silver City grew to thousands within weeks. CBSs were the first structures in these towns. The first territorial governor, James Nye, responding to Mormon conservatives, took a strong stand against gambling and the wild lifestyle of the miners. In 1861, Nye persuaded the newly elected legislature to pass a broad statute banning all forms of gambling. Gambling continued unabated in spite of the law. Eight years later (1869), gambling, except lotteries, was legalized in spite of the governor's veto. The 1869 legislation also set up a system of licensing and fees split by the counties and the state. Gambling would remain legal in Nevada until 1910, when it was once again outlawed.

In 1931 the Nevada legislature, responding to the effects of the Great Depression and the decline in the price of silver, passed two revenue-generating devices. The legislature legalized casino gambling and lowered the waiting period for divorce from three months to six weeks. The "quickie divorce" law responded to competition from other states to the Nevada marriage–divorce industry. Gambling proponents argued that the taxes would bring in sorely needed revenues and reduce property taxes. The gambling law served to make legal what had been common practice and allow the state and counties to collect fees from casino gambling. The bill's sponsor is quoted as saying:

Illegal gambling was widespread in Nevada at the time, and there was not a market, hotel, or gas station that didn't have a slot machine or two. They were in the old Golden Hotel lobby, and places like the Bank Club in Reno operated openly with casino gambling. (Galliher and Cross, 1983, 56)

As long as we don't seem to get rid of [it], we might as well derive a tax from it. (Vogel, 1991, 2B)

The 1931 Nevada "Wide Open Gambling Bill" started the modern era of legalized gambling in the United States.

CONCLUSION

The nineteenth-century reform efforts, legal and vigilante, sought to control the spectacle, disorderly conduct, and violence accompanying public and commercial gambling. Lottery scandals, particularly of the Louisiana Serpent, killed the lottery. Throughout the country the sentiment was, as in colonial times, against public gambling, including lotteries, professional gamblers, and banked commercial gambling. Private gambling was largely left untouched. By the end of the nineteenth century, wide-open public and legal gambling remained only in Nevada, where it was to become the state's largest industry. The legal gambling capital of the United States, and the world, would soon move to Las Vegas, Nevada.

REFERENCES

Bergler, Edmund. (1958). *The Psychology of Gambling*. New York: International University Press.

Blakey, Robert G. (1976). *The Development of the Law of Gambling 1776–1976*. Washington, D.C.: GPO.

Brenner, Reuven, and Gabrielle Brenner. (1990). *Gambling and Speculation*. New York: Cambridge University Press.

Chafetz, Henry. (1960). *Play the Devil: A History of Gambling in the United States from 1492 to 1955*. New York: Clarkston N. Potter.

Dunstan, Roger. (1997). *Gambling in California*. Sacramento: California Research Bureau, California State Library.

Fenich, George G. (1996). "A Chronology of (Legal) Gaming in the U.S." *Gaming Research & Review Journal* 3(2): 65–77.

Galliher, John F., and John R. Cross. (1983). *Morals Legislation without Morality: The Case of Nevada*. New Brunswick, N.J.: Rutgers University Press.

Martin, Robert J. (1996). "Historical Background." In *The Gaming Industry: Introduction and Perspectives*. New York: John Wiley & Sons.

McDonald, John. (1967). "Sport of Kings, Bums, and Businessmen." In Robert D. Herman, ed., *Gambling*. New York: Harper & Row.

Rosecrance, John. (1988). *Gambling without Guilt: The Legitimation of an American Pastime*. Pacific Grove, Calif.: Brooks/Cole.

Vogel, Ed. (1991). "Father of Nevada Gambling Remembered." *Las Vegas Review Journal* (March 18): 1B, 2B. In Donald A. Farrell and Carole Case (1995), *The Black Book and the Mob: The Untold Story of the Control of Nevada's Casinos*. Madison: University of Wisconsin Press.

Chapter 4

Sin, Vice, and Gangsters

At the time the seeds for legalized gambling were planted in Nevada, gambling as an illegal monopoly of organized crime was growing in the Northeast, particularly in New York and New Jersey. In the early 1900s, a New York City's Lower East Side crime cabal of teenage Italian and Jewish gangsters joined together in criminal pursuits. Five young toughs—Salvatore Lucania (Lucky Luciano), Maier Suchowljansky (Meyer Lansky), Benjamin Siegel (Bugsy Siegel), Francesco Castiglia (Frank Costello), and Vincent Alo (Jimmy Blue Eyes)—would change the nature of organized crime and gambling in the United States. The Lower East Side gangsters grew up with the street crap games, illegal casinos, lottery rackets (policy), and betting in cigar and candy stores flourishing in the early 1900s. The lessons these gangsters learned in managing the illegal vice rackets of liquor and gambling would be useful to them when they moved into Las Vegas in the late 1940s.

NEW YORK CASINOS

In the late 1800s and early 1900s, New York City was a gambler's paradise (Chafetz, 1960). Several well-known casinos operated wide open in the city, and a lavish casino operated at Saratoga Springs, New York, during the August racing season. These early Temples of Chance catered to cash-happy men with big fortunes and no taxes to pay— Reggy and Albert G. Vanderbilt; Payne Whitney; Louis Ehret, heir to a brewing fortune; Jessie Lewison; banker and boyfriend of Lillian Russell; Francis Kinney, maker of Sweet Caporals; Percival S. Hill, president of American Tobacco Company; Julius Fleischmann, manufacturer of yeast;

Joseph Seagram, the Canadian distiller; and William Thompson, owner of a racetrack at Glouscester City, New Jersey. The rich financiers gambled with professional gamblers like Diamond Jim Brady and Bet-a-Million Gates.

The New York casinos were plush operations unlike the rustic CBSs common in the West. Stanford White's gambling den, the Bronze Door, at 33 West Thirty-third Street, was furnished with oil paintings, velvet carpets, Persian rugs, and a $60,000 second-floor banister carved by 10 master Venetian craftsmen (Chafetz, 1960, 314). The famous $20,000 front door came from a wine cellar of the palace of a Venetian doge, where it had hung since 1498. From 1895 to 1902, White spent $25,000 a year on food for his casino. An elaborate screening system and payoffs to police and politicians kept the Bronze Door in business.

Richard Canfield, reportedly the biggest gambler in the world at that time, ran the Club House in Saratoga Springs, New York. His opulent casino made a profit of $2.5 million a year in the five- to six-week racing season (Chafetz, 1960, 323). The casino catered only to the rich out-of-towners in for the races. No year-round residents of Saratoga were allowed to gamble. The downstairs gambling room held two faro tables and nine single-end roulette wheels. The high rollers gambled upstairs at a faro table and two double-end roulette wheels.

The illegal, but wide-open, New York City and Saratoga casinos operated into the 1930s and 1940s. Under the tutelage of Arthur Rothstein, a legendary 1920s New York City gambler, who owned parts of the illegal lake house casinos in Saratoga, New York, teenagers Meyer Lansky and Lucky Luciano were introduced into casino operations and management. Meyer Lansky ran a Saratoga Springs casino for several years early in his gambling career.

GAMBLING AS A BUSINESS: ORGANIZED CRIME

The term *Mafia* has become a metaphor for organized crime. Today, terms such as *Russian Mafia, Dixie Mafia, Mexican Mafia, Japanese Mafia,* and *Chinese Mafia* are used to describe ethnic or cultural groups' involvement in crime as a business. The term *Mafia* used in this context may be useful in the sense that it dispels the myth that all organized crime, particularly illegal gambling, in the United States is, and has been, controlled by a bureaucratic corporation of Italian American crime families. Gambling as an illegal business was not, and is not, under the sole control of any one ethnic or cultural group. However, organized crime in the United States did get its start with the Great Experiment—Prohibition—and the Italian gangsters played a huge part in its growth and development. The temperance movement, culminating in Prohibition, resulted in the greatest expansion of criminal activity in U.S. history (Davis, 1993). Prohibition was the biggest moneymaker for organized crime that the government ever conceived. Prohibition demonstrated that making a widely demanded vice illegal and not vigorously enforcing the law inevitably turns the supply side of the supply-demand equation over to the crooks and gangsters. Gambling fits into the same pattern.

During the last years of Prohibition, Lucky Luciano, in an effort to stop the internecine warfare of the Italian/American gangsters, created a national syndicate of Italian gangsters as members with Jewish, Irish, German, and Polish gangsters as nonmember associates (Davis, 1993). Luciano fashioned this crime syndicate on the model of the old Sicilian Mafia. The Siegel-Lansky gang was included as an associate member. Meyer Lansky, a boyhood friend, was to become Luciano's most trusted nonmember associate. The close relationship between Lansky and the Italian gangsters would continue when Frank Costello became boss after Luciano's deportation in 1946.

In 1933, with the repeal of Prohibition, the bootleg/gangsters came out of the Great Experiment, where they had grown rich and powerful with an illegal monopoly over liquor, and sensed that another vice monopoly existed for them. That illegal monopoly was the control of gambling. Speakeasies had provided multiple forms of gambling. After Prohibition, gambling was another vice that enjoyed widespread appeal for the American public. The laws prohibiting gambling reduced the mob's competition, giving them a legally imposed monopoly. They would soon move their money and muscle into bookmaking (sports and race), policy (the poor man's lottery), gambling machines, and illegal casinos.

The gangsters brought a perfect control system to their new monopoly, one perfected in supplying liquor to a willing public: violence. The gangsters used violence to enforce contracts, eliminate competition, and defend or expand their markets. Primarily, the violence they used was against other gangsters. Some years later, the psychopathic Bugsy Siegel—a member of the equally psychopathic Albert Anastasia's Murder Inc.—after admitting 12 murders to Del Webb, the Flamingo Casino's contractor, told the shocked builder not to worry—"[W]e only kill each other (Smith, 1997a, 85). The unsolved murders of both Siegel and Anastasia are attributed to their gangster friends.

Illegal Gambling in the 1930s and 1940s

In the 1930s and 1940s, illegal gambling flourished throughout the country with casinos in Palm Beach, Florida, Hot Springs, Arkansas, and Cleveland, Ohio, to mention a few cities. However, illegal gambling as a business became prominent with the northeastern influence where Jimmy Blue Eyes and Lucky Luciano built up a huge Harlem policy, Bugsy Siegel developed bookmaking and the race wire, Frank Costello became known as the King of Slots, and Meyer Lansky became the casino King.

In 1934, the young Lansky in a joint-venture partnership with Lucky Luciano, Frank Costello from New York, and Joe Adonis from New Jersey ran the most successful casino in Saratoga Springs, New York—the Piping Rock. Meyer Lansky would later say, "There's no such thing as a lucky gambler. There are just the winners and the losers. The winners are those who control the game" (Lacy, 1991, 33). Lansky also learned from his experiences in Saratoga that secret ownership and corruption of public officials were a necessary part of the control of gambling—legal and illegal. The necessary paperwork for the Saratoga club's liquor and restaurant licenses were in the name of a local businessman, who was also responsible for arranging the fix.

Carpet Joints

Robert Lacy (1991), Meyer Lansky's biographer, reports that Lansky and his Italian partners made gambling available throughout the United States from 1933 until after World War II through gaming roadhouses known as carpet joints. The carpet joints, modeled after the Saratoga lake houses, were a combination of speakeasies and Nevada casinos. Most were located in rural areas, with the local police and politicians as silent partners. Gambling, liquor, restaurants, and big-name entertainment were provided.

The carpet joints gaming tables—housed as in Saratoga, discreetly separate from the rest of the establishment—subsidized the ingredients of the great American roadhouse night out: a good dinner, some dancing, and a Copacabana-style floor show that featured a magician, a comedian, and a big-time entertainer, the whole package topped and tailed by a chorus line of a dozen or so leggy beauties, generally known by a name that ended in—ettes. (Lacy, 1991, 98)

The carpet joints run by Lansky and his partners in Hallandale, Florida—10 miles from Miami Beach—became known as a "little Las Vegas before its time." Paul Whitman, Sophie Tucker, Harry Richman, and Joe E. Lewis appeared at the Florida carpet joints, the Farm, the Beach Club and the Colonial Inn (Lacy, 1991, 105).

Other former speakeasy operators ran carpet joints in Hot Springs, Arkansas, Cincinnati and Cleveland, Ohio, Covington and Newport, Kentucky, Omaha, Nebraska, Houston, Texas, Council Bluff, Iowa, and New Orleans. Many of these carpet joint owners/partners, such as Moe Sedway, Moe Dalitz, and Benny Binion, would resurface along with Meyer Lansky and his Italian friends in Las Vegas in the 1950s. Moe Dalitz, an associate of Detroit's Purple Gang, owned or had "points" in Mound Club, the Pettibone Club, and the Jungle Inn, near Youngstown,

Ohio; the Beverly Hills Club in Miami; and the Lookout Club and the Beverly Hill Country Club in Kentucky (Reid and Demaris, 1963). Reflecting on his speakeasy days before the Kefauver Committee, Dalitz testified:

Kefauver: As a matter of fact, you have been making a great deal of money in recent years, so I suppose from your profits from one investment you would then go ahead and make another investment. Now, to get your investment started off you did get yourself a pretty good little nest-egg out of rum running didn't you?

Dalitz: Well, I didn't inherit any money, Senator. . . . If you people wouldn't have drunk it, I wouldn't have bootlegged it. (Smith, 1997b, 37)

Bugsy Siegel and the Flamingo

Contrary to popular fiction and the entertainment industry, Bugsy Siegel didn't build Las Vegas. The highly acclaimed movie *Bugsy*, starring Warren Beatty as Bugsy and Annette Bening as his Alabama-born lover, Virginia Hill, are like the Mafia story *The Godfather*, entertaining and inaccurate. Bugsy, or more accurately his murder, made Las Vegas famous.

Benny, as Meyer Lansky called him, had been on the West Coast since 1936 pursuing his favorite illegal pursuit: bookmaking. Siegel and his back East gangster friends wanted to solidify their control of the Trans-America horse-racing wire service—a radio transmission service that transmitted racing information nationwide. Bugsy was also evading investigation/arrest for the murder of a Jewish gangster, Henry Greenberg. Furthermore, the flamboyant gangster was drawn to Hollywood by the movie celebrities and aspirations to become an actor (Carpozi, 1992; Lacy, 1991; Smith, 1997a).

When Bugsy made his first trip from Los Angeles to Las Vegas in 1941, casino gambling had been legal in Nevada for a decade. Several months before his arrival the Nevada legislature legalized betting on horse races coming over the wire. Siegel came to Las Vegas to expand the race-wire business. There was already a luxurious hotel-casino operating when he arrived. The El Rancho Vegas hotel-casino, a 61-acre landscaped and waterfalled resort complex, was located in the desert outside of town in an area that would become known as the Las Vegas Strip. The next year the Last Frontier was built on the Strip. The Last Frontier was even more luxurious. When completed, the new hotel-casino had a swimming pool, sun deck, tennis courts and riding stables, a showroom and casino, and 170 individually air-conditioned rooms (Lacy, 1991, 150).

Siegel's first attempt to enter into the Las Vegas hotel-casino business was an offer in 1943 to buy the El Rancho Vegas. Tom Hull, the owner, aware of Siegel's gangster reputation, was quoted in the *Las Vegas Review Journal* as saying, "[T]he people of Las Vegas have been too good to me to repay them that way. Mr. Siegel has contacted me several times with an offer to purchase, but I have told him I was not interested—and that goes for all time" (Lacy, 1991, 151).

In 1945, Siegel was able to purchase a downtown gambling hotel—the El Cortez. Meyer Lansky, unimpressed with the desert town of Las Vegas and whose major interest was in the Broward County, Florida, carpet joints, invested a modest $60,000 for a 10 percent stake. Lansky was helping out his boyhood friend. The other investors came from the former bootleggers, bookies, and carpet joint operators who had come to Las Vegas to escape their pasts: Gus Greenbaum, Arizona bookmaker; Willie Alderman and the Berman brothers, Dave and Chickie, carpet joint operators in Minneapolis. The last investor was Moe Sedway, who had come west with Siegel to set up the race-wire business (Lacy, 1991, 152). Six months later the group sold the El Cortez for a $166,000 profit and decided to reinvest their monies in a new hotel-casino being built on the Las Vegas Strip: the Flamingo.

The Flamingo was actually the brainchild of Californian Billy Wilkerson, the founder of the *Hollywood Reporter*. Wilkerson was also the creator of the Cafe Tracadero, Ciro's, and La Rue's on the Sunset Strip. He wanted to build a casino with a glamorous Beverly Hills theme, not the Old West theme popular in Las Vegas. His casino would feature movie stars and Hollywood starlets. Wilkerson bought the land, drew up the plans, and began construction. Unfortunately, he ran out of money before he could complete the project. He approached Ben Siegel, who he had met in Hollywood, as a possible investor. Siegel jumped at the chance to finally get his Las Vegas casino, especially one with a Hollywood theme. Siegel convinced his El Cortez partners to invest in the Flamingo. They reinvested the $650,000 from the sale of the El Cortez into 66 percent holdings in the Flamingo (Lacy, 1991; Smith, 1997a).

The mercurial Siegel's hands-on approach to the construction of the casino led to numerous overruns and delays in construction. The construction costs originally estimated to be $1.5 million ballooned to $6 million. His partners, running short on money and patience, demanded that the Flamingo open. When the Flamingo opened on December 26, 1946, the hotel rooms were not finished. This would turn out to be a costly mistake. The high-rolling gamblers who attended the gala opening won steadily the first hours and into the night. The gamblers and their tired wives or girlfriends took their winnings to the neighboring El Rancho Vegas and the Last Frontier, where they had rooms for the night. The high rollers deposited their Flamingo winnings at these casinos after their female companions went to bed. The gambling losses, combined with the construction overruns, left Siegel and his partners without the monies to complete the rooms. The casino closed. Strapped for cash, Ben Siegel flew to Florida to ask Meyer Lansky and Frank Costello for money, leaving his grumbling, paranoid partners behind. Benjamin "Bugsy" Siegel was a marked man.

Siegel returned to Las Vegas with the loans from Lansky and Costello, and room construction continued. When the Flamingo reopened in March 1947, "Benny Siegel was under notice. This time the Flamingo would have to work—and it would have to show a profit" (Lacy, 1991, 156). The reopened casino showed a profit that year and the following years, but Bugsy never knew it. He was brutally murdered on June 20, 1947, in the Los Angeles home of his lover Virginia Hill.

Gangsters have always used murder as a management tool. Bugsy's shares in the Flamingo were divided among his partners. The truth surrounding Bugsy Siegel's death will never be known. However, the most plausible explanation is that his Las Vegas partners, having grown tired of his flamboyant lifestyle, temper tantrums, and extravagant manner of spending their money, killed him or had him killed.

Ben Siegel did not invent the luxury resort hotel-casino. He did not found the Las Vegas Strip. He did not buy the land or first conceive the project that became the Flamingo. But by his death he made them all famous. (Lacy, 1991, 158)

1950s Crime Commissions

The publicity surrounding Bugsy Siegel's death—and the wide-open gambling, illegal bookmaking, and carpet joint casinos—led to a resurgence of citizen crime commissions popular during the 1920s. By 1950, crime commissions were operating in Chicago, California, Kansas City, Dallas, St. Louis, New York, Miami, and Gary, Indiana. Senator Estes Kefauver's Special Committee to Investigate Organized Crime in Interstate Commerce was a national response to the growing interest in organized crime and gambling. The televised Kefauver Commission, along with the citizens' crime commissions, would have two effects on gambling: Nevada would be forced to develop a strong licensing and regulatory process for casino gambling. In addition, the national publicity increased the movement of gambling and gamblers to Las Vegas.

Changes in Nevada

The notorious Bugsy Siegel and other well-known gangsters were licensed by Nevada to open casinos for very practical reasons. The casino industry was considered immoral and corrupt; therefore, legitimate investment money was not available. Banks and other investment firms were not going to loan money to reputed gangsters to build gambling casinos, legal or illegal. Nevada licensed Siegel for the potential reward of development, employment, and expansion of tourism (Cabot, 1996, 318–319). Although all those coming to Las Vegas were not gangsters, most had engaged in illegal gambling elsewhere. In testimony before the Kefauver Commission, Nevada's lieutenant governor and a part owner in the Thunderbird casino, Cliff Jones, stated:

Halley [committee counsel Rudolph Halley]: Wouldn't you say that prior to 1949 a great many undesirable characters with bad police records were engaged in gambling operations in the state of Nevada?

Jones: Well, of course. I would say that as long as they conduct themselves properly that I think probably no harm comes of it. . . . There were some people that you might say had police records and reputations of gambling in other places. But this seems to hold true, that people who came here when the state started to grow, they weren't particularly Sunday school teachers or preachers or anything like that. They were gamblers. (Lalli, 1997b, 5)

Unfortunately, for Lieutenant Governor Cliff Jones his secretly taped conversations with an undercover agent hired by a crusading publisher-editor of the Las Vegas *Sun* revealed what the Kefauver Commission was worried about: corrupt collusion between the gamblers and politicians. The editor and the undercover agent worked with the Clark County district attorney during the taping and investigation.

Jones [Nevada's lieutenant governor talking to the undercover agent, seeking a gambling license]: You're all right but not until after the first of the year when Pittman [gubernatorial candidate of the Democratic political machine. His election was considered in the bag.] takes office. After the election we're going to be stronger than ever. To make an application for a gambling license during election time would be poor judgement, especially for you with your criminal record. Wait until the first of the year; then we're going to boot Robbins Cahill out of his job. After that everything is going to be smoothed out.

Tabet [the undercover agent]: Cahill?

Jones: He's the secretary of the State Tax Commission. He's the big boss in Carson City. He says whether you get a gambling license or not. And what he says goes up there right now, but it's going to change quick after the election.

Tabet: Well, I've taken care of the county. I've got Harley Harmon, Colton [Clark County commissioner], and Sheriff Jones [Clark County sheriff, no relation to Cliff Jones].

Jones: You're with the right people. Louie Weiner, my partner [law partner], takes care of the legal end of the deals and finances. (Reid and Demaris, 1963, 136)

The resulting scandal led to the indictment of Sheriff Jones and County Commissioner Rodney Colton on charges of accepting gifts and offers of money to further the welfare of a self-proclaimed hoodlum. Lieutenant Governor Cliff Jones, the recently elected Democratic National Committeeman for Nevada, submitted his resignation as Democratic National Committeeman. It was accepted.

The Kefauver Commission, in addition to pointing their finger at Nevada for licensing former "criminals" as casino operators, introduced the term *Mafia* to describe organized crime in the United States: "[T]here exists in the United States a crime syndicate known as the Mafia, operating Nationwide under centralized direction and control. . . . The Mafia is a direct descendent of a criminal organization of the same name originating in the island of Sicily" (Lacy, 1991, 201). The committee went on to say that two Mafia syndicates dominated organized crime and gambling—"the Accardo-Guzik-Fischetti syndicate, whose headquarters are Chicago; and the Costello-Adonis-Lansky syndicate based on [*sic*] New York" (Lacy, 1991, 201). However, the committee, as Lacy points out, failed to explain the presence of two Jews—Jake Guzik and Meyer Lansky—in these criminal syndicates.

The Kefauver Committee's investigation and the threat of federal intervention in Nevada gambling, by either shutting it down, regulating it, or taxing it (Kefauver did propose a 10 percent federal gaming tax), led to changes in Nevada. There had also been talk of a national casino ban law similar to Prohibition. In 1955, the governor closed the Thunderbird after it was revealed that the casino had been secretly financed by Meyer Lansky and his brother. He also imposed a 90-day moratorium on new gambling licenses and created a three-member Gaming Control Board within the Nevada Tax Commission. The Gaming Control Board would conduct investigations into applicants and oversee the enforcement of the state's gaming regulations (Farrell and Case, 1995, 27).

Gamblers Move to Nevada

The effects of the reform efforts by the Kefauver Committee and the other citizens' crime commissions speeded up the movement of professional gamblers to Nevada where gambling was legal. The outlaws moved to where their crimes were legal. The lake-house casinos in Saratoga Springs, New York, and the Broward County, Florida, casinos were shut down, closing the major gambling palaces of Meyer Lansky and his Italian partners. The wide-open carpet joints in New Orleans and virtually every other American city were also closed (Lacy, 1991, 197). Many of the gambler/operators, dealers, and other workers of these illegal gambling operations moved to Nevada. Nevada needed their investment dollars and their gambling expertise. Las Vegas's "live and let live" attitude toward the gamblers who moved to the desert city to legally pursue their chosen occupation is best expressed by Sheriff Ralph Lamb, a Mormon and sheriff of Clark County in 1962:

As far as I know, everyone in the gambling business out here has been a gentleman. Maybe they got caught elsewhere doing the same thing they do here legitimately, but that don't make them wrong, just the laws where they come from. (Reid and Demaris, 1963, 6)

This movement was not without its problems for Nevada's growing gambling industry. The gamblers without legitimate sources of investment capital and prior mob connections turned to the Teamsters Central States Pension Fund. The Teamsters "cookie jar" was a mixed blessing. The investment capital was sorely needed. Las Vegas would not be what it is today without the Teamsters Union (Lalli, 1997b, 14). The Desert Inn, the Stardust, the Fremont, the Tropicana, Caesars Palace, Circus Circus, and Dunes received close to $250 million in loans from the Teamsters Pension Fund. Unfortunately, these investments had strings attached. There were kickbacks to Teamster officials—Jimmy Hoffa, then Frank Fitzsimmons and Jackie Presser—who voted in favor of the loans. Mobsters controlling the union and the officials, unable to meet the new Gaming Control Board's background investigations, became "secret partners" in the casinos. Silent partners/hidden owners in the Las Vegas casinos were a well-known secret. When the Sahara opened in 1954, a national magazine printed the following:

Today, the big mystery is the identity of the owners of the Sahara Hotel, newest of the multimillion-dollar casino palaces along the Strip. Listed owners of the Sahara are A. F. Winter, Milton Prell, and Barney Morris. All are small-time gamblers out of Oregon, where they ran upstairs dice tables, poker games, and race books. Such minor operators don't move in on a territory dominated by the Flamingo, Desert Inn and Sands outfits just because they feel like it. The only thing that figures is they're backed by somebody big. (Reid and Demaris, 1963, 60)

The hidden fees, kickbacks, and silent partners were paid in cash skimmed from the casino profits prior to being reported to the state. The simplest form of the skim was to take cash out of the counting rooms every night. The former owner/operators of the carpet joints and the mobsters were familiar with secret partners and skimming.

The first concrete evidence of the mob's involvement in Nevada casino skimming occurred in 1957 (Lalli, 1997a). An assassination attempt on mob boss Frank Costello sent him to the hospital. The police searched Costello's clothes and found a slip of paper listing the gross receipts, the table game income, and the markers from an unnamed Las Vegas casino.

Gross casino wins as of 4/27/57	$651,284
Casino wins less markers	434,695
Slot wins	62,844
Markers	153,745

Mike $150 a week, totaling $600; Jake $100 a week, totaling $400; L. —— $30,000; H. —— $9,000.

The subsequent investigation led to the recently opened Tropicana as the unnamed casino. The casino supervisor lost his job and was forced to sell his shares in the Tropicana. Another major Tropicana investor was denied a gaming license because of his previous associations with Costello.

CONCLUSION

The gangsters weren't out yet. Other evidence of mob skimming at the Flamingo would be uncovered by Federal Bureau of Investigation (FBI) wiretaps in 1961 and 1967. The owners, Morris Lansburgh and Sam Cohen, pleaded guilty to skimming $36 million in untaxed income from the Flamingo between 1960 and 1967 (Lalli, 1997a). Meyer Lansky was charged in this case but never brought to trial. There would be another mob skimming scandal revealed in 1976 at the Stardust Casino; however, by this time large-scale mob influence in Nevada gambling, particularly Las Vegas, was coming to an end. A new investment source—Wall Street—would replace the Teamsters Central States Pension Fund.

REFERENCES

Cabot, Anthony N. (1996). *Casino Gambling: Policy, Economics and Regulation*. Las Vegas: University of Nevada Press.

Carpozi, George. (1992). *Bugsy: The Bloodthirsty, Lusty Life of Benjamin "Bugsy" Siegel*. New York: S.P.I. Books.

Chafetz, Henry. (1960). *Play the Devil: A History of Gambling in the United States from 1492 to 1955*. New York: Clarkston N. Potter.

Davis, John H. (1993). *Mafia Dynasty*. New York: Harper Paperbacks.

Farrell, Ronald A., and Carole Case. (1995). *The Black Book and the Mob: The Untold Story of the Control of Nevada's Casinos*. Madsion: University of Wisconsin Press.

Lacy, Robert. (1991). *Little Man: Meyer Lansky and the Gangster Life*. Boston: Little, Brown.

Lalli, Sergio. (1997a). "Howard Hughes in Vegas." In Jack Sheehan, ed., *The Players: The Men Who Made Las Vegas*. Reno: University of Nevada Press.

Lalli, Sergio. (1997b). "A Peculiar Institution." In Jack Sheehan, ed., *The Players: The Men Who Made Las Vegas*. Reno: University of Nevada Press.

Reid, Ed, and Ovid Demaris. (1963). *The Green Felt Jungle*. New York: Trident
    Press.
Smith, John L. (1997a). "The Ghost of Ben Siegel." In Jack Sheehan, ed., *The
    Players: The Men Who Made Las Vegas*. Reno: University of Nevada Press.
Smith, John L. (1997b). "Moe Dalitz and the Desert." In Jack Sheehan, ed., *The
    Players: The Men Who Made Las Vegas*. Reno: University of Nevada Press.

Chapter 5

Gambling as a Legitimate Industry

THE PHANTOM ARRIVES

A reclusive, unkempt, emaciated drug addict with a broken body was
wheeled across the lobby of the Las Vegas Desert Inn Casino in the
predawn hours of Thanksgiving Day in 1966. Few saw the phantom
arrive. Those that did would not have recognized him. However, in the
next four years Howard Hughes became Nevada's largest private employer, the state's largest private property owner, and the state's largest
owner of mining claims (Lalli, 1997). His Summa Corporation, the parent
company of Hughes's Nevada holdings, owned seven Nevada casinos—
the Desert Inn, the Sands, the Frontier, the Castaways, the Silver Slipper,
the Landmark in Las Vegas, and Harold's Club in Reno—when the reclusive phantom slipped out of Las Vegas on Thanksgiving Eve in 1970.
The majority of these casinos had mobsters as major investors and "point
holders" (shareholders) when Hughes purchased them. The gambling
industry had a special appeal to the wealthy hermit. He wrote, "I have
decided once and for all. I want to acquire even more hotels and to build
this operation to be the greatest thing in the U.S. This is a business that
appeals to me" (Lalli, 1997, 133). Hughes's vision for Las Vegas was a
"family vacation" area for middle-income Americans. A peculiar idea for
a man who detested children and referred to them as "ever lovin' little
darlings" and stopped the annual Desert Inn Easter egg hunt (136).

Just as Nevada needed Bugsy Siegel and the infusion of Teamsters'
investment capital, Las Vegas needed Hughes and his "honest" investment money. No matter how eccentric, Howard Hughes was a shrewd
businessman with a deep pocket. Nevada Governor Paul Laxalt saw in

Table 5.1
Licensees/Investors, Las Vegas Casinos, April 1, 1962

Casino	Number of Licensees
Dunes Hotel	10
Desert Inn	17
Flamingo Hotel	9
Fremont Hotel	22
Hacienda	25
The Horseshoe Club	20
The Mint Casino	25
New Frontier Hotel	4
Riviera Hotel	21
Sahara Hotel	34
The Sands	17
Silver Slipper	3
Stardust Hotel	12
Thunderbird Hotel	5
Tropicana Hotel	17

Source: Reid and Demaris, 1963, appendix.

the phobia-ridden tycoon a way to repair Nevada's image, recently tarnished by national crime commissions and mob skimming scandals. Governor Laxalt hoped Hughes's presence would give the state a Good Housekeeping Seal of Approval (Lalli, 1997, 142).

The state made numerous concessions for Hughes and his reclusive behavior. Hughes's 1967 gaming license was approved by the Gaming Control Board without Hughes's filling out a financial background report, being photographed or fingerprinted, or appearing in person before the Control Board. This violation of gaming regulations had never occurred before and has not occurred since.

Just as Benjamin "Bugsy" Siegel didn't make Las Vegas—Howard Hughes didn't run the mob out of Las Vegas. Nevada's relaxed attitude toward corporate investment had more of an effect on mob ownership of casinos than Howard Hughes. Prior to 1969, casino ownership rested in the hands of a few wealthy partners or small corporate groups (see Table 5.1). Mob/tainted money supplied the major source of capital for these partners/groups. In order to screen out mob associates, all casino shareholders/investors had to undergo a background investigation and be licensed by the Gaming Control Board (Lalli, 1997, 18). This restriction precluded publicly traded corporations from investing in casinos. There was no practical way to examine the backgrounds and license hundreds, perhaps thousands, of stockholders. Personal appearances by stockholders before the Gaming Control Board were out of the question.

In 1954, one enterprising "former" gangster, Tony Cornero, did come up with the idea of selling stock publicly to build the largest resort hotel in the world, the Stardust. He, while waiting for approval from the Securities and Exchange Commission (SEC), started selling stock all over the country. He advertised in newspapers and on billboards. Operating out of a leather valise, Cornero sold stock until he was told by the governor that the state would not grant him a casino license, and the SEC informed him that he could not sell stock in interstate commerce until the issue was registered with the commission. The SEC told him that he could sell stock in state as long as the investors were Nevada residents (Reid and Demaris, 1963). The stock issue became a moot point when Tony had a heart attack while shooting craps at the Desert Inn. However, the idea of publicly traded stock to finance casino construction had been planted.

Casino owners recognized that the monies needed to buy, construct, and expand casinos in the expanding Nevada gaming industry could not be supplied by private investors, especially mobsters. Lobbying pressures from Las Vegas casino owners led to the Nevada legislature passing the Corporate Gaming Act in 1969 (Farrell and Case, 1995). This act allowed for corporate ownership requiring licensing of only the major stockholders, those owning 10 percent or more of the stock. Individuals holding 5 to 10 percent of the stock could be called in for licensing if the Gaming Control Board thought it was necessary. Those who owned less than 5 percent of the stock—the majority in publicly traded corporations—did not have to be licensed. The legislature felt that oversight by the SEC would bring legitimacy to casinos and provide "clean" sources of monies for casino development. Within six years of the act's passage, Hilton, Hyatt, and Metro-Goldwyn-Mayer had invested in Nevada casinos.

Howard Hughes's four-year sojourn in the desert did not, by itself, bring corporate ownership of casinos to Nevada. The eccentric phantom didn't drive the mob out of Las Vegas. However, the "Hughes Effect" did boost a sagging Las Vegas economy, attracted a new class of tourists, and sparked an influx of corporate investors. These new investors followed Hughes's example and bought up casinos reported to have mob connections (Skolnick, 1978, 136). Hughes's presence and investments increased respectability of a pariah industry and stimulated corporate investment in gambling. By 1980, the 20 largest publicly owned casinos in Nevada were generating 50 percent of the gross gaming revenues and employing 50 percent of the gaming employees (Eadington, 1982, 54).

WILLIAM F. HARRAH OF RENO

The University of Nevada, Las Vegas (UNLV) International Gaming Institute is located within the William F. Harrah College of Hotel Administration at the University of Nevada, Las Vegas. The modern-day gambling operations run by corporate business executives with M.B.A.s, managing the investments of public shareholders, owe much of their success to a Reno, Nevada, casino owner—William "Bill" Harrah. If the gambling, or "gaming," industry truly deserves the label of a gaming entertainment industry run by gaming entertainment professionals (casino developers, casino operators, casino regulators, lottery managers, racetrack owners, etc.), as claimed by the American Gaming Association, Bill Harrah was one of the creators of that image.

When the hard-drinking young Bill Harrah first arrived in Reno, Nevada, he found a wide-open town where gambling was legal 365 days a year, 24 hours a day. Bill had been running the "Circle Game" for his lawyer father in Venice, California, for several years (Moe, 1996, 80–86). The game, where the players rolled a ball in a hopper, was legal as a game of skill or illegal as a game of chance, depending on the whim of the district attorneys.

Harrah, sensing the opportunities in Nevada where gambling was legal, opened his first gambling business in Reno, a bingo parlor, on October 29, 1937, and built a gambling empire that still bears his name—Harrah's Entertainment, Inc. (corporate headquarters—Memphis, Tennessee). William Harrah, not a transplant from Chicago or Detroit, was well known for running clean, profitable gambling operations untouched by mob influence (Lalli, 1997, 145). John L. Smith, Steve Wynn's biographer, calls Bill Harrah "one of the founders of the modern, image conscious casino industry" (1995, 28).

Harrah's aim was to erase the stigma of gambling and make it morally and legally acceptable (Skolnick, 1978, 109). His businesslike approach to gambling included market research, use of consultants, and advertising. As a result of his market research, Harrah instituted the first casino bus charter in the country at Harrah's Lake Tahoe in 1955. A 1957 study "An Investigation of Factors Influencing Bus Scheduling" by the Stanford Research Institute found that the people using the buses were "elderly, in a low occupational status, unmarried, a renter rather than home owner, and without a car" (Mandel, 1982, 99). The bus riders had their fare refunded and received a complementary dinner and a split of champagne. Twenty buses a day arrived from Oakland, California, alone.

William Harrah was also the first to use the "eye in the sky" casino surveillance (Mandel, 1982). His fear of federal intervention, following the Kefauver Committee's revelations, led him to champion the move toward tighter control over gambling.

William F. Harrah was the first to take gambling stock public. After his death, the Southern Baptist–controlled Holiday Inn, Inc., bought his company. The president, L. M. Clyner, resigned because he opposed gambling. In 1998, Harrah's casinos were located in 15 cities throughout the United States—Phoenix, Arizona, Joliet, Illinois, Topeka, Kansas, Shreveport, Louisiana, New Orleans, Louisiana, Tunica, Mississippi, North Kansas City, Missouri, St. Louis–Riverport, Missouri, Lake Tahoe, Nevada, Las Vegas, Nevada, Laughlin, Nevada, Reno, Nevada, Atlantic City, New Jersey, Cherokee-Smoky Mountains, North Carolina, and Skagit Valley, Washington. Harrah's Entertainment, Inc. also manages a casino in Auckland, New Zealand. Although Bill Harrah of Reno was instrumental in ushering in the modern-day gaming entertainment industry, its real growth would occur in Las Vegas.

LAS VEGAS: ADULT DISNEY WORLD

Nevada is gambling; and the undisputed gambling capital of the world is Las Vegas. The Mouse transformed Orlando, Florida, into the entertainment center east of the Mississippi, and gambling changed the little town in the middle of the desert into the adult entertainment center west of the Mississippi—gambling's Disney World.

During the 1950s, Las Vegas moved from a stopover in the desert to a real destination point and entertainment center. The most famous entertainers of that decade appeared in the shows and lounges—Edgar Bergen and Charlie McCarthy, Red Skelton, Anna Maria Alberghetti, Ray Bolger, Liberace, Maurice Chevalier, Cab Calloway, Sophie Tucker, Lionel Hampton. Then, as now, the showroom was a major draw for the casinos. There was nothing to compare to the extravagance and glitz of a Las Vegas show. The Desert Inn Tournament of Golfers drew the best professional golfers and celebrity golfers like Bing Crosby, Bob Hope, and Walter Winchell. The Hacienda Hotel/Casino even presented itself as a "family resort" and offered miniature golf and family-oriented shows (Moe, 1996, 76).

In 1966, Caesar's Palace became the first themed (Imperial Rome), self-contained, all-recreation entertainment resort in Las Vegas. In the late 1970s and early 1980s Las Vegas became a national/worldwide entertainment center with the influx of publicly traded stock investment monies, college-educated casino managers, and family-oriented casino construction. In the leisure-time pursuits–oriented society of the period, gambling was seen by more and more Americans as one more form of entertainment to be engaged in with discretionary monies. Then, Steve Wynn, chairman of Mirage Resorts, and his new casino erupted on the Las Vegas Strip.

On November 22, 1989, Steve Wynn opened The Mirage, the first new

Las Vegas casino in 15 years. The new 87-acre, $690 million megaresort "family entertainment center" with a rainforest, an erupting volcano in front, white tigers in a glassed-in habitat, and sharks swimming by the front desk was extravagant even by Las Vegas standards. The five dolphins swimming in their $14 million, 1.5 million-gallon lagoon came the next year. Wynn said that The Mirage was a resort hotel that included a casino, not a casino that included a hotel. Steve Wynn, like Meyer Lansky, learned the truth about casino gambling at a young age: "But one thing my father's gambling [his father was a compulsive gambler] did was that it showed me at a very early age that if you wanted to make money in a casino, the answer was to own one" (Demaris, 1986, 227).

Five months after The Mirage opened, Circus Circus opened the largest casino hotel to date. The 4,000-room, $290 million Excalibur, with a storybook castle with a medieval theme, had live jousting and medieval feasts. Las Vegas now had "must see" attractions comparable to Orlando. The adult Disney World flavor of Las Vegas had begun. This "new" Las Vegas was more than gambling. It was luxury, families, and themed attractions.

Melissa Cook (1998) states that the construction of The Mirage and the Excalibur was the first wave in the creation of the "new" Las Vegas. The second wave occurred in 1993 when the megaresorts the Luxor (Egyptian land of the pharaohs theme), Treasure Island (pirate theme complete with a pirate battle every 90 minutes in a moat in front), and the 5,000-room MGM Grand (Wizard of Oz theme) opened. The MGM Grand was the largest hotel in the world. The 2,000-room megaresort the Manhattan, themed New York–New York, complete with the Empire State Building and the Statute of Liberty, opened three years later to usher in the third wave. Cook predicts that the opening of Steve Wynn's $1.8 billion Bellagio is the fourth wave in the "new" Las Vegas of megaresorts and family-oriented entertainment centers.

The Bellagio, which opened on October 15, 1998, has 3,000 guest rooms, 150,000 square feet of gaming space, 10,000 square feet of meeting space, and a collection of retail shops and restaurants. The restaurants and retail shops include Olives, Le Cirque, Chanel, Giorgio, Armani, Tiffany, and Gucci, reflecting the move toward a total entertainment center. The new entertainment center has a 12-acre man-made lake (water is a major problem in the desert city of Las Vegas) complete with a water, light, and sound show. The entertainment/casino includes a gallery of fine art complete with a $300 million collection of nineteenth- and twentieth-century paintings. It will take a lot of players getting entertained in the casino to pay for this extravagance. Steve Wynn says that the Bellagio is an alternative to a weekend in Paris.

The new Las Vegas casinos are a "special kind of commercial gaming" that includes fantasy architecture, spectacular floor shows, inexpensive or free food and alcoholic beverages, and golf courses, swimming pools, tennis courts, and other outdoor activities (Christiansen and Brinkerhoff-Jacobs, 1997, 12). Las Vegas is "one vast and glorious movie set surrounded by a halo of neon" (Faragher, 1995, 5). Admittedly, all this glitz, glamour, and entertainment have one goal: to attract the visitors to the tables and machines. Mario Puzo (1977), an admitted degenerate gambler, stated the Basic Truth about Gambling over 20 years ago:

REMEMBER ALWAYS: The money to build that billion-dollar gambling plant came from *Losers*.

However, much, if not all, of the "new" Las Vegas entertainment image can be seen as a response to the geographic expansion of casino gambling to Atlantic City (1978). Nevada's, particularly Las Vegas's, monopoly on casino gambling was already at an end when The Mirage opened.

ATLANTIC CITY: GAMBLING ON THE BOARDWALK

Bye the sea, by the sea
By the beautiful sea,
You and me, you and me
Oh how happy we'll be

(Harry Carroll, 1912)

The first expansion of legalized casino gambling outside Nevada occurred in New Jersey. In 1976, New Jersey, in an effort to revitalize the decaying resort city of Atlantic City, legalized "Las Vegas–style" casino gambling. Years of population decreases, deteriorating facilities, and unemployment had reduced Atlantic City, the Queen of Resorts, to a South Bronx by the seashore populated by the poor (elderly and minorities). In 1960, Atlantic City had the second-highest percentage of people 65 or older in the country (Demaris, 1986). The once-great hotels were refuges for senior citizens. The famous Steel Pier visited by millions of tourists (including one of the authors as a child), had been closed for years. Legalized casino gambling was hailed as a "magic bullet" that would spur growth, lower unemployment, and restore the blighted resort city to its previous glory (Sternlieb and Hughes, 1983).

Casino gambling was added to the list of state-sanctioned (legalized) gambling: parimutuel betting, 1939; bingo and raffles by nonprofit groups for charitable purposes, 1953; amusement park and resort games of chance, 1959; and lottery, 1970. The new law restricted casino gambling to Atlantic City in spite of its reputation as one of the most corrupt cities in the nation (Sternlieb and Hughes, 1983). The city also had a long history of wide-open gambling during its heyday through the 1960s, often with organized crime and city officials working together. Demaris (1986) says that locating casino gambling in Mafia-infested and corrupt Atlantic City was "tantamount to dropping the chicken coop into the heart of fox country." Admittedly, this is an exaggeration; however, the city's history of corruption and the presence of organized crime would present unique problems for the state and the city.

Revenue monies from the casinos were earmarked for state-sponsored programs for the elderly and handicapped. Then-Governor Byrne said on the day the law was signed in Atlantic City, "Our efforts will not be deemed a success unless we carry out the constitutional mandate that the proceeds be used for senior citizens and the disabled. I've committed myself, over the next several months, to regional conferences with senior citizens and the disabled as to how the money should be spent in their behalf" (Demaris, 1986, 11). He finished his speech with a message to organized crime, "I've said it before and I will repeat it again to organized crime. Keep your filthy hands off Atlantic City! Keep the hell out of our state." The law he signed that day required all casinos to have at least 500 hotel rooms, 25,000 square feet of meeting space, and a 40,000-square-foot entertainment center. The hours of casino operation were limited to 18 hours daily and 20 hours on weekends.

The first Atlantic City casino, Resorts, owned by the Bahama's casino operator Resorts International, opened on May 28, 1978. Resorts International had been the largest contributor—20 percent of the total—to the Committee to Rebuild Atlantic City, the committee sponsoring the casino legislation campaign. The hotel Chalfonte-Haddon, where the casino was located, was the second largest contributor. Sixty percent of the contributors had Atlantic City addresses. Resorts International was also buying up land bordering the Boardwalk and spending money of its own in a media campaign during the campaign. They were also helping to draft the legislation authorizing casino gambling. The rush to open a casino in Atlantic City led the state to grant a temporary license to Resorts International. There was not sufficient time to complete the required licensing reviews and investigations. When it was revealed later that Resorts International had mob ties (Meyer Lansky and his Italian/American partners who had been forced out of Cuba by Fidel Castro), the hurried licensing became a source of embarrassment for the state's newly created regulatory agency.

The abandoned Boardwalk hotel the Chalfonte-Haddon, once the largest hotel in the world, was refurbished by Resorts International for $42 million. It wasn't long before it was demonstrated that there was a huge market for gambling in the Northeast. The total $77 million debt for the opening of the casino was repaid in 11 months. Resorts's success was unprecedented. Thousands stood in line for three or four hours, waiting for the casino to open. When it opened, gamblers stood 10 deep waiting for a table or machine. The first year's gross revenue was $224.6 million and a win of $62.8 million. Resorts International as a corporation doubled its net worth and total assets in one year. The State of New Jersey collected $18 million in taxes (Fenich, 1996, 72). Eight more casinos were built by the end of 1981.

Within two years of the first casino opening on the Boardwalk, an FBI sting called Abscam (Abdul Scam) revealed public official corruption in the granting of casino licenses. The FBI as part of a national investigation of public official corruption sent an undercover agent to New Jersey, posing as an emissary for an Arab sheik interested in building a casino in Atlantic City. The sting operation implicated Camden, New Jersey, Mayor Angelo Errichetti (also a state senator); U.S. Senator Harrison Williams, Jr.; Joseph Lordi, chairman of the Casino Control Commission; Kenneth MacDonald, vice chairman of the Casino Control Commission; seven congressmen; and Howard Criden, a Philadelphia lawyer with ties to Meyer Lansky (Demaris, 1986; Sternlieb and Hughes, 1983).

Mayor Errichetti told the sheik, on film and tape, that for $400,000 he could guarantee the casino license. The mayor bragged that he owned the vice chairman of the Casino Control Commission (MacDonald) and through him Lordi, the chairman. The mayor and Criden assured the FBI operatives that they would talk to Meyer Lansky and get his approval of the deal. Senator Harrison bragged that he had convinced Lordi to waive construction specifications that had saved a casino developer millions of dollars. He said he could do the same for the sheik because Lordi was "his man."

It is hard to distinguish the facts from the phoney name dropping and bragging about political muscle; however, when the videotapes were aired on national TV, scandal rocked New Jersey. The resulting scandal led to MacDonald's resignation from the Casino Control Board and changes in the board's composition from part-time to full-time appointments and a tightening of the regulations on commission members receiving perks from the casinos (Demaris, 1986). Lordi survived the scandal and was reappointed chairman of the reorganized Casino Control Commission. He later resigned before finishing his term.

The viewing public was left with the impression that political corruption was inevitable with casino gambling. The Abscam scandal slowed down the spread of casino gambling to other states. In fact, Abscam and political corruption associated with casino gambling reared its head in New York, the first state to consider casino gambling after the scandal. Dr. Gerald Lynch, the president of New York City's John Jay College of Criminal Justice, stated, "The thread of casino money influence was woven throughout the fabric of ABSCAM" (Dombrink and Thompson, 1990,

105). The Abscam scandal was also brought up in 1981 when Connecticut considered casino gambling.

The scandal did not slow down the growth of casino gambling in Atlantic City. Following the success of Resorts International, Atlantic City casino expansion was accelerated by high-yield (junk) bonds in the 1980s. Christiansen and Brinkerhoff-Jacobs (1997) state that the success of Resorts International brought the lucrative economics of the gaming industry to the attention of the investing public and provided the industry access to public equity markets. However, Atlantic City and its casinos have not matched the entertainment megaresorts of Las Vegas. Atlantic City is still the "other kid on the block" in comparison to Las Vegas. However, this may change in the future.

Steve Wynn, the Las Vegas dream maker, is set to make his second intrusion into the Atlantic City casino market. After several years of litigation funded primarily by Donald Trump and Hilton—the major casino owners in Atlantic City—to stop casino construction in the Brigantine Marina District (approximately one mile from the city), groundbreaking on an Atlantic City–Brigantine Connector has begun. The tunnel once built would result in the "second wave" of casino development in the Atlantic City area (Gros, 1999). Current plans call for building two megaresorts in the Marina District by the year 2002. This "second wave" of casino development will, in all probability, affect the casinos on the Boardwalk and Atlantic City.

At this time, there are 12 casinos in Atlantic City. Only 5 of these casinos have over 1,000 rooms: Bally's Park Place, 1,064 rooms; Caesars Atlantic City, 1,138 rooms; Tropicana Casino & Resort, 1,370 rooms; Trump Plaza Hotel and Casino, 1,331; and Trump Taj Mahal Casino Resort, 1,013 rooms (*American Casino Guide*, 1998). Atlantic City, at this time, has no family-oriented entertainment megaresorts. Available land, climate, building restrictions, and construction costs have worked against the construction of entertainment-oriented megaresorts. Future plans for construction would add 7,500 rooms in 2002: MGM Grand Atlantic City, 2,500 rooms; Mirage Atlantic City, 2,000 rooms; Circus Circus Atlantic City, 2,000 rooms; and Stardust Atlantic City, 1,000 rooms (Bear Stearns, 1998).

Atlantic City, for the most part, is pure-product gambling, with the overwhelming majority of its clientele being 50-plus "day-trippers" (funbuses and walk-ins). The day-trippers spend 3 or 4 hours in the casino, eat at the casino, and then go home. Nevertheless, Atlantic City's location in the densely populated mid-Atlantic metropolitan corridor provides for a large number of day-trippers. Philadelphia is 60 miles away; Newark and New York City are 100 miles away. When the first casinos opened in Atlantic City, there "were 50 million people who could leave their homes in the morning, spend the day at the casinos, and return home the same night" (Sternlieb and Hughes, 1983, 10). *International Gaming & Wagering Business* (*IGWB*) reports that in 1997 the 34.1 million visitors to Atlantic City stayed an average of 6.5 hours. The 30.4 million visitors to Las Vegas stayed an average of 3.5 days (1998, 14). Las Vegas's clientele are "overnighters"—out-of-towners who stay in the hotels. Hotels are in Atlantic City because the law requires them. There are few rooms available for overnight stay, and they are expensive. Las Vegas had 105,347 hotel rooms in 1997; Atlantic City had 11,316. The available Atlantic City hotel rooms are primarily for complimentary stay by "high rollers" or junkets. Las Vegas is a convention city; Atlantic City is not at this time. Furthermore, for the most part, social problems exacerbated by Las Vegas gambling are exported out of town; they are kept at home (or in the communities within driving distance) by Atlantic City.

Atlantic City's casino industry burst on the scene a little over 20 years ago, literally a gambling boomtown. On the other hand, Las Vegas's casino industry was the result of a slow-growth process that began almost 70 years ago. Atlantic City's accelerated growth has not been without its problems, many severe, because of its boomtown nature. Three million people visited Atlantic City in 1976. Nine years after the casinos opened, 30 million people a year were visiting Atlantic City. Most of these visitors were repeat visitors, some 20 or more times. Real estate taxes and tax assessments skyrocketed, forcing out most small businesses. The poor and elderly were evicted or burned out (arson or "Jewish lightning" as it came to be known) of their residences by slum landlords as land speculation increased. Crime doubled, tripled, and quadrupled in the first years after the casinos opened (see Table 5.2). The millions who visited Atlantic City were gamblers, not tourists. By 1985, almost 90 percent of the city's businesses had left, along with 8,000 inhabitants (Demaris, 1986).

Atlantic City's location in close proximity to major urban areas raises issues that must be addressed by the gambling industry and the nation. The 1976 Commission on the Review of the National Policy toward Gambling had cautioned that "legalization of casino gambling be restricted by the state to relatively isolated areas where the impact on surrounding populations can be minimized" (Commission on the Review, 1976, 102). The 1996 National Gambling Impact Study Commission's deputy executive director arrived at the same caution:

It may be that large cities with their relatively extensive and permanent criminal class, may experience higher rates of crime following the opening of a casino than would be the case with smaller towns and rural communities. (Seay, 1998)

Furthermore, the effect of pure-product gambling's appeal on Atlantic City's future development as legalized gambling, particularly casino and

Table 5.2
Atlantic City Crime Index Change, 1977–1981

Year	Crime Index	Number	Percent Change from Previous Year
1977	4,391	−298	−6.4
1978 (casino)	5,738	1,347	30.7
1979	7,010	1,272	22.2
1980	11,899	4,889	69.7
1981	12,594	695	5.8

Note: Crime Index (1983): The sum total of seven major offenses used to measure the extent, fluctuation, and distribution of crime in a geographic area. The seven crimes that made up the index at that time were murder, forcible rape, robbery, aggravated assault, burglary, larceny-theft, and motor vehicle theft.
Source: Adapted from Sternlieb and Hughes, 1983, 191, table 22.

machine gambling, expands in its market area, remains to be seen. We will return to these issues later.

CONCLUSION

Approximately 130 private sector companies conduct casino gaming somewhere in the world (Christiansen and Brinkerhoff-Jacobs, 1997, 29). Examples include Mirage Resorts, Inc.; MGM Grand Inc.; ITT Sheraton Caesars World Inc.; Circus Circus Enterprise Inc.; Hilton Hotels Corporation; Harrah's Entertainment Inc.; Hyatt Hotels International; Trump Hotels & Casino Resorts, Inc.; Sun International Hotels Ltd.; and Rank and President Casino Inc. Hilton, the world's largest casino operator, has casinos in Las Vegas, Atlantic City, and Mississippi.

The growth of the U.S. gambling industry has been phenomenal since publicly traded corporations entered the market. The industry forecast for the new millennium is further expansion and development. Bear Stearns (1998) reports that 29 casinos will be expanded or built in the United States in the years 1999, 2000, 2001, and 2002: 1999, 1 in Mississippi, 2 in Louisiana, 2 in Indiana, 1 in Colorado, 1 in Iowa, 5 in Nevada; 2000, 1 in Connecticut, 2 in Mississippi, 1 in New Jersey, and 5 in Nevada; 2001, 3 in Michigan (Detroit) and 1 in Nevada; and 2002, 4 in New Jersey.

Publicly traded corporations, more than any individual/s, regulatory agency, or law enforcement efforts, drove the mob out of casino gambling and changed the nature of the gambling/gaming industry. Socially sanctioned gamblers (speculative investors) now provide the monies for the construction and expansion of casino gambling. It would be a mistake to conclude that casino gambling is totally free of organized crime. Organized crime has been heavily involved in the construction and casino service businesses (garbage hauling, trucking, junket operations, laundry, limousine service, security personnel, vending machines, liquor, cigarettes, food service) and labor unions. Atlantic City mob boss Nicky Scarfo's construction company, Scarf, Inc., was involved in the construction of five of the first nine Atlantic City casinos. The sheer volume of cash money handled by casinos will always make them a target for organized crime. However, gambling regulatory agencies have attempted to reduce the presence of criminal elements in the service industries. New Jersey requires "[a]ny business doing regular or continuing business with a casino licensee to be licensed" (New Jersey Casino Control Commission, 1998). Since 1978, the New Jersey Casino Commission has prohibited over 1,500 enterprises from doing business with Atlantic City casinos. The business undergoes the same rigorous examination as the licensee. Publicly held corporations have lessened the threat of organized crime involvement in casinos and their operation (Albanese, 1997, 352–353). Organized crime does not appear to dominate the casino industry because of the SEC's extensive monitoring and accounting requirements, the exacting rules for corporate reporting, and the need to avoid negative publicity to avert falling stock prices. Gaming has moved from hands-on operators to boards of directors, with their attorneys, accountants, and corporate chief executive officers (CEOs). A Merrill Lynch vice president succinctly stated the investment market's new view of "the gaming industry" in 1978:

There can never be any guarantee that the industry has completely outgrown its tainted roots, but because of close scrutiny and regulation by various governmental agencies, and because of the need to rely on public capital for expansion, we believe that for most of the major companies in the industry this concern is no longer a primary consideration. (Vogel, 1978, 3–4)

The current National Gambling Impact Study Commission (NGISC) has not received any testimony concerning organized crime's connection to the gambling industry. Commission member Bill Bible, the former chairman of the Nevada Gaming Board, attributes this to the "integrity of the regulatory systems" put in place since the last national commission on gambling 25 years ago (*National Gaming Summary*, 1998). Doug Seay, the NGISC's senior policy director, takes the position that organized crime's "operation and ownership of casinos in Las Vegas and elsewhere is a thing of the past" (Seay, 1998, 177). The 1976 U.S. Commission on the Review of the National Policy toward Gambling arrived at the same conclusion. However, that commission has been criticized for underestimating and underplaying the importance of hidden ownership and organized crime in the Nevada gambling industry (Eadington, 1982, 62).

The gaming (casino gambling) industry originated in Nevada, matured in Las Vegas, and then moved eastward to Atlantic City. It has now spread throughout the nation, even to the heart of the southern Bible Belt. The Native Americans and the riverboats are responsible for the latter geographic expansion.

REFERENCES

Albanese, Jay S. (1997). "Predicting the Impact of Casino Gambling and Law Enforcement in Windsor, Ontario." In William R. Eadington and Judy A. Cornelius, eds., *Gambling: Public Policies and the Social Sciences*. Reno: Institute for the Study of Gambling and Commercial Gaming, University of Nevada, Reno.

American Casino Guide. (1998). Dania, Fla.: Casino Vacations.

Bear Stearns Equity Research. (1998). *1998 Global Gaming Almanac*. New York: Bear Stearns & Co.

Christiansen, Eugene, and Julie Brinkerhoff-Jacobs. (1997). "The Relationship of Gaming to Entertainment." In William R. Eadington and Judy A. Cornelius, eds., *Gambling: Public Policies and the Social Sciences*. Reno: Institute for the Study of Gambling and Commercial Gaming, University of Nevada, Reno.

Commission on the Review of the National Policy toward Gambling. (1976). *Gambling in America*. Washington, D.C.: GPO.

Cook, Melissa. (1998). "The 10 Year Century." *Casino Player* (September): 44–46.

Demaris, Ovid. (1986). *The Boardwalk Jungle*. New York: Bantam Books.

Dombrink, John, and William N. Thompson. (1990). *The Last Resort: Success and Failure in Campaigns for Casinos*. Reno: University of Nevada Press.

Eadington, William R. (1982). "The Evolution of Corporate Gaming in Nevada." In Kathryn Hashimoto and Sheryl F. Kline (1996), *Casino Management for the 90's*. Dubuque, Iowa: Kendall/Hunt.

Faragher, Scott. (1995). *The Complete Guide to Riverboat Gambling*. New York: Citadel Press.

Farrell, Ronald A., and Carole Case. (1995). *The Black Book and the Mob: The Untold Story of the Control of Nevada's Casinos*. Madison: University of Wisconsin Press.

Fenich, George. (1996). "A Historical Analysis of Casino Gambling in the United States." Conference Proceedings of the Second Annual Gaming Educators Conference, UNLV International Gaming Institute, May 13–15, 1996.

Gros, Roger. (1999). "Groundbreaking Progress." *Casino Journal* (January): 58–61.

International Gaming & Wagering Business (IGWB). (1998). "The United States Gross Annual Wager—1997" (August). Special supplement.

Lalli, Sergio. (1997). "Howard Hughes in Vegas." In Jack Sheehan, ed., *The Players: The Men Who Made Las Vegas*. Reno: University of Nevada Press.

Mandel, Leon. (1982). *William Fisk Harrah: The Life and Times of a Gambling Magnate*. Garden City, N.Y.: Doubleday.

Moe, Albert W. (1996). *Nevada's Golden Age of Gambling*. Reno: Nevada Collectables.

National Gaming Summary. (1998). November 16.

New Jersey Casino Control Commission. (1998). *Casino Gambling in New Jersey: A Report to the National Gambling Impact Study Commission*.

Puzo, Mario. (1977). *Inside Las Vegas*. New York: Grosset & Dunlap.

Reid, Ed, and Ovid Demaris. (1963). *The Green Felt Jungle*. New York: Trident Press.

Seay, Doug. (1998). *Testimony before the National Gambling Impact Study Commission*. September 10–11.

Skolnick, Jerome H. (1978). *House of Cards: Legalization and Control of Casino Gambling*. Boston: Little, Brown.

Smith, John L. (1995). *Running Scared: The Life and Treacherous Times of Las Vegas Casino King Steve Wynn*. New York: Barricade Books.

Sternlieb, George, and James W. Hughes. (1983). *The Atlantic City Gamble: A Twentieth Century Fund Report*. Cambridge, Mass.: Harvard University Press.

Vogel, Harold. (1978). *Gaming Industry Commentary: Prospects and Perspectives. Institutional Report, Securities Research Division, Merrill Lynch Pierce Fenner and Smith, Inc.*, August 9. Cited in John Dombrink and William N. Thompson (1990), *The Last Resort: Success and Failure in Campaigns for Casinos*. Reno: University of Nevada Press.

Chapter 6

The Dam Bursts: Indian Gambling and Gambling Vessels

The mobster Meyer Lansky praised the expansion of casino gambling to Atlantic City.

Today with the opening of casinos in Atlantic City, I think the American government has realized that you can't stop people from gambling. Now I read that Japanese businessmen are buying their way into hotels in Atlantic City, and that *Penthouse* magazine has acquired another hotel on the Boardwalk, and I can't help smiling. . . . It seems a long time ago that Bugsy [Siegel] and I were driving back and forth across the desert trying to get the first casino built. (Eisenberg et al., 1978, 229, in Dombrink and Thompson, 1990, 91)

Following the opening of Atlantic City's casinos until the late 1980s, 17 states considered casino gambling either by public referenda or legislative actions. All of these efforts to legalize casino gambling were defeated (see Table 6.1). Even Lansky, had he lived, would have been surprised by the geographic expansion of casino gambling that occurred when the bubble burst and casino gambling spread to Indian reservations and gambling vessels (riverboat and dockside). Since 1988, there are Indian casinos operating in 7 of the 17 states with earlier failed casino gambling initiatives. One of these, Connecticut's Pequot Indian's casino, Foxwoods, is the largest and most profitable in the world. Riverboat casinos operate in 2 of the states that rebuffed earlier efforts at casino gambling: Louisiana and Illinois. Indian gambling and the competition it spawned rapidly expanded casino gambling throughout the United States.

Table 6.1
Rejected Casino Efforts, 1978–1988

Arizona	Hawaii	New York
Arkansas	Illinois	Pennsylvania
California	Louisiana	Rhode Island
Colorado	Massachusetts	Texas
Connecticut	Michigan	Washington
Florida (2)	New Hampshire	

THE RED MAN ENTERS

The Native Americans after removal, by purchase or force, from their lands were moved to reservations where they were considered outcast members of sovereign alien nations. Historically, reservation living for Native Americans, as wards of the federal government, can best be described as extreme poverty marked by low incomes, unemployment, poor education, inferior housing, and high incidences of suicides, alcoholism, and drug abuse. The reservations, on lands the white man did not want, were cut off from the outside societies, except for government employees and occasional tourists. The isolation and poverty have changed on many reservations with Indian gambling.

The proliferation of gambling on Indian lands has been called the Red Man's revenge, the return of the buffalo, a godsend, an economic boon, and the most disastrous event since the arrival of the U.S. Calvary on Indian lands. Support for these tags can be found in the voluminous literature written on Indian gambling as well as the multiple lawsuits filed since 1988. Donald Trump, echoing the sentiment of many states, sued the federal government for supposedly giving the Indians a "free ride" and special gambling regulatory considerations. His argument had some merit, but his lawsuit was unsuccessful. However, one fact stands out: Indian gambling, up to 1996, was the fastest-growing segment of the gambling industry.

In 1997, Bear Stearns, the Wall Street investment banking firm, provided data on 115 federally recognized tribes operating what are known as Class III (house-banked) gambling casinos in 10 states (Bear Stearns, 1998, 338; see Table 6.2). (The classification system of Indian gambling will be discussed later.) The Bear Stearns analysis does not include all Indian casinos. For example, Mississippi's Silver Star Hotel & Casino operated by the Choctaw Indians in Philadelphia, Mississippi, is not listed in the Bear Stearns analysis. Silver Star Hotel/Casino, an atypical Indian casino, is an opulent gambling facility offering slots, video gam-

Table 6.2
Tribal Casinos: Bear Stearns 1998 Analysis of Regulatory Issues

State	No.	Gaming Restrictions	Other
Connecticut	2	None.	Slot revenue taxed at 25%; no tax levied on table game revenue.
Arizona	16	Tribal casinos have table games, but reel slots, video poker, and video keno are allowed.	Number and size of casino each tribe is permitted to operate are dependent upon size of tribe.
California	30+	Class III compacts in existence limited to offtrack wagering.	Predominant operation of "gray area" gaming devices by tribes operating casinos without negotiated Class III compacts.
New Mexico	11	Full range of casino gaming permitted, with the exception of reel slots.	Current law requires casinos to contribute 16% of profits to the state; however, the law is being contested.
Kansas	3	None.	
North Carolina	1	Games restricted to video poker, video blackjack, and video craps.	
Washington	18	Compacts limit casinos to table games only; no electronic devices of any kind are permitted.	Six tribal casinos in eastern Washington operate casinos with slot machines without compacts.
Minnesota	16	Casinos can offer video machines and blackjack but no traditional reel slots or other table games.	Compacts have no expiration date and do not require tax payments to the state.
Wisconsin	15	tribal casinos offer slots, video poker, and blackjack. No other table games are permitted.	Existing compacts begin expiring this year and are up for renegotiation.
New York	1*	None.	No taxes are levied.

* One pending.
Source: Bear Stearns, 1998, 339.

bling machines, and table games. The "Las Vegas style" Silver Star has several restaurants, a showroom, and two golf courses and took in $200 million in 1998 (*National Gaming Summary*, 1999, 7).

Fifteen of the Indian casinos examined by the Bear Stearns report are managed by nontribe public corporations. Nontribe entities can manage Indian casinos; however, they are forbidden by federal law from owning the casinos. Casino management by nontribe corporations has been costly to the tribes. Some corporations have charged up to 40 percent of the gross revenues as management fees.

The 1997 handle for Indian casinos (Class III) was over $77 billion, a 22.2 percent increase over 1996 (*IGWB*, 1998, 3). They had a gross gambling revenue of $5,779 million in 1997, representing 3 percent of the total casino market. The total gambling market share for Indian gambling, all classes, was 13.12 percent for the same year. Indian gambling is the seventh largest employer in Minnesota.

In spite of its success, gambling has not been embraced by all Native Americans. Less than one-third of the tribes operate gambling operations. Many members of the Cherokee Nation do not participate in gambling operations because of religious and moral objections. The Navajo and Hopi of Arizona voted not to allow gambling on their reservations. The internal dispute over gambling led to murder and bloodshed on the St. Regis Mohawk reservation in New York and the Cattaraugus Indian reservation (Seneca) in the same state (Davis and Otterstrom, 1996).

The principal opposition to Indian gambling has come from state governments (loss of sovereignty), the gambling industry (loss of revenue), and Nevada and New Jersey (competition). Nevada is particularly vulnerable to competition from Indian gambling.

If one state ever had the capacity to destroy the economy of another state, it would be California. The victim would be Nevada. The weapon would be legalized gambling. Nevada's economy is essentially a one-product economy [gambling]. Tourism and gambling account for approximately one-half of the income of the people and one-half of the governments of the state. Californians provide a substantial share of the dollars that flow into the Nevada economy. [Estimates range from 50 to 80 percent.].... The legalization of casino gambling by the state of California could doom Nevada to economic oblivion comparable to that faced by the state in the 1880s and 1890s when silver mining died out. (Dombrink and Thompson, 1990, 162)

International Gaming & Wagering Business shares this view.

If Native Americans in California win their initiative to keep Class III games, at least one-third of the $1.5 billion Californians currently gamble in Nevada would stay in the Golden State. (*IGWB*, 1998, 26)

In spite of a large infusion of Nevada casino money (Mirage Resorts Inc., $9.5 million; Hilton Corp., $6.5 million; Circus Circus Enterprises, $6.5 million) to the opponents, the initiative passed in the November 3, 1998, election (Yes, 62.6 percent; No, 37.4 percent). No doubt, there will be numerous court challenges. The California Supreme Court in December 1998 blocked the implementation of the initiative until they had time to study the constitutional questions raised by its opponent (*National Gaming Summary*, 1998b).

The phenomenal success of Indian gambling is the result of two events: the 1987 U.S. Supreme Court decision *California v. Cabazon Band of Mission Indians* and the Indian Gaming Regulatory Act (IGRA) passed by Congress in 1988. These two events opened the floodgates for the geographic expansion of legalized casino gambling in the United States.

Of particular interest is that this expansion has been largely the movement of casino gambling into rural areas and has been of a pure-product nature (gambling). Eighty-five percent of the reservations are located west of the Mississippi River; only six states—Connecticut, Florida, Maine, Mississippi, New York, and Wisconsin—east of the Mississippi River have more than one reservation within their borders. Indian casinos are concentrated in several regions: the upper Midwest (the Dakotas, Minnesota, and Wisconsin), the Pacific Coast (California, Oregon, and Washington), and the Southwest (Arizona and New Mexico) (Davis and Otterstrom, 1996, 57). As mentioned earlier, few Indian casinos are "Las Vegas style" entertainment centers. They are not destination resorts for vacationing families. The visitors to Indian high-stakes bingo halls and casinos are mainly "day-trippers," often bus loads of non-Indian gamblers, similar to what takes place in Atlantic City.

California's Little Big Horn: *California v. Cabazon*

The antecedent for the *Cabazon* decision began with high-stakes bingo in Florida. In the late 1970s, Florida had a $100 limit on charitable bingo prizes. Facing competition from other bingo halls, the Seminole Indians began offering high-stakes bingo with $10,000 prizes in 1979. Florida, in an attempt to bring the Seminoles in line with state law, challenged the Indians in court. The U.S. Fifth Circuit Court of Appeals, using the criminal-prohibitory and civil-regulatory test, ruled that Florida could ban Indian bingo by banning it statewide, but they could not regulate bingo on Indian reservations. The court said that the regulation of Indian activities was the jurisdiction of the federal government, not the states (*Seminole Tribe of Florida v. Butterworth* 658 F. 2d 310). The court held that state bingo regulations did not apply to Indian operations without their consent.

After the decision, over 100 tribes throughout the United States began offering high-stakes bingo, angering many state governments. From their experiences with the profitability of high-stakes bingo, some tribes developed a desire to move into other forms of gambling. The Pequot Indian's (Foxwood Casino in Ledyard, Connecticut) gambling efforts began as a high-stakes bingo parlor in 1986. The first year they made $2.6 million in bingo profits.

The Cabazon Band of Mission Indians started offering bingo prizes more than 200 times higher than the California limit. California sued in federal court, claiming that the state had the authority to enforce California law on Indian lands. The resulting litigation went all the way to the United States Supreme Court. In *California v. Cabazon*, the Supreme Court considered the same issue, criminal-prohibitory or civil-regulatory, presented in the *Seminole v. Butterworth* case. The Court said that the criminal-prohibitory or civil-regulatory test was clear. Since California permitted other forms of gambling (state lottery, horse racing, charitable bingo, card rooms), the state intended to regulate, not prohibit, gambling. State regulatory laws did not apply on Indian lands. Therefore, the state could not regulate gambling on Indian lands without their permission. The Supreme Court's decision said that federally recognized tribes were sovereign nations with the right to govern themselves, and the tribes could offer any form of gambling already offered in the states where they were located. The Court also stated that if Congress wanted to limit Indian gambling, they could do so through legislation. Their decision had unforeseen consequences. Fourteen states allowed charities to have limited "Las Vegas" nights. The door was open for Indians in these states to open casinos. The states, now without the authority to regulate Indian gambling or to collect taxes from it, turned to Congress for help.

Indian Gaming Regulatory Act, 1988

The stated purpose of the Indian Gaming Regulatory Act was to regulate the operation of Indian gaming as a means to promote tribal economic development, self-sufficiency, and strong tribal governments. The act was intended to be a compromise between the states and the Indian tribes within their borders. When Congress passed the Indian Gaming Act, they had the following goals in mind (Eade and Eade, 1997, 17):

GOAL 1. To provide a legal and statutory foundation for sovereign tribes to be involved in gambling/gaming.

Congress formally recognized that gambling could be an effective tool for economic development on Indian reservations.

GOAL 2. To ensure that the tribes would be the beneficiaries of gambling/gam-
ing revenues and ensure their right to sole ownership of gambling/
gaming operations.

The IGRA dictates that tribes and not individual members can have
gambling operations. Indian gambling is tribe-sponsored gambling, just
as lotteries are state-sponsored gambling. Decisions about profits must
be made by the tribes. Decisions about profits from privately owned
casinos are made by the individuals or corporations that own them.
However, IGRA rules said that an outside company that invested in
reservation casinos could receive up to 40 percent of its profits for seven
years.

The act established the National Indian Gaming Commission (NIGC)
to regulate and oversee tribal gaming operations. Two of the NIGC's
responsibilities were to assess the fairness of casino management contracts and judge the suitability of casino managers. The NIGC had to
give final approval to all Indian casino management contracts.

GOAL 3. To provide a framework to prevent organized crime's potential infiltration into tribal gambling/gaming.

Congress was fearful that organized crime would move on to the reservations. They hoped that the IGRA and the National Indian Gaming
Commission would prevent this. In spite of unsubstantiated claims that
organized crime has moved into Indian gambling, the act appears to
have been successful in preventing this.

GOAL 4. To establish a framework for state-negotiated compacts that define the
types of games played, payoff percentages, internal control procedures,
and other enforcement concerns.

The states lobbied extensively for IGRA and the compacting provisions. A *compact* is an agreement between sovereigns similar to a treaty.
The states argued that compacts were a way for the states to have some
control over Indian gambling, particularly casino-style gambling. Under
the act, a tribe would advise the state of their intentions to offer casino
gambling on Indian lands and enter into a compact with the state. The
tribe and the state would then negotiate the terms of the compact (contract). The intent of the act was to force the two parties to come to some
compromise between opposing views: Tribes—the states have no regulatory power on Indian lands; states—all state and local laws should
apply on Indian lands. Since 1990, 147 tribes have entered into 158 compacts with 24 states (www.legislate.com/ftdir/tribes1.htm).

The compacts may include the laws (criminal and civil) and regulations covering the gambling activity; the allocations of criminal jurisdictions between the state and the tribe for the enforcement of such laws and regulations; the state's revenue assessment necessary to defray the regulation costs; taxation by the tribe in amounts comparable to amounts assessed by the state on similar gambling activities; remedies for breach of contract; and the standards for the licensing, operation, and maintenance of the gambling facility. Many tribes have complained the compact areas infringe on their sovereignty and right to self-govern.

As often happens, when the federal government gets involved, things don't work out as planned. Often, the states have been uncooperative, feeling that IGRA infringes on states' rights and further demonstrates "big brother's" (federal government) assumption of powers over local issues. The IGRA created a battleground where three distinct sovereigns—federal, state, and tribal communities—renewed their centuries-old conflict.

The states have been particularly incensed over the section of the act that allows the tribes to have any forms of gambling when the state permits "such gaming for any purpose by any organization, or entity" (Kelly, 1997, 216). This has been used by the tribes to introduce casinos and slot machines into states where they were illegal. The tribes have been able to offer casino-banked games when the states have allowed charity "Las Vegas" nights of low-stakes roulette and blackjack. The Pequots were able to open up a casino in Connecticut because the state allowed "Monte Carlo Nights" for nonprofit organizations. After negotiations between the state and the tribes broke down, a federal court imposed a compact on Connecticut.

The act also created another problem for the states: Negotiate in good faith or be sued. Congress, in IGRA, gave the Indians the right to sue the states in federal court if the states did not negotiate in "good faith" with the tribes. If the courts found against the states, the court could order negotiations, which could include a court-appointed monitor. If the states refused the recommendations of the mediator, the secretary of the interior could impose a compact on the state consistent with the law and the mediator's recommendations. Numerous lawsuits resulted.

GOAL 5. To establish regulatory tiers based on the type of gambling/gaming offered.

The act created three classes of Indian gambling.

Class I. Social games solely for prizes of minimal value or traditional forms of Indian gambling engaged in as part of tribal ceremonies or celebrations.

Class I gambling is regulated solely by the tribes.

Class II. All forms of bingo and other games similar to bingo, such as pull tabs and punch boards, provided that they are played in the same location as bingo games. Nonbanking card games are also included.

Class II gambling/gaming is permitted on tribal lands if (1) the tribal lands are in a state that permits these forms of gambling "for any purpose" by any person, organization, or entity, and (2) the activity is approved by the Indian tribe's governing body and the chairman of the National Indian Gaming Commission (regulatory body created by IGRA). Class II gambling is regulated solely by the tribes if they meet the conditions set forth in the Indian Gaming Regulatory Act.

Class III. Includes all forms of gambling that are not Class I or II, including slots, casino card games, banked card games, horse and dog racing, parimutuel wagering, and jai-alai.

Class III gambling can be conducted on tribal lands if the conditions of Class II gambling are met and there is a tribal-state compact in existence. Class III gambling is regulated by the tribes, by the National Indian Gaming Commission, and by compact, the state. The following are examples of Authorized Class III games in the Michigan and New Mexico compacts:

MICHIGAN

Section 3: Authorized Class III Games.

A. The Tribe may lawfully conduct the following Class III games on Indian lands:

1. Craps and related dice games;
2. Wheel games, including "Big Wheel" and related games;
3. Roulette;
4. Banking card games that are not otherwise treated as Class II gaming in Michigan pursuant to 25 U.S.C. & 2703 (7) (C) and nonbanking card games played by any Michigan tribe on or before May 1, 1988;
5. Electronic games of chance featuring coin drop and payout as well as printed tabulations, whereby the software of the device predetermines the presence or lack of a winning combination and payout. Electronic games of chance are defined as a microprocessor-controlled electronic device that allows a player to play a game of chance, which may be affected by an element of skill (rules out slot machines), activated by the insertion of a coin or currency, or by the use of a credit card, and awards game credits, cash, tokens, or replays, or a written statement of the player's accumulated credits, which written are redeemable for cash; and
6. Keno

NEW MEXICO

Authorized Class III Gaming:

The Tribe may conduct, only on Indian Lands, subject to all the terms and conditions of this Compact, any and all forms of casino-style gaming, including but not limited to slot machines and other forms of electronic gaming devices; all forms of poker, blackjack and other casino-style card games, both banked and unbanked; roulette; craps; keno; Wheel of Fortune; Pai Gow; and other games played in casino settings; and any form of a lottery.

The compacts give states limited regulatory power over Indian gambling. However, the federal government through the National Indian Gaming Commission and agencies such as the U.S. Department of Justice, the FBI, the Internal Revenue Service (IRS), and the Bureau of Indian Affairs has the primary responsibility for government-to-government relations with sovereign Indian nations.

According to the National Indian Gaming Commission, there are 186 tribes operating 276 gambling operations of all classes (Class I, II, and III) with compacts in 28 states (www.legislate.com/xp/p-spec). Seventy of the gambling operations are Class III casinos, 68 are Class II high-stakes bingo parlors, and the remainder are a combination of Class II and Class III operations.

GOAL 6. To ensure that tribal gambling/gaming is fair and reasonable for both the tribes and the customers.

The IGRA was an attempt by Congress to set up a system of tribal-state cooperation that would protect state and Indian rights. It was an attempt to find a middle ground between two competing views: Indians—the states have no right to interfere with gambling activities on tribal lands; states—state and local gambling laws apply on Indian lands.

The Future of Indian Gambling

In 1991, the Seminole Tribe of Florida sued the state and its governor for refusing to enter into a tribal-state compact for Class III gambling, including slot machines, which were illegal in Florida. Florida agreed to negotiate poker and similar games allowed under state law. The state balked at negotiating gambling machines and any other forms of casino-style gambling forbidden by state law. As stated earlier, under the IGRA, Congress granted the tribes the right to sue in federal courts if the states did not negotiate in "good faith" with the tribes. Florida asked the federal district court to dismiss the suit as violating the state's sovereign immunity granted by the Constitution. The district court dismissed the state's request. However, the Eleventh Circuit Court of Appeals reversed the district court, holding that the Eleventh Amendment of the Constitution barred the Seminoles from suing the state.

Eleventh Amendment: The Judicial power of the United States shall not be construed to extend to any suit in law or equity, commenced or prosecuted against one of the United States by Citizens of another State, or by Citizens or Subjects of any Foreign State.

In 1996, the U.S. Supreme Court held: "Notwithstanding Congress' clear intent to abrogate the State's sovereign immunity, the Indian Commerce Clause does not grant Congress that power, and therefore Section 2710(d)(7) cannot grant jurisdiction over a State that does not consent to be sued" (*Seminole Tribe v. Florida et al.*). The decison did not end the controversy. Still unsettled is whether the secretary of the interior and Congress can authorize Class III gambling and prescribe regulations when the states refuse to negotiate a compact. The Senate, in March 1998, barred Interior Secretary Bruce Babbitt from enforcing procedures that would impose a gaming compact on the states until the issue was resolved (*National Gaming Summary*, 1998a). Nevertheless, some states and tribes have still entered into compacts. Fourteen tribal-state compacts have been approved since 1996, resulting in 10 new Indian gambling facilities. The decision and Congress's reluctance to move on reform of the Indian Gaming Regulatory Act have slowed the spread of Indian gambling. Whether or not it will accelerate again in the future remains to be seen. However, one issue is clear: "Indian gambling has evolved from high-stakes bingo at a few reservations to the potential for Las Vegas style casinos all over the United States that generate billions of dollars in revenue" (Flatt, 1998).

Unresolved Issues

The Indians' claim that their gambling is the most regulated form of legal gambling is not supported by the facts. No single body has complete authority for the regulation of Indian gambling. The states have a role in the regulation of Indian gambling based on tribal-state compacts. However, the primary regulation efforts rest with the National Indian Gaming Commission. The NIGC has only been in operation for the last five years and has a staff of 40 employees with a budget of $5 million in 1998. The Arizona Department of Gaming alone has 65 full-time employees and an annual budget of $4.5 million.

Ten years after the passage of IGRA, a bill has been introduced into Congress to strengthen Indian gambling regulation. The bill—The Proposed Indian Gaming Regulatory Act of 1998—would "promulgate minimum standards relating to background investigations, internal control systems, and licensing standards." The Department of the Interior states that such minimum standards would "help address concerns relating to preventing infiltrations of organized crime and other corrupting influences on Indian gaming." The cynical might say, "Well! It's about time. Every state that has legalized any form of gambling has promulgated these minimum standards prior to issuing licenses."

States are also not allowed to take criminal action against Indian tribes that are operating gambling activities without a compact or in violation of a compact. The federal government has jurisdiction in these matters, and it often has been reluctant to act. This has been a real issue in California where at least 39 tribes have engaged in uncompacted and illegal (according to California) gambling activities.

Labor relations between Indian employers and non-Indian employees is another issue that must be resolved in the future. Many tribes claim that their employees are exempt from federal and state labor laws. However, employees pay federal and state taxes. In Connecticut, the Pequots (Foxwoods Casino) say that their employees are not covered by state and federal labor laws; however, the Mohegans (Mohegan Sun) say their employees are. The Hotel Employees and Restaurant Employees International Union is fighting the results of the California Proposition 5 vote because it has no provisions for collective bargaining by tribal casino employees.

ROLL 'EM ON THE RIVER: RETURN OF THE RIVERBOATS?

One can argue that the return of riverboat gambling was a reaction to IGRA and Indian gambling (Faragher, 1995). It is more than coincidence that Iowa, with three Indian casinos, became the first state to legalize riverboat gambling in 1989, one year after the passage of IGRA. A domino effect was created as several other states followed Iowa's lead. Illinois and Mississippi legalized riverboat gambling in 1990, with Louisiana and Missouri following in 1991. The Indiana legislature's override of the governor's veto in 1993 made that state the sixth to legalize riverboat gambling. Riverboat gambling is the primary means for the spread of legalized gambling into the Midwest.

Riverboats conjure up an image of legendary flat-bottomed "sternwheelers" and "sidewheelers" leisurely meandering down the Mighty Mississippi, loaded with gleeful travelers enjoying lavish entertainment, dancing, and fine dining. The travelers interrupt their conversations and sipping of mint juleps and mimosas to try their luck at the tables. That image is a will-o'-the-wisp "Gone with the Wind" seen only in old movies and on the History Channel. Furthermore, riverboat gambling is a misnomer, a term not appropriate to reality. Depending on state law, the modern riverboat may be a lavish converted motorless barge secured to pilings that never leaves the dock, a refurbished cruise vessel forever dockside, or a riverboat that cannot permit gambling dockside; a few are even riverboat replicas. The latter are seaworthy, meeting all Coast Guard regulations; others never sailed and never will. We prefer the term *gambling vessels* to describe both riverboat and dockside gambling.

Iowa

In 1989, after a failed attempt in 1987, both houses of the Iowa legislature (by one vote) legalized riverboat gambling. Iowa became the first state to legalize riverboat gambling. The first riverboat opened on April Fool's Day in 1991 (*American Casino Guide*, 1998). The original intent of the legislation was to deemphasize gambling and emphasize the excursionary, historical, and tourism aspects of riverboat gambling (Delva, 1995). The boats were to resemble, as close as possible, Iowa riverboat's history and have a section where Iowa-made arts, crafts, and gifts could be sold. When the boats first opened, they had a $5 per wager bet limit and a maximum loss of $200 a person. The Iowa legislature thought that such restrictions would minimize the negative effects often associated with gambling. The historical theme and the bet and loss limits were an attempt to "draw a line in the sand between riverboat gambling (a tourist attraction for families from as far away as Chicago, Milwaukee and Minneapolis) and casinos (magnets for mobsters, loan sharks, hookers and high-rolling drunks)" (Guskind, 1991, 90).

The loss limit was enforced by a tear-off voucher system (Faragher, 1995). Each passenger was given a sheet with 10 tear-off vouchers totaling $200. The player presented the voucher to the casino cashier and received chips or slot tokens. Once the $200 was lost, the gambler was finished; it was against the law to share vouchers, even between spouses. This system lasted until 1994, when riverboat competition from Illinois and Mississippi forced its removal. Several of the original Iowa riverboats pulled up their anchors and paddled to Illinois and Mississippi where the rules were less stringent.

The first gambling boats had to "grow the market," that is, create new gamblers as clientele. The midwesterners were not casino gamblers, few had traveled to Las Vegas, and most were unfamiliar with the casino table games (Thompson and Comeau, 1992, 247). At the time, many midwesterners considered gambling to be a "sin." Therefore, the riverboat managers had to, within the law, modify many games and award special prizes. The roulette rules were interpreted to allow a vertical wheel of fortune, and blackjack rules were modified to include an even money over and under 13 on the first two cards (Thompson and Comeau, 1992,

246). It was not long before the new gamblers were returning huge revenues to the riverboat owners.

The 11 seaworthy Iowa riverboats operate on the Mississippi and Missouri Rivers. By law, gambling was only allowed while the boats were cruising; however, because of the Iowa weather conditions, dockside gambling was permitted from November 1 through March 31. The 1994 legislative changes also allow the boats to be open 24 hours a day with only one daily 2-hour cruise required, clearly more time gambling while dockside.

The largest riverboat, the *Lady Luck Casino Bettendorf* at Bettendorf, Iowa, is a 2,500-passenger old-fashioned paddle wheeler on the Mississippi River. The boat cruises daily from 7:30 A.M. to 9:30 P.M., Monday through Friday. The rest of the time it is dockside and open 24 hours a day (*American Casino Guide*, 1998, 184).

Illinois

Illinois, suffering from the 1980s economic declines in manufacturing, mining, and agriculture, turned to riverboat gambling as a source to create jobs and generate revenues (Truitt, 1997). The success of the Iowa riverboats, especially those across the Mississippi River from Chicago, played a significant part in Illinois's decision to legalize riverboat gambling. The "foreigners" from Illinois were stimulating the economy of Iowa. Riverboats by their very nature, located on the rivers that form the boundaries between states, create competition for revenues between states. "Keep the money at home" campaigns are powerful arguments in gambling initiatives, especially when accompanied by a financial crisis. The riverboat gambling act would also deposit the taxes and fees (after deducting administrative and law enforcement costs) into an Education Assistance Fund, another persuasive argument in gambling initiatives.

Illinois legalized riverboat gambling in 1990 (Illinois Riverboat Gambling Act of 1990) and trumped Iowa by allowing unlimited bets and no loss limits. The law had the desired effect, as several of the Iowa boats moved over to the Illinois side of the Mississippi River. The act allowed riverboats to operate on any navigable river within the state or one that served as it boundary. The act did prohibit riverboat gambling within a county having a population in excess of 3 million (Truitt, 1997). This, in effect, prohibited riverboat gambling in Chicago and the suburban Cook County municipalities.

There are 10 licenses authorized for the entire state, with each license allowed to have two boats. In 1998, there were nine riverboats operating (*American Casino Guide*, 1998). The maximum gambling time on most boats is three hours—a two-hour cruise and a half hour before loading and after docking. If the weather prevents sailing, gambling is conducted dockside. The gambling tax was a flat 20 percent; however, as of January 1998, Illinois taxes its riverboats' revenues on a range of 15 to 35 percent, depending on monies taken in. The tax revenues go to public education.

Mississippi: Dockside Casinos

Mississippi legalized dockside gambling in 1990. However, Mississippi has a long history of illegal casino gambling. In the 1960s, illegal, but wide-open, casinos were operated by what became known as the "Dixie Mafia." Biloxi, Mississippi, which has more casinos and casino gambling space than Atlantic City, has a long history of public official corruption and illegal gambling that would rival, or surpass, that of Atlantic City (Humes, 1997).

House Bill 2 in the 1990 Special Legislative Session of the Mississippi legislature legalized dockside casino gambling. Casinos were limited to the waters along the coast (including the Bay of St. Louis and the Back Bay of Biloxi), along the Mississippi River, and in navigable waters that border the river. Since that time the Mississippi gambling industry has grown phenomenally.

Mississippi is the second largest gaming jurisdiction in the United States with 1.3 million square feet of gaming space, 33,876 slot machines, and 1,370 table games. The MGC [Mississippi Gaming Commission] regulated 29 casinos with over 30,000 employees during FY 1997. The state realized a total revenue of $231,687,575 with $154,458,383 dedicated to the general fund and $77,229,192 directed towards the local governments in the cities and counties where there are legal gaming operations. This is a 9% increase over the previous year. (Mississippi Gaming Commission Annual Report, 1998)

Calling Mississippi's casinos "riverboats," as is popular in the literature, is a humorous fiction to those who have visited the Mississippi casinos. The law does not require them to be seaworthy or look like boats; however, they must be dockside floating vessels. They are prohibited by law from leaving the docks. Although some are converted vessels (The Copa Casino in Gulfport is a converted 1,500-passenger cruise ship.), most are converted barges. The barges are a foundation for the multistoried casinos built on them. The hotels, restaurants, and other supporting facilities are located on land. Several of the casinos located in Tunica (called the "Ethiopia of the United States" by Jesse Jackson before the advent of legalized gambling) and Robinsonville, Mississippi, are converted grain and oil barges "which have been pulled out of the river and laid up on the land in predug pits" (Faragher, 1995, 32). The dockside casinos range in size from 14,300 square feet (Lady Luck

Casino Hotel-Natchez) to 140,000 square feet (Grand Casino Tunica), surpassing the gambling space of many casinos in Las Vegas and Atlantic City.

Louisiana

Louisiana, the fourth state to legalize riverboat gambling in 1991, allows a maximum of 15 boats with no more than 6 in any one parish. By law the boats must be newly constructed replicas of the old-fashioned turn-of-the-century riverboats, fully operational, a minimum of 120 feet long, and carry a minimum of 600 people (Faragher, 1995). The boats must be constructed in Louisiana. All the boats are required to sail, except those located on the Red River, which is too dangerous to navigate. However, a ship's captain can order any boat to remain dockside during inclement weather. Gambling is permitted when the boats are dockside under these conditions.

As of August 1997 there were 14 riverboats operating in 12 different locations (*American Casino Guide*, 1998). The largest, Casino Magic–Bossier City, is a 1,925-passenger paddle wheeler with 28,000 square feet of casino space. Since it is located on the Red River, the casino remains dockside 24 hours a day. Louisiana levies an 18.5 percent tax on riverboat revenues.

Missouri

Missouri, the fifth state to legalize riverboat gambling, amended the 1992 law legalizing riverboats in Missouri, leaving it up to the individual cities where the boats were located to decide if the boats cruised or remained dockside. However, all the boats located on the Missouri River must remain dockside because of navigational problems. The boats (cruising and dockside) conduct two-hour gambling sessions/cruises with scheduled starting and stopping times. According to the *American Casino Guide* (1998), there is a $500 loss limit on all sessions/cruises. The loss limit is enforced by a voucher system. Each passenger is issued a set of vouchers as he or she boards. The vouchers, along with the cash, must be exchanged for chips or slot tokens. No sharing of vouchers is allowed. If a passenger loses the $500 dollars, he or she is finished until the next session.

There are 15 gambling vessels in Missouri. Only 1 of the gambling vessels is actually a cruising paddle wheeler, the Casino Aztar at Caruthersville, Missouri (*American Casino Guide*, 1998). Similar to Mississippi, the remainder of Missouri's riverboats are converted vessels (boats and barges) that remain dockside. Nine of the "riverboats" are "boats in moats" located in man-made moats outside the mainstream of the Mississippi and Missouri Rivers. In 1997, the state supreme court ruled that games of chance (slot machines) were illegal. The issue was resolved through a statewide referendum in November 1998, allowing slots on the "boats in the moats."

Indiana

The Indiana legislature voted to override the governor's veto in 1993, making Indiana the sixth state to legalize riverboat gambling. The original statute approved 11 boats in the state: 5 on Lake Michigan, 1 on Lake Pakota, and 5 on the Ohio River (*American Casino Guide*, 1998). The boat on Lake Pakota was later disallowed when it was discovered that the U.S. Army Corps of Engineers owned the rights to Lake Pakota. The boats must cruise, except during bad weather, when dockside gambling is permitted. There are 7 riverboats operating, with more to be approved, up to 11.

CONCLUSION

The spread of legalized gambling lay dormant after the casinos opened in Atlantic City. No doubt Abscam and the social disaster that occurred in Atlantic City immediately after legalized gambling arrived affected its spread to other states. "Look what happened to Atlantic City" is still an anti-gambling slogan. The unanticipated spread of Indian gambling in the late 1980s and early 1990s put these thoughts to rest as Indian gambling, particularly casino gambling, spread to areas of the country and states where it had been illegal—at least the states thought it was illegal. The 1988 Indian Gaming Regulatory Act, with its compacting process, allowed the Indians to have any form of gambling when the state permits "such gaming for any purpose by any organization, or entity." The Indians charged into legalized gambling.

The Indians were followed by states legalizing riverboat gambling. It wasn't long before the riverboat sham became clear. The majority of the "riverboats" were barges, forbidden to sail. Riverboat gambling was/is, for the most part, dockside gambling. However, of particular concern to the students of legalized gambling is that the riverboats—not the elaborate dockside casinos—located in small rural areas, in their attempts to "grow the market," may end up drawing money from local populations, leading to an end of economic prosperity and community growth. Unfortunately, riverboat gambling, particularly in the Midwest, has not existed long enough to resolve this issue. Also at issue is how the spread of Indian gambling and riverboat and dockside gambling, particularly in Mississippi, will affect the Nevada and Atlantic City casinos, already feeling pressure from lotteries and racinos and each other.

REFERENCES

American Casino Guide. (1998). Dania, Fla.: Casino Vacations.

Bear Stearns (1998). *1998 Global Gaming Almanac*. New York: Bear Stearns & Co.

Davis, James A., and Samuel M. Otterstrom. (1996). "Constraints to the Growth of Native American Gaming." *Gaming Research & Review Journal* 3(2): 43–47.

Delva, Paul. (1995). "The Promises and Perils of Legalized Gambling for Local Governments: Who Decides to Stack the Deck?" *Temple Law Review* 68: 847–873.

Dombrink, James, and William N. Thompson. (1990). *The Last Resort: Success and Failure in Campaigns for Casinos*. Reno: University of Nevada Press.

Eade, Vincent H., and Raymond H. Eade. (1997). *Introduction to the Casino Entertainment Industry*. Upper Saddle River, N.J.: Prentice-Hall.

Eisenberg, Dennis et al. (1978). *Meyer Lansky: Mogul of the Mob*. New York: Paddington Press. Quoted in John Dombrink and William N. Thompson (1990), *The Last Resort: Success and Failure in Campaigns for Casinos*. Reno: University of Nevada Press.

Faragher, Scott. (1995). *The Complete Guide to Riverboat Gambling*. New York: Citadel Press.

Flatt, Allison. (1998). *Testimony before the National Gaming Impact Study Commission*.

Guskind, Robert. (1991). In Kathryn Hashimoto and Sheryl Fried Kline (1996), *Casino Management for the 90's*. Dubuque, Iowa: Kendall/Hunt.

Humes, Edward. (1997). *Mississippi Mud*. New York: Pocket Books.

International Gaming and Wagering Business (IGWB). (1998). "The United States Gross Annual Wager—1997" (August). Special supplement.

Kelly, Joseph M. (1997). "American Indian Gaming Law." In William R. Eadington and Judy Cornelius, eds., *Gambling: Public Policies and the Social Sciences*. Reno: Institute for the Study of Gambling and Commercial Gaming, University of Nevada, Reno.

Mississippi Gaming Commission Annual Report. (1998).

National Gaming Summary. (1998a). July 13.

National Gaming Summary. (1998b). December 7.

National Gaming Summary. (1999). February 1.

Thompson, William F., and Michele Comeau. (1992). *Casino Customer Service: The Win Win Game*. New York: Gaming and Wagering Business.

Truitt, Lawrence J. (1997). "The Regulation and Economic Impact of Riverboat Casino Gambling in Illinois." In William R. Eadington and Judy Cornelius, eds., *Gambling: Public Policies and the Social Sciences*. Reno: Institute for the Study of Gambling and Commercial Gaming, University of Nevada, Reno.

Chapter 7

Gambling-Lotteries: State-Run Games of Chance

The modern state-run lotteries are different in many ways from earlier chance drawings, even from the public lotteries that were a part of our nation's history from settlement until the death of the Louisiana Serpent. The modern-day state lottery is first and foremost a gambling lottery, not "choosing by lots" to fairly distribute (by chance) good or bad things. There are no explicit references to gambling in the Bible; however, there are 21 biblical references to "choosing by lots," including selecting Judas's replacement as one of 12 apostles (Karcher, 1992, 14). In these cases, the outcome was not due to chance but the revelations of divine will (Brenner and Brenner, 1990, 51). Choosing by lots occurs in sports drafts and in jury selection, and in previous years, it has been used to determine selection for military service (World War II and Vietnam in the later years). However, these drawings by chance are not gambling-lotteries. Gambling-lotteries, unlike choosing by lots, involve chance, consideration (something of value), and a prize/reward. The player purchases a chance to win a prize, based on a random drawing. Lotteries are considered different from other forms of gambling because the outcome of the game is determined solely by chance, with no skill involved.

Gambling-lotteries are state-run monopolies staffed by career-minded bureaucrats, often more interested in revenue generation than the player's welfare or benefit. The modern lotteries are political creations, and their mandates, goals, and revenue potentials change with each session of the legislature and new administration. Lottery directors in states where the lotteries are viewed as "cash cows" feeding into the state's general fund sometimes find themselves under pressure from politicians to increase profits by introducing new games or lowering the payback

("Lottery Directors Roundtable," 1998). State-run lotteries, particularly three- and four-number picks, are the movement of the "numbers racket" from the neighborhoods to the state capitals, often with less favorable odds, convenience, and payout. The state-run "brass ring" confuses the state's proper role in public policy and gambling. The state in initiating a gambling-lottery moves from the prohibition of gambling-lotteries—Thou Shalt Not—to permission—You May—to promotion—Please Do.

NATURE AND EXTENT

As stated earlier, 38 states, including Washington, D.C., have gambling-lotteries. The lottery is also a worldwide from of gambling—100 countries. The games played in the U.S. gambling-lotteries include instant and pull-tabs, lotto, three- and four-number daily games, five number games, multistate Powerball (21 states), and Big Game (6 states) lottos, keno, and video lottery terminals. In 1997, the combined VLT and ticket sales for lotteries was a record $46,268 billion (*IGWB*, 1998). This was a 7.7 percent increase over 1996. The VLT handle in 5 small states (Delaware, Oregon, Rhode Island, South Dakota, West Virginia) was responsible for the greater part of the increase. These 5 states took in one-third (34.4 percent) of the dollar amount of all lottery sales in the United States (*IGWB*, 1998, 29).

International Gaming & Wagering Business (*IGWB*) reports that the long-term decline in consumer price (what players spent and what they got back in prizes) of lottery games continued in 1997. For every dollar spent on lotteries (tickets and VLTs), the players got back 35.8 cents. From the players' standpoint, VLTs, often referred to as the "crack cocaine of gambling," have the lowest payback percentage. Slot machines are the most profitable games in casinos. VLTs are the most profitable lottery games. In 1997, Delaware's VLTs revenue accounted for 83.8 percent of the lottery revenue. West Virginia's VLTs accounted for 54.1 percent of the state's lottery revenues and South Dakota's VLTs were the largest source of lottery revenues ("The Hands-on Approach," 1998, 44).

Nationwide, 44.9 cents of every dollar spent on lottery tickets is returned to the players. However, as shown earlier, this varies by state. Governments retained as revenues 32 cents of every dollar bet. *IGWB* states, "Casinos and racetracks make greater contributions to employment, but in terms of direct contributions to government budgets, lotteries stand alone" (*IGWB*, 1998, 30).

Patricia McQueen (1998b), the lottery editor for *IGWB*, reports that the Massachusetts Lottery is the effectiveness king of traditional lotteries. She defines *effectiveness* as the ability to penetrate the marketplace, and it "is the percentage of personal income [states] extracted by lottery sales" (44) (see Table 7.1). According to McQueen, a lottery's efficiency

Table 7.1
Fiscal 1997 Sales as a Percent of Personal Income

Rank	Traditional Lottery	Total Sales as a Percent of Personal Income
1	Massachusetts	1.658%
2	D.C.	1.066%
3	Georgia	0.959%
4	Ohio	0.843%
5	Texas	0.822%
6	New York	0.716%
7	Maryland	0.707%
8	Kentucky	0.703%
9	Michigan	0.650%
10	Connecticut	0.648%
11	New Jersey	0.594%
12	Florida	0.561%
13	Vermont	0.558%
14	Rhode Island	0.557%
15	Pennsylvania	0.546%
16	New Hampshire	0.540%
17	Maine	0.531%
18	Virginia	0.520%
19	Delaware	0.492%
20	West Virginia	0.474%
21	Illinois	0.467%
22	Oregon	0.420%
23	Indiana	0.420%
24	Idaho	0.349%
25	Colorado	0.344%
26	Wisconsin	0.341%
27	Missouri	0.339%
28	Louisiana	0.311%
29	Kansas	0.295%
30	Minnesota	0.293%
31	Washington	0.271%
32	Iowa	0.262%
33	Arizona	0.247%
34	New Mexico	0.241%
35	California	0.240%
36	Nebraska	0.191%
37	South Dakota	0.175%
38	Montana	0.161%

Source: McQueen, 1998b, 46, table 2.

can be measured as the "government revenue as a percentage of personal income" (46). The top three states (Massachusetts, the District of Columbia, Georgia) are effective and efficient. The monies taken in by the individual states include an unknown number of out-of state ticket buyers. Nevertheless, it is clear that Massachusetts, the District of Columbia, and Georgia are very effective and efficient, according to *IGWB*, in extracting monies from their citizens. Massachusetts lottery director Sam De-Phillippo reports that the lottery has $500 per capita sales with a $175 net ("Lottery Directors Roundtable," 1998, 122). The VLTs in South Dakota, Delaware, Oregon, and Rhode Island are also very efficient in generating government revenue as a percentage of their state's personal income (see Table 7.2).

PERMISSION: YOU MAY

Casino gambling had been legalized in Nevada (1931) and 26 states had legalized horse racing by 1963. Gallup polls from 1941 to 1963 revealed that popular support for government lotteries was strong and growing (Clotfelter and Cook, 1989). In fact, there was a general softening of public opinion toward all forms of gambling. However, lotteries were prohibited by all the states. The policy was Thou Shall Not. This changed with the New Hampshire Lottery.

Development of the Modern State Lottery

The First Modern Lottery: New Hampshire Lottery, 1964

The New Hampshire legislature prior to 1963 had considered lottery bills, one passed in 1955, but it was vetoed by the governor. However, in 1963 New Hampshire, without a sales or income tax, needed additional revenues for public services, particularly education, then ranked lowest in the nation in state aid. Pro-lottery forces pointed out that a state-run lottery could provide revenues and support education without resorting to new taxes. Then, as now, the principal selling point for state-run lotteries was revenue generation. Revenue is the raison d'être of state lotteries. A "painless" means to raise public revenues without increasing taxes. The bill was passed by the legislature, signed by the governor, and approved in a 1964 statewide referendum (Clotfelter and Cook, 1989).

The first lottery in the twentieth century was primitive when compared to the modern multimillion-dollar lotteries of today. The 1964 New Hampshire Lottery resembled the early colonial sweepstakes/lotteries: Winning tickets were drawn from a pool of tickets purchased, originally twice a year. Like the common church, school, and civic group raffles of today, a purchaser wrote his or her name and address on one side of a

Table 7.2
Fiscal 1997 Government Revenue as a Percent of Personal Income

Rank	Traditional Lottery	Government Revenue as a Percent of Personal Income
1	Massachusetts	0.375%
2	D.C.	0.364%
3	Georgia	0.317%
4	New York	0.277%
5	Ohio	0.275%
6	Maryland	0.266%
7	Texas	0.259%
8	New Jersey	0.247%
9	Michigan	0.242%
10	Pennsylvania	0.224%
11	Florida	0.222%
12	Connecticut	0.213%
13	Virginia	0.193%
14	Kentucky	0.190%
15	Rhode Island	0.176%
16	Illinois	0.175%
17	Vermont	0.171%
18	New Hampshire	0.166%
19	Delaware	0.164%
20	Maine	0.152%
21	West Virginia	0.132%
22	Indiana	0.128%
23	Louisiana	0.113%
24	Wisconsin	0.109%
25	Missouri	0.102%
26	Oregon	0.097%
27	Kansas	0.090%
28	Colorado	0.090%
29	California	0.084%
30	Arizona	0.083%
31	Idaho	0.074%
32	Minnesota	0.065%
33	Minnesota	0.065%
34	Washington	0.063%
35	New Mexico	0.060%
36	Nebraska	0.051%
37	South Dakota	0.040%
38	Montana	0.038%

Source: McQueen, 1998b, 46, table 3.

ticket and held the stub until the drawing. The winning ticket was chosen from among all the tickets sold. The $3 tickets were purchased from state agents at racetracks and state-liquor stores. New Hampshire returned 31 cents of every dollar bet back to the players. The New Hampshire Lottery was an instant success—$58.6 million in sales the first year, largely due to the influx of out-of-state ticket buyers. However, it went into a five-year ticket sales decline. In 1968 the lottery was running a poor second to horse racing in terms of money wagered (Clotfelter and Cook, 1989). The passive nature of the lottery was the prime reason for its decline. Lottery players did not "play" the game as in horse racing, and they had to wait a long time to find out if they won.

Less than Neighborly Competition: New York, 1967

New York, seeing the success of the New Hampshire Lottery, began operating a lottery in 1967. The number of New York residents playing the nearby New Hampshire Lottery was also a big factor in the lottery's passage in the New York legislature. Lotteries are an example of what we saw in the spread of riverboat gambling: the domino effect. Neighboring states pass lotteries to keep their citizens' money at home. In order to compete against New Hampshire, New York increased drawings to once a month but also required players to write their names and addresses on the ticket. New York's $1 lottery tickets were sold at banks and certain public offices. The payout was set at 40 cents per dollar bet, 9 cents higher than New Hampshire. A portion of the lottery revenues was designated as supplemental aid to public schools. However, the current comptroller for the State of New York in testimony before the National Gambling Impact Study Commission stated, "In New York, as in many other states, lottery earnings have been earmarked for education primarily as a public relations device." Lottery monies have never supplemented state aid for education. Lottery revenues are deducted from the general revenues allocated to schools, according to the comptroller.

The New Game in Town: New Jersey, 1970

The success of state lotteries as "money" machines came with New Jersey's introduction of computer-numbered tickets, 50-cent tickets, weekly drawings, and modern marketing techniques. The New Jersey legislature designated the lottery net proceeds (after prizes and expenses) to be used for state institutions and state aid for education, including higher education and senior citizen education. New Jersey's lottery was an instant success ($1.1 billion), and its revenues did not decline as they had in New Hampshire and New York.

The Lotto Arrives: New York, 1978

Prior to the lotto, preprinted lottery tickets were matched to the numbers drawn. New York's lotto game allowed players to pick their own numbers from a selected field (6 out of a field of 42) through networks of computer terminals at retail outlets. Lotto allowed for the player's active involvement in the game (choosing the numbers). Even more significant to the lotto's appeal was that it allowed jackpots to "roll over" until a player/s won. In effect, lotto is a parimutuel game, with the jackpot set equal to a percentage of the amount bet. This amount varies by state. If there is no jackpot winner in a drawing, the set percentage "rolls" over to the next drawing (Clotfelter and Cook, 1989, 113).

Following New York's lead, New Jersey began using the lotto in 1980, with other lottery states soon making the switch. These states used a form of the lotto with the field, of numbers to choose from ranging from 30 to 50. The larger the field, the more combinations of numbers to choose and an increased likelihood of a rollover. The lotto is a game of long odds and huge jackpots. The odds of picking the correct six numbers dramatically increase with the field of numbers to select from (see Table 7.3). However, the lotto innovation made possible the astronomical jackpots of the 1990s. The rollover feature of the lotto, and its potential to produce large jackpots, is the one characteristic that sets the lotto apart from all other lottery games. It is strictly a "going for the dream" game.

Instant Success: Massachusetts, 1974

The development and introduction of the world's first "secure" instant tickets, "paper slot machines," by Scientific Games International (SGI) (headquarters in Alpharetta, Georgia), was the next lottery innovation. The instant ticket first used in Massachusetts in 1974 allowed the player to know immediately whether or not he or she had won a prize. Tickets were winners if they matched a combination of numbers, letters, or words hidden under a vinyl cover the player scratched off. The instant tickets developed by Scientific Games made it impossible to counterfeit tickets, see through the rub-off layer, or alter the tickets once sold. By 1982 all state lotteries were using some form of instant games (Clotfelter and Cook, 1989).

Instant games have been useful for states in the start-up phase of their lotteries. Scratch-offs can be easily distributed to retailers, and they are quick and easy to play. Instant tickets are the most cost-effective means of establishing a retailer network and player base. States often begin their lotteries with the sale of instant tickets until they raise enough revenue to set up the interconnected computer terminals for the sale of lottery tickets. The South Dakota (1987) Lottery repaid the $1.5 million start-up

Table 7.3
Approximate Odds of Matching All Lottery Numbers

Format	Approximate Odds
6 out of 30	1:600,000
6 out of 34	1:1.3 million
6 out of 36	1:1.9 million
6 out of 38	1:2.8 million
6 out of 39	1:3.3 million
6 out of 40	1:3.8 million
6 out of 42	1:5.2 million
6 out of 44	1:7.1 million
6 out of 45	1:8.1 million
6 out of 46	1:9.4 million
6 out of 48	1:12.3 million
6 out of 49	1:14.0 million
6 out of 50	1:15.9 million
Powerball and Big Game	
5 out of 50 field and 1 out of 25 Powerball or Big Money Ball field	1:53 million

loan plus interest to the state in three months by selling instant tickets (South Dakota Lottery, 1997). Florida repaid its $15.5 million start-up loan plus interest to the General Revenue Fund 17 days after it began the sale of instant tickets (Florida Lottery, 1997). Georgia payed back its start-up loan in 11 days. According to the Scientific Game's website, "[I]n the early 1980s, SGI was often also called 'the start-up company,' having served as a start-up consultant for 13 of the 14 U.S. lotteries in existence at that time" (Scientific Games International, n.d.). Scientific Games is the instant ticket supplier for 26 of the 38 lottery states.

In 1983, instant games accounted for over $50 million of Massachusetts Lottery sales; three years later, the games' yearly sales climbed to $300 million. The instant games' success established the Massachusetts Lottery agency as "the guru of instant games" (Clotfelter and Cook, 1989, 174).

The Legal Numbers Game: New Jersey, 1975

Clotfelter and Cook (1989) call the state lotteries' Pick 3 and 4 numbers game the "Sincerest Form of Flattery" to the illegal numbers game run by organized crime. That statement is not too far from the truth. The legal and illegal numbers games share a number of common character-istics. Furthermore, when the New Jersey legislators instituted the Pick 3 numbers game, they thought they would drive the illegal games out of business.

The illegal numbers games that became popular in the Northeast during the 1920s were based on simple three-digit number selection, usually the last three numbers in the handle from local racetracks. The bettor could choose a straight bet, all three numbers in exact order; a boxed bet, six combinations of the three numbers; a single bet, one of the numbers; or two digits. The bets could be for as low as a nickel and often on credit. The collectors sold door to door, in stores and newsstands, or by phone. Typically, the bet was payed off at 500 or 600 to 1. The true odds were 1,000 to 1.

The legal numbers games offer no credit and allow no bet less than 50 cents. Straight bets and boxed bets are allowed but not single- or two-number bets; however, Florida and Missouri allow players to choose the first two or the last two digits of their CA$H 3. Payoff odds are 500 to 1. Numbers are randomly drawn from the field 0 through 9, with replacement, by the lottery commission, usually on a daily basis. Trust in the random selection by the state and the instant publication of results—TV and radio—have led the illegal numbers games to use the same numbers. The first televised lottery drawing was in 1977 (Delaware).

The legal numbers games have not appeared to impact the illegal games that operated before the state lotteries instituted the numbers game (Clotfelter and Cook, 1989). The illegal games are still more convenient to the players and offer credit, a smaller minimum bet, and no payment of taxes. Often, the payouts are higher than the legal games. Nevertheless, Pick 3 and 4 numbers games are popular and profitable for the states.

THE GAMES PEOPLE PLAY: THE MODERN LOTTERY

State lotteries since their legalization in 1964 have come a long way. Today lotteries are much more than players risking a small amount against long odds to win a big prize. The innovations of lotto, instant games, and numbers have made the modern state-run lotteries quite different from earlier lotteries. State-run gambling lotteries are a major part of the U.S. gambling industry. The lotteries, like the "gaming" industry, claim they are part of the entertainment industry: One of the Michigan Lottery's missions is to: "Provide quality entertainment to the public" (Michigan Bureau of State Lottery, 1997, 3). The mission of the Missouri Lottery is "to maximize revenues for public education through the creation and sales of fun and entertaining products" (Missouri Lottery, 1996). Georgia seeks "[t]o maximize revenues for specific education programs by providing entertaining lottery products." Nebraska states that "players and winners alike enjoy the high quality entertainment option provided by Nebraska scratch games and lotto games" (Nebraska Lottery, 1997).

Lotteries are the most popular (based on participation) and widely and conveniently available form of legalized gambling in the United States. California has a network of 22,000 retailers statewide and recently joined 14 other states in allowing in-state residents to subscribe to the lottery for six months or a year in advance (California Lottery, 1996). Michigan has 9,300 retailers statewide. Missouri has 4,900. South Dakota has 672 instant ticket retailers and 386 lotto retailers statewide.

Lottery retailers have a vested interest in lottery sales. In Missouri, retailers receive 2 percent of all online redemptions and 2 percent of all cash redemptions on instant tickets. They also receive $50,000 for selling a Powerball jackpot ticket and 1 percent of a Missouri Lotto jackpot prize for selling the winning ticket (Missouri Lottery, 1996). In South Dakota, instant ticket retailers are paid a 5 percent commission. They also receive a 1 percent bonus on all prizes over $100 sold in their stores and a 1 percent bonus for cashing any winning ticket, no matter where it was sold (South Dakota Lottery, 1997). Massachusetts conducts an Agent Incentive Drawing every year based on the number of instant ticket books sold. Massachusetts blatantly encourages instant ticket sales by its agents: "And remember this is an Agent Incentive Contest, which means the more books you sell and settle, the better your chances of winning. Simply sell and settle your Instant Tickets and we'll take care of the rest" (Massachusetts Lottery, n.d.). Five agents won $10,000 each in one drawing in 1998. Washington, D.C.'s 552 lottery agents received $11.9 million in commissions and bonuses in 1995 (D.C. Lottery & Charitable Games Control Board, 1995–1996). That was almost three times the $4.7 million raised for worthy causes through charitable gaming (sic) activities.

Lotto: Traditional Draw Lottery

Prizes are life-changing events. The procedures for selecting the winning lottery numbers are very elaborate and closely monitored.

Instant Tickets

Thirty-one states have instant ticket vending machines, some located in supermarkets. Instant tickets game prizes can range from free tickets to $50,000 or more in some states. Massachusetts's "Take Home Millions" $5 instant game has a "take home" prize of $1,005,000 after withholding taxes. California's "Dream Home" instant game allows winners to choose cash or a new home. Florida's WIN FOR LIFE game offers top prizes of

$1,000 per week for life, paid in annual installments of $52,000 (Florida Lottery, 1997). The payouts vary by state. Florida law requires a minimum of 50 percent to players with an average payout of 56.24 percent. From January 12, 1988, to October 31, 1997, Florida had introduced 167 different instant games.

The New Jersey Lottery has partnered with the Sands Hotel and Casino in Atlantic City on one of their instant games. The $5 instant ticket has a top prize of $25,000, and all players get a chance to pull a special $1 million slot machine at the casino.

The instant games provide immediate gratification for the players, are virtually "cheat proof," and provide the states a means to make regular changes to the games. Every state with instant games makes frequent changes by varying the themes and game details. They can also be sold in vending machines, which require fewer employees. However, vending machine sales increase the possibility of sales to minors.

Pick 3 and Pick 4 Numbers

Pick 4 players choose four-digit numbers from 0000 through 9999. Tickets are $0.50 or a $1, with prizes ranging from $100 to $5,000, depending on the type of play (straight, exact order; 4-way box, any order; 6-way box; 12-way box; 24-way box) and the amount bet. There are 10,000 possible four-number combinations. Therefore, the odds of matching all four numbers in a single straight play are 1 in 10,000. Pick 3 players choose their numbers from 000 through 999. Again, tickets are $0.50 or $1. Prizes range from $20 to $500 in most states. There are 1,000 three-number combinations. The odds of matching three winning numbers in a single straight play are 1 in 1,000.

Multistate Drawings

Powerball

In 1992 Powerball replaced the multistate lottery Lotto America. It is run by the Multi-State Lottery Association. The Powerball jackpot starts at $10 million and keeps building until someone wins. Six numbers are drawn from two sets, five from a set of 1 to 49 and one (the Powerball) from a set of 1 to 42. The overall odds of hitting the jackpot are 1:80,089,128; however, there are eight other ways of winning from $3 to $100,000. As of this writing, there are 21 states, all members of the Multi-State Lottery Association, that sell the game: Arizona, Connecticut, Delaware, Idaho, Indiana, Iowa, Kansas, Kentucky, Louisiana, Minnesota, Missouri, Montana, Nebraska, New Hampshire, New Mexico, Oregon,

Rhode Island, South Dakota, Washington, D.C., Wisconsin, and West Virginia.

In May 1998, the Powerball went eight weeks without a winner and produced a record jackpot of $195 million. A few weeks later, the Powerball set another record with a $295 million jackpot in July 1998. The last jackpot led to a record $592 million in ticket sales (McQueen, 1998a, 1).

Big Game

The multistate Big Game (Georgia, Illinois, Maryland, Massachusetts, and Virginia) began operating in 1997. The jackpots start at a guaranteed $5 million and offer eight other ways to win cash prizes. The jackpot reached $93 million the weekend of Easter 1999. One ticket holder won the whole amount.

Tri-State Megabucks and WinCash

The states of Vermont, Maine, and New Hampshire have three multistate games, Megabucks, WinCash, and 5 Card Cash. Megabucks is a two-night a week, 6 out of 40 lotto game with a guaranteed $500,000 jackpot. With rollovers the highest Megabucks jackpot has been $16.4 million. WinCash is a 6 out of 36 game with a rolling jackpot. The two-night a week WinCash has slightly better odds than the Megabucks game.

Wild Card Lotto

The Tri-West Lotto composed of the states of South Dakota, Montana, and Idaho used a 6 of 33 game with four different all-cash prize levels. In February 1998 this game was replaced by the four-state (Idaho, Montana, Nebraska, South Dakota) Wild Card Lotto. The multistate lotto use a 6/38 game with a wild card picked from a 52-card deck ("Game News," 1998, 51). These four states are also members of the Multi-State Lottery Association.

Five-Number Draws: Little Lotto Games

The state lotteries offer a variety of five-number lottos with varying odds, payoffs, and sets of numbers to choose from. For example, the Florida Fantasy Five: 5 of 5 numbers out of a set of 26 numbers; odds of matching 5 of 5 are 1:65,780; and prizes range from $12,000 to $30,000 for a jackpot. Florida reduced the range of numbers from 1 through 39 to 1 to 26 to reduce the odds of winning and create more winners. This virtually eliminated the possibility of a rollover, but it created more winners. The first nine draws of the new Fantasy 5 produced 490 jackpot winners, with prizes ranging from $12,000 to $30,000 each.

Cash4Life

Eleven states, all members of the Multi-State Lottery Association, launched a four-number game, Cash4Life, in March 1998. Cash4Life is offered in the District of Columbia, Indiana, Iowa, Kansas, Minnesota, Montana, Nebraska, New Hampshire, South Dakota, West Virginia, and Wisconsin. Players choose four two-digit numbers from 00 to 99. The top prize is $1,000 a week for life. In addition, players receive 14 random sets of numbers to win at other prize levels ("Game News," 1998, 51).

Other Games

Television Game Shows

Florida's Lottery has a television game show—*Flamingo Fortune*—where players are chosen from entries submitted by winners in instant games and randomly generated lotto and Fantasy 5 tickets. Chosen on-stage contestants play for hundreds of thousands of dollars (Florida Lottery, 1997). California's *Wizard of Odds* instant game gives players a chance to appear on a TV game show and compete for $50,000 (California Lottery, 1996). Michigan's *Road to Riches* weekly television game show offers cash prizes up to $50,000, bonus cash prizes, and a Caribbean cruise for two (Michigan Bureau of State Lottery, 1997). Contestants chosen from Missouri's "Fun and Fortune" instant game vie for $100,000 on the *Fun and Fortune* TV game show. Players on Massachusetts's *Bonus Bonanza* game show can win up to $640,000. Illinois's *Instant Riches* game show is tied to the instant ticket game of the same name. The Massachusetts and Illinois game shows were created by the game show producer of *The Price Is Right, To Tell the Truth, Password,* and *Family Feud,* Mark Goodson Productions ("Massachusetts Lottery," 1995).

Break-Open Tickets (Pull-tabs)

Oregon, Washington, and Iowa sell break-open tickets (also known as pull-tabs) in taverns and neighborhood shops. The prizes generally run from $0.50 to $50. Pull-tabs have a fixed number of wins in each batch of tickets. The odds of winning increase after each person buys a losing ticket. Massachusetts's "Sizzling Cherries" pull-tabs, mostly sold as charity games at veteran's clubs, offer prizes from $1 to $250. There is a $1,003 profit on each set of 3,983 tickets; the lottery's share is $331. The retailer keeps $620.00. The pull-tabs are purchased from the distributor through the Massachusetts State Lottery Commission. Texas allows the sale of state-approved pull-tabs at charitable bingo establishments.

Quick Draw Keno

The ancient Chinese lottery game has become Americanized and computerized into keno by gambling lotteries. Quick draw keno online games are operated by New York, Georgia, and Massachusetts. The online game allows the player to select 1 to 12 numbers from a field of 80 numbers. The lottery randomly selects 20 numbers from the same field. Depending on the numbers matched, the player wins a prize.

Georgia's Quick Cash game allows the player to bet from $1 to $10 per game and mark from 1 to 10 numbers (spots) per game. Hitting all 10 spots on a 10-spot ticket has a prize of $100,000. Zero hits on the same ticket win $5. Games are played every five minutes over computer terminals in selected locations.

Video Lottery Terminals

Many gambling terms are confusing and subject to different interpretations, depending on the spokesperson and state statute. However, the term *video lottery terminal* is the most confusing gambling term. Looking at the machines leads to the conclusion that VLTs are gambling machines—video and slot—found in any Las Vegas, Atlantic City, or Mississippi casino. Playing VLTs manufactured by the same companies that make casino gambling machines, often with the same games, leads to the inescapable conclusion that they are the same machines found in casinos. However, they are different according to the states that allow them.

States allowing VLTs argue that the classic casino gambling machines (video and slot) are house-banked and coin-in, coin-out machines. Video lottery terminals, on the other hand, are state-banked (banked by the state's lottery commission) and dispense redeemable tickets to winners, not coins. Some states also point out that VLTs have buttons, not the pull levers of one-armed bandits found in casinos.

South Dakota

South Dakota was the first state to use video lottery terminals in 1989. They were shut down in August 1994, following a state supreme court decision that they were unconstitutional. A referendum was held to reauthorize them that same year. It passed 53 percent to 47 percent, and video lottery restarted on November 22, 1994 (South Dakota Lottery, 1997). Currently, the games of poker, keno, blackjack, and bingo are played on the VLTs. There are 8,000 VLTs in approximately 1,416 establishments. Each location is allowed to have up to 10 machines (Rzadzkl, 1998, 44).

The state receives 50 percent of the revenues from the machines and divides the remaining amount between the owner of the machine and the owner of the establishments where the machines are located. The state's central computer system automatically polls each video lottery terminal every night to collect accounting and game-play statistics. The governor has authorized a study of the impact of gambling in South Dakota and the possibility of a VLT repeal.

Oregon

Oregon has 8,900 VLTs. They are located mostly in bars and pubs, playing only video poker. Each establishment can have a maximum of 5 machines (Rzadzkl, 1998, 44).

Racinos

According to a retired CEO of International Game Technology, the largest slot machine manufacturer in the United States, "From a business standpoint, the ideal casino is a slot house [no table games]" (O'Brien, 1998, 40). The states of Rhode Island, West Virginia, and Delaware have created slot houses—ideal casinos—at their racetracks by placing VLTs at theses sites. Patricia McQueen, the lottery editor for *International Gaming & Wagering Business* magazine, predicts "that racinos may soon become the rule rather than the exception" at racetracks ("Reeling Them In," 1998, 60). The traditional VLT games do not generate the profits that coin-in, coin-out slot machines do; therefore, these states are moving in traditional reel slot machines and calling them VLTs because they are regulated by the state's lottery commission.

Rhode Island

Rhode Island has VLTs located at a greyhound racetrack and a jai alai fronton, which offers daily dog and horse racing. The VLTs are programmed to play blackjack, keno, slots, and three versions of poker (jacks or better, joker poker, and deuces wild). According to the *American Casino Guide*, "These machines are the same as regular gaming devices but are called lottery terminals because they are regulated by the state's lottery commission which receives a share of each machines revenue" (1998, 296). The machines also accept cash but don't pay out in cash. The machine prints out a receipt, which must be taken to a cashier for payment.

West Virginia

West Virginia's video lottery games are authorized at Mountaineer Park, Wheeling Downs, Tri-State Greyhound Park, and Charles Town Racetrack (West Virginia Video Lottery, 1998). The racetracks install and service the terminals, and the West Virginia Lottery regulates them (security, license approvals; ensures expenditures in accordance with law). In April 1998, there were 2,914 VLTs in these four facilities. Bets run from a $0.05 minimum to $0.25, with a $2.00 maximum bet. The lottery collects 34 percent of the net machine income, with the rest of the money going to the state's racing industry for purses and vendors ("Racing for Growth," 1998, 25). The games offered include blackjack, keno, video poker, and "video slot" games. Each VLT is tied into a central computer system at the West Virginia Lottery Headquarters and monitored 24 hours a day. The VLTs at Mountaineer and Charles Town communicate with the lottery central system via dial-up phone lines. Wheeling Downs and Tri-State are online with the central system.

According to West Virginia law, a "Video lottery game" is a commission-approved, -owned, and -controlled electronically simulated game of chance that is displayed on the screen or video monitor of a video lottery terminal and that

(7) [d]oes not use the following game themes commonly associated with casino gambling: Roulette, dice, or baccarat card games: *Provided*, That games having a video display depicting symbols which appear to roll on drums to simulate a classic casino slot machine, game themes of other card games and keno may be used. (Article 22 A. RACETRACK VIDEO LOTTERY, 29–22 A-3 Definitions.)

Delaware: Casinos Sans Table Games

In December 1995, Delaware Downs and Dover Downs racetracks began video lottery operations (1,000 machines each track). The Harrington Raceway installed VLTs in August 1996 (702 machines). The mission of Delaware's video lottery is:

• To maximize Video Lottery revenue contributed to the State's General Fund by providing entertaining and secure Video Lottery products.

• To operate all games and facilities in a highly secure environment and in compliance with all legislation, internal control requirements and Video Lottery Rules & Regulations, in keeping with the Delaware Lottery's quality image and high level of integrity. (Delaware Video Lottery, n.d.)

Delaware's coin-in, coin-out VLTs are a mix of spinning-reel slots and video machines, making the three racetracks in effect state-run casinos without table games. The three racetracks are advertised as "state-of-the-art SLOTS facilities." *National Gaming Summary* (1998) reports that "Delaware Slots," not video lottery terminals, had an August 1998 revenue of $35.9 million. Delaware's total VLT revenue was 83.3 percent of the state's 1997 lottery's total revenue of $305.4 million (Rzadzkl, 1998, 47).

PLEASE DO: ADVERTISING

The states are accustomed to raising money from taxes and regulating private activities. However, running a lottery is selling a product. The states use two marketing techniques to sell lottery tickets: (1) the introduction of new games and (2) advertising (Karcher, 1992, 73). New games—lotto and instant tickets—are continuously being introduced by the states having gambling-lotteries. The December 1998 issue of *International Gaming & Wagering Business* listed eight new games in five states. The Iowa Lottery offered a "Design a Game from Scratch" promotion, which gave players a chance to submit ideas for new instant games. The top prize was $3,000 ("Lottery News," 1998, 45).

In his seminal work on lotteries, Karcher (1992, 75) quotes a Maryland State Lottery public relations and advertising consultant's 1984 Senate testimony on marketing and advertisement.

Since it is ineffective and most often counter productive to advertise a lottery ticket as a product, we have created a series of television and radio commercials which highlight the fun of playing the game and take away the onus from gambling. We want to feed the consumers' need for fun and excitement propelling the fantasy which motivates them to buy the next ticket.

The following statement from the Florida Lottery demonstrates that the same strategy exists today.

Q. *Why is advertising important to the lottery?*

A. Lottery products are popular with Florida residents and visitors and creative, tasteful advertising is the best way to market them. Lottery products are not necessities and, like many entertainment products, are bought on impulse. The Lottery competes in the consumer marketplace with many other widely advertised products including soft drinks, candy, movies, video tape rentals and amusement parks. In short, well-spent advertising dollars generate sales and revenue for the Educational Enhancement Trust Fund. (Florida Lottery, 1997)

Gambling-lotteries ads appear in every possible mass-marketing venue, television, radio, newspapers, Internet, billboards, buses. Giant jackpots, happy winners, and changed lives are news events. State-run lotteries are not subject to federal "truth in advertising" laws and are not subject, along with Indians, to Federal Communications Commission (FCC) bans against advertising (Plume, 1999). Advertising what was formerly sinful (betting) and illegal when conducted by individuals and is now lawful and "moral" when conducted by the state places the state in a strange and contradictory position. The state finds itself promoting a behavior, gambling, that is potentially dangerous for its citizens, or some of its citizens. The goals of lottery advertising are to increase the number of people who play the lottery and increase the amount of money that current players bet. The state is open to criticisms of truth in advertising if the advertisements are false and misleading, as they often are.

Lottery advertisements in the past have led to numerous criticisms: They target those audiences that will spend (and lose) more, target the poor, play off the fears of habitual players, dupe players into believing that profits go to good causes, foster a get-rich-quick mentality while belittling the work ethic, and misrepresent the true odds of winning and the true value of annunitized jackpots. Karcher (1992) recommended that five lottery advertising techniques that exist, or have existed in the past, be eliminated.

1. Any advertising that denigrates the work ethic should be banned.
2. There should be no tearjerker advertisement that exploits the handicapped, the disabled, or elderly; the recipients of lottery revenues in some states should not be used.
3. No false-hope or fantasy types of appeals should be sponsored by the state.
4. Lottery commercials should advertise the true odds of hitting the lottery and not belittle or make light of the odds.
5. Lottery advertisements should not be timed to run when government checks are being received—the first of the month.

The advertising problems have been recognized by the lottery industry and the states. The director of the New York State Lottery is quoted in Hill (1998, 25) as saying in a May 1997 speech to fellow lottery directors:

Although most lottery advertising is responsible in its claims, some ads are so farfetched and fanciful that they would not stand up to the same "truth-in-advertising" standards to which advertising conducted by private industry is held. Add to that the fact that our advertising is often relentless in its frequency, and lottery critics and even supporters are left wondering what public purpose is served when a state's primary message to its constituents is a frequent and enticing appeal to the gambling instinct. The answer is none. No legitimate purpose justifies the excesses to which some lottery advertising has resorted.

According to Patricia McQueen (1999), the lottery editor for *International Gaming & Wagering Business*, "Current lottery advertising has shifted markedly in favor of reality." McQueen also reports that lottery advertising budgets have been reduced, Massachusetts, with the second largest sales (behind New York), had seen its advertising budget decline from $12 million in 1992 to $400,000 in 1998 (the lowest among the lottery states). New Jersey's Lottery had its advertisement budget cut by 50 percent last year. Texas implemented a cap on lottery advertisement in 1998. Virginia, Minnesota, and Wisconsin ban ads that are designed to induce people to play.

Also complicating the advertising issue are the vendors' involvement in promotion and advertising. They have a financial interest in lottery sales. Their profits are a percentage of sales.

CONCLUSION

Other than charitable bingo, state-run gambling-lotteries are the most popular and widespread form of legal gambling. Unlike casinos, most people have experience with lotteries. States are actively seeking ways to increase this experience or, as they would say, penetrate the market. The Colorado Lottery will soon have an online lottery ticket sales system—"Player Express"—at 2,000 check-out stands at the registers in 200 multilane supermarkets (Jones, 1998, 14). This will eliminate the need to go to the service desk to purchase lottery tickets. GTECH, the developer of the system, proclaims, "GTECH's self-service Player Express terminals can bring the excitement of lottery to supermarket check-out lanes around the world making impulse purchases easier." Mass merchandisers like Wal-Mart and K-Mart may be the next step in online lottery ticket sales. Instant ticket sales have existed at registers in mass merchandisers for years.

Political pressure to increase profits leads to the introduction of new games that are not lotteries, for example, scratch-offs, Quick Draw Keno, and video lottery terminals. Video lottery terminals operated and managed by the state lottery commission are expanding gambling opportunities under the lottery rubric, eliminating the distinction between casino gambling and lotteries. Some states argue that VLTs are not slot machines because they do not pay out in coins or currency. Some states expressly forbid this practice in the lottery statutes. For example, "In games utilizing computer terminals or other devices, no coins or currency shall be dispensed to players from these computer terminals or devices" (California Lottery, 1996, 10). Coin-free slots, which began in the VLT market, are being adopted by casinos for some games. VLC's (slot manufacturing company) coin-free slot machine was nominated as one of the Top 20 Innovative Products for 1998 in the gaming industry (*National Gaming Summary*, 1998b). Some racinos, recognizing the profitability of machine gambling, would like to offer table games ("Racing for Growth," 1998, 25). They probably will in the future, leading to full-blown state-run casinos.

We would expect that gambling-lotteries will continue to be used as a source of revenue by the states. As Massachusetts Attorney General Scott Harshbarger said before the NGISC: "In a time when no politician of any party will even talk about raising taxes, the lottery has become a truly irreplaceable source of income" (*National Gaming Summary*, 1998b). At the present time, only 10 states earmark lottery revenues to go into their general fund. The most common earmarking is for education—16 states. The other states designate lottery revenues to a variety of public projects. However, there is no practical way to prevent a state legislature from diverting general funds away from the earmarked source when general expenditures exceed lottery revenues available.

REFERENCES

American Casino Guide. (1998). Dania, Fla.: Casino Vacations.
Brenner, Reuven, and Gabrille Brenner. (1990). *Gambling and Speculation*. Cambridge: Cambridge University Press.
California Lottery. (1996). "1996 Report to the Public."
Clotfelter, Charles T., and Philip J. Cook. (1989). *Selling Hope: State Lotteries in America*. Cambridge, Mass.: Harvard University Press.
D.C. Lottery & Charitable Games Control Board. (1995–1996). "Annual Report 1995 & 1996 Fiscal Years."
Delaware Video Lottery. (n.d.). http://www.state.de.us/lottery/video.html.
Florida Lottery. (1997). "Public Information Guide—1997."
"Game News." (1998). *IGWB* (April): 51.
Hill, John. (1998). *Theft by Consent*. Rev. ed. Birmingham: Alabama Family Alliance.
International Gaming & Wagering Business (IGWB). (1998). "The United States Gross Annual Wager—1997" (August). Special supplement.
Jones, Michael. (1998). "Checking It Out." *IGWB* (October). Supplement: "Ticket to the Future: IGWB's Lottery Technology Review."
Karcher, Alan J. (1992). *Lotteries*. New Brunswick, N.J.: Transaction Publishers.
"Lottery Directors Roundtable." (1998). *IGWB* (September): 116–122.
"Lottery News." (1998). *IGWB* (December): 45.
Massachusetts Lottery. (n.d.). "Sales Agent Information."
"Massachusetts Lottery Launches Bonus Bonanza." (1995). *Public Gaming International* (March): 12–15.
McQueen, Patricia A. (1998a). "Powerball Gets Star Treatment." *IGWB* (September): 43–47.
McQueen, Patricia A. (1998b). "The Quest for Efficiency." *IGWB* (April): 43–47.
McQueen, Patricia A. (1999). "It All Ads Up." *IGWB* (January): 39–41, 46.
Michigan Bureau of State Lottery. (1997). "1997 Annual Report."
Missouri Lottery. (1996). "1996 Annual Report."
National Gaming Summary. (1998a). March 16.
National Gaming Summary. (1998b). October 5.
Nebraska Lottery. (1997). "1997 Annual Report."
O'Brien, Timothy. (1998). *Bad Bet*. New York: Random House.
Plume, Janet. (1999). "Ad Ruling Breaks Ground, Opens Abyss." *Casino Journal* (January): 66–68.

"Racing for Growth: The Future of Parimutuel Technology." (1998). *IGWB* (December). Special supplement.
"Reeling Them In: While VLTs Have Limited Appeal, Slots Slay 'Em at the Tracks." (1998). *IGWB* (May): 57–60.
Rzadzkl, John. (1998). "The Hands-On Approach." *IGWB* (November): 43–47.
Scientific Games International. (n.d.). www.scigames.com/history.htm.
South Dakota Lottery. (1997). "1997 Annual Report."
West Virginia Lottery. (1998). April.

Chapter 8

The Web of Gambling

In the 1960s, the U.S. Department of Defense created an emergency system that would allow communication and data transfer in the event of a national disaster or nuclear war. This system, known as ARPANET (Advanced Research Projects Agency Network), linked scientific and academic researchers and was the precursor for the modern Internet. Since that time, both electronic data transfers and wireless communications have blossomed. Virtually millions of Americans have access to technological communication devices—and the number is growing. Indeed, many politicians—led by Vice President Al Gore—have expressed intentions of subsidizing low economic areas, so that all levels of American society would have access to the virtual marketplace. At the same time, the Supreme Court has ruled against online censorship—allowing a virtual cornucopia of vice to take root.

Traditional efforts at censorship were directed at Internet pornography. However, religious Right organizations have leveled their sites at a more popular target—gambling. Supported largely by community leaders from gambling jurisdictions and the gaming industry itself, these groups argue that online gambling is unregulated, potentially fraudulent, enforcement retarded, and accessible to minors. They suggest that the sheer availability of online connections will lead to an increase in pathological gambling, youth involvement, and illegal wagering. While their arguments have some merit, current legislation is unable to address the legality of online gambling, and it is unclear whether traditional statutes are applicable. In addition, jurisdictional regulation is questionable, as many sites operate out of areas that support such endeavors.

WHAT IS THE INTERNET?

As early as 1961, communication between computer users has been possible. Original methods of communication relied on "modulator-demodulators" (i.e., modems). This basic system allowed computers to transmit data images to foreign terminals. At the smallest level, local access networks (LANs) enable users within a company or small location to communicate among themselves. Wide access networks (WANs) extend this capability to national and international levels by establishing links between LANs. Online service providers, on the other hand, enable users to communicate via personal computer with a variety of seemingly unconnected foreign and domestic locations. Though similar in concept, methods of data transfer vary from location—presenting law enforcement and legislators with a multitude of problems.

The oldest, and subsequently most simplistic, method of communication is, of course, copper wire. Indeed, it is this medium that was specifically addressed in the much-debated Wire Act of 1961 (discussed later). The introduction of modems has enabled users to telephonically communicate with others. Implementing fiber optic technology, which relies on light rather than electric impulses, has decreased the vulnerability to broken signals and is more appropriate for data purity. However, the increasingly mobile nature of society has encouraged the development of alternative, less restrictive technologies. Indeed, the advent of cellular technology has ensured the mobility of personal computers and greatly enhanced the efficiency of business travelers. As they essentially mimic the technology of two-way radios, cellular products tend to be more susceptible to geographical characteristics. Thus, other strategies have attempted to eliminate such shortcomings. In fact, the latest methods of data transfer include technologies that have long been employed in other capacities by government agencies—such as the Department of Defense and the Central Intelligence Agency. The emergence of satellite technology into the private sector has allowed data transfer at unprecedented speeds, locations, and clarity.

Attractive Nature

As discussed, the advent of technology has radically changed traditional methods of communication. The accessibility and inexpensive nature of the Internet have greatly enhanced knowledge transfer and the availability of information to businesses and consumers alike. Low operating costs and a greater exposure have led many traditional land-based establishments to relocate portions of their commerce to this borderless realm. In addition, many new businesses have emerged. Virtually all sectors of capitalism are now represented. Gambling is no exception.

In 1996, slightly more than 20 online casinos could be found. Currently, that number is between 200 and 300, with no signs of decreasing opportunities. In fact, Internet gambling, mirroring America's consumption of cyberspace technology, has skyrocketed in recent years and may reach profits of $7 billion by the year 2002 (Karleff, 1998). This surge may be attributed to the negligible start-up costs associated with such a venture. By setting up shop on the Internet or within "cyberspace," companies are not anchored to a particular jurisdiction. In fact, operators may float their headquarters or work from home. As such, companies could actually create data havens to escape taxes and, ultimately, regulation. This includes gambling companies that have set up operations outside the boundaries of the United States. Although the government has made limited attempts to identify and eradicate certain operations, their efforts have been largely unrewarded.

The proliferation of opportunity to engage in gambling activities is inherently beyond the management of current government personnel. Individual bettors no longer have to travel to legitimate venues nor seek out illegitimate means. They do not have to bear the expense or invest the time necessary to secure a reliable babysitter for their children while engaging in purely adult entertainment. They are available for household emergencies and calls from the office. They are invisible to others, so personal hygiene considerations can wait. In essence, they can have all of the excitement without the accompanying headaches of crowds, lines, drunks, and annoying tablemates. As such, the soft hum of a computer monitor, found in the majority of homes or businesses, may become the medium for gambling activity. Such accessibility greatly enhances the likelihood of partaking. In 1998, over $600 million was illegally wagered on sports through cybertechnology. Although not yet close to the $100 billion wagered through traditional means, it is clear that Internet gaming has made an impact (Crist, 1998).

Cybercurrency

Like the Home Shopping Network, Internet gaming sites (IGSs) have created easy payment plans for consumers. Recognizing the American principle of nonpaper money, Internet gaming sites have enhanced their appeal by offering a variety of recognizable currency for bettors. Interested individuals may obtain cash advances or maintain open lines of credit with little collateral other than their credit card numbers. *Cybercurrency*—a term used for credits redeemable online—may be issued by wins, promotions, or converted cash and is not unique to online casinos. For example, many casinos offer a specified number of credits for first-time visitors. These credits are only redeemable at the promotional site and are not cash convertible. Such cybercurrency may also be collected as online credits when individuals successfully win a wager placed. Finally, cybercurrency or cybercredit may be issued after an individual bettor deposits cash funds or provides credit card numbers for an online account.

A final avenue for monetary exchange in cyberspace casinos poses the greatest concern for government officials. Offshore accounts, long popular for the purchase of illegal commodities, has now emerged as a source of funds for individuals concerned with government monitoring. Perhaps anticipating the jackpot, many individuals have channeled their money into offshore institutions free from IRS scrutiny. In addition, many individuals, uncertain of the legality of online wagering, have attempted to protect themselves and their "investments" from forfeiture or other civil or criminal penalties.

Gambling Sites

As previously discussed, gambling has become so much a part of American life that gambling opportunities can be found on land, over water, in the air, and even in cyberspace. While the millions wagered electronically in 1998 pale in comparison to the billions legally wagered in casinos, lotteries, and parimutuel venues, it appears to be the wave of the future (Crist, 1998). In fact, over 600 gaming-related sites may be found on the Internet. These sites, including simulated casinos, informational pages (i.e., injury reports, latest line, etc.), and gaming advertisements, are expected to increase exponentially in the near future. Currently, sites may be grouped into five distinct categories: (1) *downloading*, in which comers play independently by buying only the right to purchase casino-type software (some of these sites require *interactive*-type play); (2) *interactive*, in which promissory notes and methods of payment are exchanged for "real-time" casino action; (3) *propagandized*, in which Internet and nonelectronic gaming venues are advertised and excursions planned; (4) *educational*, in which site operators promote "guaranteed" programs or mechanisms for winning; and finally, (5) *informational*, in which interested parties can solicit knowledge on gambling opportunities from sports betting to local lotteries. It is perhaps the latest of these that is the most common and the most significant.

The proliferation of informational sites on the Web mirrors the increasing interest of the American public in gaming venues and periphery activities. Surfers interested in lotteries, for example, may check multistate results or find avenues for wagering on international lotteries. What makes these sites so unique is their sheer abundance and absolute legitimacy. It appears that many sites are taking their cue from mainstream news organizations that have long supported gambling interests by publishing information ranging from latest numbers to handicapping advertisements. Although much of this information may only be used in illegitimate avenues (sports betting is only legal in Nevada), it has traditionally received scant attention from anti-gambling activists. Such is not the case with other categories of Internet sites.

REGULATING THE WEB

With the increase in electronic casino simulation, unlikely bedfellows have emerged—each with his own highly territorialized agendas. Opponents of Internet gaming have included the American Gaming Association, the National Collegiate Athletic Association (NCAA), the National Football League (NFL), and not surprisingly, the Christian Coalition. Citing potential fraud and dishonesty on the part of site operators, the AGA has questioned the "integrity" of cybergames, whereas the Christian Coalition warns of the rapid decline of morality amidst increasing temptations (Crist, 1998). Proponents, on the other hand, include civil libertarians, bookmakers, Internet providers, and gamblers. They argue that legislation regulating or limiting Internet gambling is inherently self-serving and egocentric. They argue that attempts by lawmakers are a further example of America's heavy-handedness and gestapolike approach to international commerce (Crist, 1998). They also suggest that the movement to prohibition is an attempt by lawmakers to protect their own interests while limiting private opportunities—pointing out that legislators from states that support other forms of legalized gambling are often the first to cry foul on privately owned online gambling services.

Arguments notwithstanding, the federal government is taking note. As a consequence, the Professional Amateur Sports Protection Act (1992) forbade states from passing laws to legalize sports gambling. Though the constitutionality of such a mandate has yet to be tested, the act has been largely ineffectual as it lacks specificity of criminal violations and punishments. Thus, legislators and other opponents must use ammunition gathered in three statutes that are grossly outdated and only superficially applicable to cybergaming. These statutes, originally created to limit organized crime infiltration of legitimate venues, are also intended to contain legalized gambling within state boundaries. The application of such legislation, however, has not yet been tested.

Federal Interstate Wire Act of 1961

The first statute that may contain limited applicability to Internet gaming is the Federal Interstate Wire Act of 1961, which states:

Whoever being engaged in the business of betting or wagering knowingly uses a wire communication facility for the transmission in interstate or foreign commerce of bets or wagers or information assisting in the placing of bets or wagers on any sporting event or contest, or of the transmission of a wire communication which entitles the recipient to receive money or credit as a result of bets or wagers, or for information assisting in the placing of bets or wagers, shall be fined under this title or imprisoned not more than two years, or both. (18 U.S.C. 1084 [a] [1994])

Although the language of the statute clearly addresses telephonic wagering, application to Internet gambling is unclear in the act's current form. Traditionally, this act was not designed to punish the individual bettor but the bookmaker, individual, or organization responsible for perpetuating such activity. Thus, the law may be applied to Internet bookies but not individual bettors. Furthermore, the act specifically includes sports wagering only. Casino-type games and other forms of wagering such as bingo are not included. In addition, its current form does not allow for enforcement against the service provider. In fact, enforcement could only be directed at common carriers who are licensed by the Federal Communications Commission. At this time, Internet providers are not licensed by the FCC, nor are they required to be licensed by similar regulatory agencies. Finally, the Wire Act's language may preclude the inclusion of Internet wagering due to the antiquated nature.

By sheer definition, a "wire communication facility" only refers to information (i.e., pictures, writings, and sounds) that is transmitted "by and of a wire, cable or other like connection between points of origin and reception of such transmission." Technological advances in satellite and/or radio communications make such language obsolete and, more important, inapplicable. Until a court decision determines the applicability of such language to T1 or T3 lines necessary for ISP (Internet service provider) connection, the legality of Internet wagering under provisions set forth by the Federal Wire Act of 1961 (18 U.S.C. 1084) remains unclear (Cabot, 1998).

Further problems of application concern mens rea (the concept that one party has a specific intention or knowledge of the criminality of an activity) and jurisdictional disputes. due to the ambiguity surrounding legality and jurisdictional sovereignty, it appears virtually impossible to prove criminal intent pending concrete legislation or court decision. It is not clear if individual sites residing in a state where casino gaming is legal are violating state or federal law by extending online services to state residents or residents of other gambling states. In other words, does this law apply to corporations in Nevada who only take sports wagers from Nevadans or visitors to the state? In addition, questions arise regarding the legality of American residents wagering through interna-

Figure 8.1
Summary of the Kyl Bill

Senator Jon Kyl (R—Arizona) is one of the most vocal opponents of Internet gambling. His bill, the Internet Gambling Prohibition Act, was intended to update the Federal Wire Act of 1961. If passed, the bill would have accomplished the following:

1. Establish the creation of Section 1085 to the Federal Wire Act of 1961, which would prohibit the placing or reception of a wager through the Internet or interactive computer service.

2. Provide specific penalties for both individual bettors and Internet site operators, including fines and penalties of $2,500/six months in prison and $20,000/four years in prison for bettors and operators, respectively.

3. Provide a complex definition of "bet" or "wager"—criminalizing some activities while permitting others. Interestingly, although traditional verbiage like *chance, prize,* and *consideration* could all be applied to stock trading, these activities were excluded from prohibition.

4. Allows provisions incorporated within 1085 to be applied to state jurisdictions.

5. Requires the secretary of state to actively negotiate with international bodies to create binding agreements allowing the enforcement of 1085.

In addition, the bill would have created exclusions for state-operated gambling sites and persons physically present in licensed facilities, thereby protecting the interests of state revenues and established institutions.

Source: "Senator Jon Kyl Press Release," 1998.

tional sites. As many originators of gaming Web sites reside outside of American boundaries, does federal or state law apply to those sites operating legally within their host country when providing services to residents where sports wagering and casino gaming are legal? If so, why and in what circumstances? Thus, jurisdictional enforcement remains questionable. In fact, many of these sites are sanctioned by or actually created for sovereign governments over which the United States has no jurisdiction or in which international relations preclude enforcement concerns.

In an effort to remedy these shortcomings, the Internet Gambling Prohibition Act of 1997 was introduced by Senator Jon Kyl (R—Arizona) (see Figure 8.1). Kyl, chairman of the technology subcommittee of the Senate Judiciary Committee, argues that attempts at regulation will inevitably fail. Kyl's solution is simple—prohibition of all Internet gambling that is not state sponsored or the product of league-sanctioned "rotisserie" leagues. Many critics argue that Kyl's bill is hypocritical—targeting those businesses, organizations, or individuals lacking political power. In fact, other federal agencies have expressed concerns over the expansion of the Wire Act. More specifically, the Kyl bill's provision for civilly penalizing and criminally prosecuting individual bettors is contrary to the attorney general's mission, which has denied that federal remedies are appropriate at this level—suggesting that the Wire Act was only intended for those promoting or soliciting wagers. However, this bill, which closed legal loopholes regarding Internet wagering and included language specifically directed at online sports wagering and casino gaming, died on the House floor after passing the Senate as an amendment to the yet-undecided $33.2 billion Commerce, Justice, and State Appropriations Bill ("Senator Jon Kyl Press Release," 1998).

Although the Kyl bill remains in limbo, the implications of its defeat are clear. Specifically, the Wire Act, in and of itself, does not apply to non-sports-related gambling. The outdated language only applies to sporting events and/or contests. In addition, federal remedies may not be jurisdictionally appropriate, as gambling laws have traditionally fallen under state supervision.

The Travel Act

The second federal statute that may be applied to Internet gambling prohibits interstate and foreign travel in aid or furtherance of racketeering enterprises. More specifically, the Travel Act states

whoever travels in interstate or foreign commerce or uses the mail or any facility in interstate or foreign commerce, with intent to 1) distribute the proceeds of any unlawful activity; or 2) otherwise promote, manage, establish, carry on, or facilitate the promotion, management, establishment, or carrying on, of any unlawful activity, and thereafter performs or attempts to perform (A) an act described in paragraph (1) or (3) shall be fined under this title, imprisoned not more than 5 years, or both (b) As used in this section (I) "unlawful activity" means (I) any business enterprise involving gambling.

This act, significantly broader than the Interstate Wire Act (IWA), may be implemented to prosecute those residents of the United States who establish offshore casinos. This act, unlike the IWA, may also be used to specifically target the individual gambler. However, enforcement of such activity is virtually impossible, as casinos would have to engage in self-defeating collusion with American authorities engaging in wiretapping to trap such violators (Gordon, 1996). This factor, coupled with the considerable monetary expense of enforcement, protects would-be experiments and hardcore gamblers alike.

The Crime Control Act

A final avenue for enforcement resides in the Crime Control Act (18 U.S.C. 1955 [1994]). According to this act:

(a) Whoever conducts, finances, manages, supervises, directs, or owns all or part of an illegal gambling business shall be fined under this title or imprisoned not more than five years, or both. (b) As used in this section—(1) "illegal gambling business: means a gambling business which (I) is a violation of the law of a State or political subdivision in which it is conducted; (ii) involves five or more persons who conduct, finance, manage, supervise, direct, or own all or part of such business; and (iii) has been or remains in substantially continuous operation for a period in excess of thirty days or has a gross revenue of $2,000 in any single day. (2) "gambling" includes but is not limited to bookmaking, maintaining slot machines, roulette wheels or dice tables, and conducting lotteries, policy, bolita or numbers games, or selling chances therein. (3) if five or more persons conduct, finance, manage, supervise, direct, or own all or part of a gambling business and such business operates for two or more successive days, then, for the purpose of obtaining warrants for arrests, interceptions, and other searches and seizures, probable cause that the business receives gross revenue in excess of $2,000 in any single day shall be deemed to have been established.

Assuming that the site has been in operation for the minimum time specified (i.e., 30 days) and assuming that it has been visited by at least five people, the above statute can be applied to gambling sites, Internet providers, and individual gamblers. It is not likely, however, that this act will result in more comprehensive enforcement approaches than the two previously mentioned. As it is currently situated, penalties for violators are much more severe than with the preceding two. Under the Crime Control Act, offenders could be punished criminally and civilly, with severe repercussions However, like the others, it does not appear to be a law enforcement priority (Gordon, 1996). Insufficient technology, personnel, and budget make enforcement of Internet gambling pragmatically impossible.

At the present time, the question of the legality of Internet gambling remains unanswered. There has been virtually no ruling from a federal court that remedies the situation. As such, it is unclear as to, if any, enforcement agency has jurisdiction over Internet gambling. Due to this ambiguity, states have been slow to take action against activities that violate anti-gambling statutes. However, there are some exceptions.

ACTION BY THE STATES

Many states are dissatisfied with the lack of federal regulation concerning cybergaming. Missouri Attorney General Jay Nixon obtained a civil injunction and damages totaling over $65,000 against Interactive Gaming and Communications, Inc. Similar cases are pending in New York and Minnesota. In fact, the Las Vegas–based Granite Gate resort is under fire from Minnesota Attorney General Hubert Humphrey III for utilizing false advertising techniques to solicit customers with assurances that Internet gaming was entirely legal in their jurisdiction. Idaho, not traditionally known for its gambling industry, has also entered the fray— rescinding support from the Coeur d'Alene Indian tribe when it established itself on the Internet. The tribe, arguing that their remote location handicapped them against other Native American initiatives, established a national Web site advertising lottery and eventual video poker accessibility. Their case, in particular, garnered interest from state legislators concerned with competition from the private sector. However, the legality of Native American–owned Internet wagering sites has not yet been decided.

One case that may serve to provide more immediate legislation concerns a civil case in California by Cynthia Haines. The plaintiff, a Marin County, California, resident, filed a countersuit in response to a civil action seeking compensation for $70,000 worth of gambling debts incurred on Haines's credit card. Haines contends that lending institutions violate anti-gambling laws by extending credit to gaming institutions and by making a percentage off gaming transactions (i.e., cash advances). Her suit, filed under the California Unfair Business Practice Act, likens such credit card companies to electronic loansharks. She is seeking monetary damages and, more important, an injunction barring lending institutions from extending credit in the furtherance of Internet gaming. Though as yet undecided, Haines won the first round when a motion to throw the case out was refused. If successful, her case would dramatically impact the viability of Internet gaming, as most wagering is accomplished through open lines of credit on bank-issued cards.

ACTION BY THE FEDERAL GOVERNMENT

Perhaps buffered by state cases, the first federally prosecuted case of its kind was initiated in New York in March 1998. Unlike the previous cases, federal agents charged individuals from five non-American companies. Some of the affected parties include the Global Sports Network/ Dominican Republic, Grand Holiday Casino/Caracas, and World Wide Telesports/Antigua. Although some of the 21 defendants have already pleaded guilty, some have chosen to argue the legality of prosecution while the application is unclear. More specifically, they argue that since they required bettors to establish offshore accounts in Antigua, the site's home, bets received and money wagered occurred not in the United States but in a country embracing companies of this sort. In addition, they argue that the Wire Act may only apply if one of the parties was behaving illegally. As their operations are legal within the boundaries of their residence and since the bets were placed in New York where it is legal to place such wagers over the phone, no party involved was in violation of federal law. Though the first of its kind, the as-of-yet-undecided case may not establish the clarification of illegal Internet wagering, as each defendant has at least one charge involving telephonic wagering. Thus, international or federal sovereignty may remain questionable.

One of the major questions facing administrators is the administration of localized legislation. In fact, it appears impossible to enforce jurisdictional regulations when the Internet is an international enterprise that ignores community boundaries and local legislation. And so the issue of jurisdictional appropriateness may not lie in either federal or state realms. Rather, in the absence of an international consortium, it would appear that attempts at censorship (oops, regulation) are inherently ethnocentric and doomed to fail. Does it seem logical to assume, for example, that legislation by the U.S. government will be recognized by foreign countries, especially those poised to greatly enhance previously empty coffers at minimal expense?

THE BUSINESS OF ONLINE WAGERING

Although the federal government has introduced legislation to limit or eliminate Internet gaming, some state governments have openly supported online endeavors in their gambling enterprises. For example, the creation of Capital OTB may signal a new era in governmentally sponsored gambling. Created by the New York State legislature, Capital OTB is designed to increase revenue earned from offtrack betting. Ostensibly, this agreement revitalizes a dying industry (i.e., horse racing) while providing funding for local programs. However, it remains unclear as to who is the primary beneficiary. Not surprisingly, state acceptance or tolerance has been limited to endeavors that fatten government coffers. (The Kyl bill would not interfere with such state-supported initiatives.)

Government ambiguity is not unique to the United States. Other countries are either reluctant to expend limited resources on such an endeavor or have been defeated in initial regulatory attempts. Canada, for example, attempted to regulate online gambling, but the defeat of Bill C-353 has left the future of legislation in limbo. While Canada's approach has been similar to the United States', some countries have actually allowed online wagering or utilized the World Wide Web to forward their own gambling interests. Tote, the state-run English gambling firm, is heavily promoted and, with governmental backing, may outpace privately held telephone betting services. Indeed, Britain's approach has resulted in the emergence of a variety of legitimate—and highly lucrative—online companies. Some of these sites are run with corporate-like precision. BetOnLine is a prime example. Hosted by the British Sporting Life Web site, this site is open to all UK residents over the age of 18 and by all estimates is experiencing unprecedented growth. In fact, other countries may soon turn to similar measures to enhance parimutuel wagering and increase state revenue (Cabot, 1998). Australia and New Zealand are but two examples of countries actively contemplating the advantages of taxation and regulation. Utilizing regulatory oversight, these countries propose to direct revenues to the originating jurisdiction of the bettor. In the event that foreign wagers are placed, revenues would be directed to the jurisdiction hosting the site (Baker, 1999).

CONCLUSION

The advent of Internet technology has created a variety of dilemmas for policy makers around the globe. The lack of oversight and control has led several interest groups to protest certain technologically based businesses. The transfer and availability of pornographic material was the first issue tackled by policy makers and legislators. Though interest groups claimed that the protection of innocents (i.e., children) was at stake, the Supreme Court ruled that First Amendment privileges precluded censorship. However, these same administrators have now targeted Internet gambling under the ruse of protecting children and adults alike. Buoyed by support from the Christian Right and the American Gaming Association, recent legislation has attempted to curtail the onslaught of cyberspace gambling. Although the issue is still under debate, attempts to eliminate online gaming have been introduced. Though not unique in this respect, it is important to remember that powerful lobbying groups have entered the fray. As such, individual agendas have emerged.

Casinos are one of the strongest—and most vocal—opponents of Internet wagering. Their argument that the integrity of Internet gaming sites cannot be assured probably has some merit. In the absence of regulation, any operator may develop a site inherently fraudulent. However, the lucrative nature of legitimate sites and online chat room and discussion groups should minimize the risk to consumers. The same accessibility that makes this initiative lucrative may serve to police scam-oriented businesses. In fact, legitimately run enterprises would be shortsighted to cheat paying customers. The success of land-based casinos—which herald promises of integrity and fairness—indicates that the house advantage sufficiently assures economic success. Coupled with the low operating costs associated with cybercasinos, respectable entrepreneurs may expect tremendous return with minimum risk.

The factors that make online venture so attractive are the very factors that threaten land-based casinos. Although traditional entrepreneurs like Donald Trump and Steve Wynn are unparalleled success stories, their bottom lines are directly related to gaming revenues minus astronomical overheads. The multimillions that have been invested in land development and casino construction may only be profitable once gaming revenues exceed their initial investments. Quite simply, any decrease in consumer interest significantly decreases their lucrativity. No wonder, then, that these groups are opposed to establishments that only require Internet operators, site development, telephone maintenance, and computer equipment. This is not intended to vilify such entities. Indeed, principles of capitalism are much in keeping with the adage "All is fair in love and war." Thus, the land-based gaming industry is simply displaying good sense in their efforts to eradicate or cast shadows over Internet gaming. Indeed, their efforts seem to have achieved a desired response from American policy makers. However, the future of legislation remains unclear.

The legality of cybergaming remains in question as potential impacts on individuals, noncyber establishments, and local and state economies are discussed. In keeping with the give-me-more-right-now environment so common in the United States, it is anticipated that fingertip accessibility will result in a virtual cyberboom of gambling activity. Protected by its very sophistication, Internet gambling has thus far proven to be too cost intensive and too technologically advanced for local and federal authorities. In fact, both jurisdictions have refused sovereignty, and only sporadic enforcement has occurred. As a result, the legality of such enterprises remains uncertain. The language of the federal legislation that may be applicable is far too antiquated, and alternative legislation has been slow to emerge. One exception, Senator John Kyl's (R—Arizona) Internet Gambling Prohibition Act of 1997—which specifically addressed Internet wagering—has failed to bear fruit but may portend future legislation. State-level politicians have fared a little better. Minnesota, New York, and Missouri courts have all provided judgments adverse to the World Wide Web of gambling. However, the future remains unclear, and policy implications have been all but ignored.

Although recent legislation has supported an all-out prohibition of non-state- and/or non-league-sponsored Internet gambling, the viability of enforcement remains in question. One jurisdiction is not capable of enforcing an all-out ban of Internet gaming. Too many small, undeveloped countries are willing to host such endeavors for tax revenues and the like. In addition, it is impossible to eliminate cybergaming without going after individual bettors. Even if the government was successful in eliminating all American-based sites, individual bettors could still bet with international companies with little difficulty. Interested individuals could simply locate an offshore site and, with the minimal inconvenience of securing an outside line and additional telephone charges, could place their bets using a variety of payment methods.

All-out prohibition of Internet gaming activity would magnify the problems of implementation of the Volstead Act in the 1920s. It is tremendously naive to believe that inclined citizens would simply abandon such activity. Just as Prohibition—the Great Experiment—and the ban on prostitution have proved to be dismal failures, such regulation only strains available resources. Indeed, American authorities would bear the monumental expense of enforcement singularly, whereas other jurisdictions would prosper through the displaced gambling revenues. Even if the American public was willing to fund such an initiative, it is unlikely that those same Americans would agree to the constitutional violations inherently attached to a mandate that would require monitoring of citizens within their private residences.

If authorities are concerned with the potentially negative impacts on individual bettors, there are some commonsensical strategies that may be employed. As discussed, it seems illogical to suppose that any government entity acting singularly could eliminate all online gambling. Unfortunately, such commissions may initially be unpopular among American residents. Though the necessity of such a multijurisdictional, international regulatory agency is certain, the acceptance among the masses may be delayed. It should be anticipated that such an attempt may prove unpalatable to Americans skeptical of government intrusion. As unpalatable as governmental supervision appears, it may be the only feasible solution.

In this era of political instability and international conflict, it appears unlikely that a *worldwide* commission or even global compliance could be established. As much as possible, administrators must then obtain the cooperation of affected or participating international governments. In the absence of a worldwide agreement, administrators must focus on an international approach of strict regulation, licensing, and oversight. Such approaches would consolidate available resources, making legislation and enforcement much more realistic. As such, administrators may, for example, license online casinos openly, assuring that the majority of monies wagered would be directed to institutions monitored and regulated by the government. Like state commissions, this would assure the integrity of such sites and discourage patronage of nonregulated sites. The specter of dishonest operators and fraudulent sites should be enough to divert the bulk of funds to federally regulated sites.

Regulations should mirror mandates established by the various state commissions. Payout percentages and careful accounting procedures should be established and published. Game integrity should be ensured through random monitoring techniques. Penalties for violators should be immediate and severe. Such supervision should be embraced by operators, who would benefit from solid reputations, and consumers, who would be assured of a fair game.

Further control should be exerted to prevent the increase in problem gambling often associated with increased availability. Concerned government entities should provide safeguards for individuals with a propensity to gamble beyond their economic resources. This solution requires the cooperation of infrastructure businesses. As cybercasinos require electronically available funds and as consumers are unlikely to send large sums of money to be deposited in offshore accounts, governmental officials and industry executives may turn to credit card companies and banking institutions for help. For without the access of established lines of credit and the absence of protection from fraudulent activities, cybercasinos would have to seek alternative methods of payment. The government may enact legislation that would require deposit of certified funds prior to wagering. This would serve to remind individuals that cybercredits actually represent monies invested. In this way, individuals would be dissuaded from wagering irresponsibly or in a manner inconsistent with their personal finances. Though site operators may object to such disallowances, credit-lending institutions should prove an easy sell as they stand to lose substantial sums in the event of bankruptcy due to gambling debts.

Online gaming sites should also be required to develop strategies to prevent underage gambling. Regulation could include, for example, the requirement that state-issued photo identification (i.e., driver's license) and one other form of ID be presented at account opening. Individual sites could also choose to require notarized statements of identification. This would prevent children from cyberwagering, a concern voiced by many opponents, and would also ensure compliance with jurisdictional law. Thus, the interests of nongambling states would be protected. This requirement should not unduly burden individual bettors or online operators. In fact, it would protect the interests of cybercasinos by providing detailed information on their consumers and protect them from civil litigation. The issuance of passwords should further protect the integrity of e-transactions. This is not to suggest that such measures are fail-proof. There is still a possibility that some determined individual could provide false information and counterfeit identification, thereby "beating the system." Just as underage individuals find methods to obtain alcohol, tobacco, and other forms of contraband, they will inevitably devise ways to defeat security measures. These measures are intended to provide some form of barrier to keep curious children outside of their boundaries. Those individuals who deliberately violate the law by circumventing existing safeguards are criminals by definition. Strict laws and punishments should be enacted to address such violators.

Taxes generated from the regulated sites should be diverted in a manner similar to proposals in Australia and New Zealand. Monies should
be channeled to the originating jurisdiction of the wager (i.e., the bettor's
location). In the event that foreign or out-of-state wagers are placed,
revenues should be utilized by the hosting jurisdiction (i.e., site location).
Though states may differ on the distribution of such monies, some of it
should be specifically earmarked for law enforcement, treatment facilities, community revitalization, and education. In fact, administrators
should evaluate the strategies employed by those jurisdictions currently
hosting gaming venues and develop plans prior to legalization and subsequent licensing. Comprehensive planning should result in a mutually
beneficial relationship between government entities and industry representatives.

Finally, it should be apparent that state interests remain sacrosanct.
As gambling issues have traditionally been debated at this level, federal
authorities should be limited to simple oversight. Although the development of an international committee mandates the involvement of the
federal government, state legislators should not be precluded from offering this type of industry through imposition of a national ban. Indeed,
their role should be likened to that of a sports referee—posting the rules
of the game and mediating potential disputes between players. As their
constitutional mandate requires, they should protect the rights of individual states without limiting them.

REFERENCES

Baker, Debra. (1999). "Betting on Cyberspace: When It Comes to the Future of
     Internet Gambling, All Wagers Are Off." *ABA Journal* (March): 54–57.
Cabot, Anthony. (1998). *Internet Gambling Report II*. Las Vegas: Trace Publications.
Crist, Steven. (1998). "All Bets Are Off." *Sports Illustrated*, January 26: 35–40.
Gordon, Britta. (1996). "Gaming on the Internet: The Odds Are on the House,
     but How Will It Last?" *Texas Tech Law School's Cyberjournal*. http://
     www.law.ttu.edu/cyberspc/jour9.htm.
Karleff, Ian. (1998). "Cybergambling: Where She Stops, Nobody Knows: Australia
     Takes the Lead—For Virtual Casinos, the Stocks Run Wild, the Laws Run
     Loose." *Financial Post*, December 5.
Neumeister, Larry. (1998). "Prosecutors Expand Case after Finding No End to
     Internet Gambling." *Detroit News*, March 27.
Preston, Mark D. (1998). "Internet Gambling Perplexes Feds." *The Sun*, December
     3.
"Senator Jon Kyl Press Release—Kyl Bill Prohibiting Internet Gambling." (1998).
     http://thomas.loc.gov/cgi-in/query/D?c106:2:./temp/c106IO81Ay:e365.

Chapter 9

Intellectualizing the Action: Why People Gamble

Traditionally, definitions of gambling have been constructed around assumptions of economic or social repercussions, rather than a process or phenomenon in and of itself. Clinicians, focusing on the negative consequences of gambling behavior, have been quick to develop typologies and inchoate definitions that may or may not adequately clarify operational constructs. In fact, few attempts have illustrated the complexity of the phenomenon. While it has been pointed out that gambling is most appropriately situated on a continuum of activity, resolution of all behaviors has not been incorporated. Authors have consistently concentrated on the extremes while failing to meaningfully operationalize those situated in between. Unfortunately, most definitions are predicated on the assumptions of loss and negative personal consequences—reifying the need for some sort of intervention. Indeed, the vast majority of definitional approaches to gambling and its participants have been developed by individuals who actually benefit from such ambiguity.

COMPULSIVE GAMBLING

Throughout the literature, terms such as *compulsive, pathological*, and *problem* gambling are either treated synonymously or as naturally progressive with no accompanying explanation. Few authors have examined the operational discrepancies between the terms. Bergler's use of the term *compulsive gambling* remains the most widely used (1957). Bergler asserted that these individuals were driven by an unconscious wish to lose that made it virtually impossible to control their gambling behavior (Rosencrance, 1989). It was argued that gambling behavior, in and of itself, promoted self-destructive behavior that could only be controlled through professional treatment. Contemporary definitions have largely followed suit, issuing dire warnings predicated on value judgments and sweeping generalizations.

Compulsive gambling is an addictive illness in which the subject is driven by an overwhelming, uncontrollable impulse to gamble. The impulse persists and progresses in intensity and urgency, consuming more and more of the individual's time, energy and emotional and material resources. Ultimately, it invades, undermines and often destroys everything that is meaningful in a person's life. (Custer and Milt, 1985, 4)

These clinical types of definitions have proven to be most pragmatic in their design—as compulsives have developed the much-earned reputation as the gravy train of psychoanalysis. Indeed, the American Psychiatric Association formally discusses "pathological gambling" as an "impulse-control disorder"–one treatable through intensive therapy.

Nonclinical definitions have predicated definitions on pecuniary loss and personal consequences. Livingston (1974, 2), for example, defined "compulsive gambling" as "gambling more often and losing more money than one wishes or intends—usually to the point of serious financial and personal consequences. A compulsive gambler is a person who gambles compulsively." In an attempt to more clearly differentiate between compulsive and noncompulsive gamblers, Livingston stated that this definition only referred to those individuals who "spend more time gambling compulsively than others who might on occasion behave in a similar way" (2). Unfortunately, this "clarification" lacks robusticity, as would any attempt that relied upon assumptions of normalcy rather than definitive parameters. Livingston's study consisted of those

people who have on many occasions lost more than they intended and felt that their gambling was a problem. Most of them have borrowed heavily to finance gambling, and several have gone to criminal lengths to get money for gambling or to cover gambling losses. . . . [Subjects] felt that they could not quit gambling even though it was ruining their lives and even though they vowed on numerous occasions that they would never gamble again. (2)

According to Livingston, there are four distinct levels of compulsive gambling: binge gamblers, paycheck-to-paycheck gamblers, continuous gamblers , and edge gamblers. Binge gamblers, the least intense level of compulsion, involved those individuals whose gambling was punctuated with long periods of abstinence. Paycheck-to-paycheck gamblers and continuous gamblers are more consistent in their gambling habits, whereas edge gamblers are situated at the end of existence–ignoring debts, responsibilities, and significant others.

Livingston's study is filled with colorful characters and insightful anecdotes. However, it only includes self-identified "compulsive" gamblers. It may be argued that those individuals who have already self-diagnosed their gambling as an illness may have preconceived notions about the nature of addictive disorders. Indeed, these individuals may actually repeat societal or clinical definitions, unwittingly perpetuating nonempirical assumptions of compulsive behavior. In addition, his study fails to control for those individuals who have not identified their gambling as problematic.

A more current definition of compulsive gambling quite comparable to Livingston's suffers from a similar lack of differentiation among gamblers. According to Wexler (1992), compulsive gamblers are those individuals who bet until no personal belongings are left—depleting their savings, liquidating family assets, and borrowing from family, friends, and lending institutions to feed their addiction. The majority of these addicts, secretive in their habits, often deny the existence of behavioral pathologies. In fact, some of these individuals may actually graduate to illegal activity to continue their compulsion. Unfortunately, Wexler failed to differentiate between *levels* of compulsive gambling. While it may appear almost intuitive that this level of behavior clearly resides outside the realm of rationality, it does not adequately address individuals who may exhibit less severe self-destructive behavioral patterns. Furthermore, such an abstract interpretation tends to overestimate the number of individuals displaying these "symptoms" while failing to provide a schematic for empirical evaluation or an explanation for such a phenomenon.

Livingston (1974) and Wexler (1992) are not the only authors who have attempted to compartmentalize compulsive gambling into one neatly wrapped package. In fact, few attempts have been made to delineate stages of behavioral development. However, there is one notable exception. Lesieur (1984) approached gambling as a progressive phenomenon in which gambling is initially approached as a form of recreation with few adverse consequences. This honeymoon period, or "winning phase," is characterized by at least marginal successes. These windfalls self-gratify the player's perception of competence and power, whereas losses are perceived as circumstances of chance. Graduation to the "losing" phase is punctuated with periods of deceptive activity—designed to elicit funds to replenish depleted accounts and provide capital to "chase" monies lost. Finally, individuals exhibit obsessive behavior—often engaging in criminal behavior to combat their escalating financial problems. This desperation phase represents the end of the line for most gamblers. Circumstances necessitate an end to gambling activity—albeit an involuntary cessation (Lesieur, 1984).

Others have argued that gambling can only be considered to be "compulsive" when individuals forsake personal vows—as is the case when

Figure 9.1
Ten Symptoms of Pathological Gambling

---

1. Preoccupation with gambling (reliving past experiences, planning future excursions, developing new ways to make money to support their habit, etc.).

2. Inability to stop gambling when ahead due to their desire to achieve an "aroused" or "euphoric" state.

3. Steadily increasing the size of bets.

4. Intolerance of losing (i.e., chasing losses).

5. General neglect of family, occupation, or marriage.

6. Borrowing, begging, lying, embezzling, stealing, or selling drugs to finance gambling or pay back debts.

7. Gambling when frustrated or disappointed.

8. Gambling in celebration of a success.

9. Concealing losses.

10. Defaulting on loans.

Source: APA, 1994.

an individual who has previously stated an intention to avoid gambling engages in the behavior. This distinction necessarily excludes those individuals who have not yet reached a stage of recognition and identification. Indeed, many studies have identified individuals who have not yet felt the impact of their behavior or individuals who have suffered significant social, economic, and personal loss but have not yet recognized their behavior as destructive (e.g., Custer and Milt, 1985). By its definition, individuals placed in this category are those who have lost their self-control or who have had an irresistible impulse or compulsion.

PATHOLOGICAL GAMBLING

Many authors have failed to differentiate between *compulsive* and *pathological* gambling, assuming that the terms were simply interchangeable or synonymous. Indeed, a comparison between the previously discussed approaches to compulsive gambling do not appear to differ significantly from that of the American Psychiatric Association's (APA's) approach to pathological gambling. Defined primarily as "persistent and recurrent maladaptive gambling behavior that disrupts personal, family, or vocational pursuits" (APA, 1994, 615), pathological gambling seems to differ from compulsive gambling only in the sophistication of the language that defines it (see Figure 9.1). In fact, the 10 "symptoms" of such a malady are all but identical to those behaviors observed by Livingston (1974), Wexler (1992), and Lesieur (1984).

Perhaps the disparity in terminology can be explained through the motivation of such behaviors. According to the APA, individuals suffering from pathological gambling are driven by an irresistible impulse to engage in behaviors that may be harmful to them or those around them. Nonclinicians, on the other hand, suggest that compulsive gamblers behave illogically and irrationally for no apparent reason. Whatever the case may be, it appears that the differences between the two are significant only to those whose occupation necessitates such a diagnosis. As with the previously discussed approaches, the DSM–IV (APA, 1994) interpretation lacks definitive parameters. In fact, this lack of specificity may actually encourage disparate diagnoses—not altogether a bad idea if intended for commercial (i.e., capitalistic) pursuits. For both clinicians and nonpractitioners, the question of how many interludes into compulsion are required for diagnostic purposes remains unanswered. Further criticisms have focused on the subjective nature of the medicalization model and the evolving nature of the definition. (As clinical diagnosis is predicated on individual decision-making processes and outcomes, many have suggested that the model lacks definitive parameter.) More specifically, two of the criteria focus on resolutions previously stated by self-identified "addicts."

Further critics have pointed to the inability of the APA to adequately clarify the phenomenon in question. Original attempts mandated arrests, illegal business transactions, and absenteeism. The contemporary model (listed above) does not require any of these earlier factors but provides broader categories of inclusion. While some deviations are tolerated— even expected—in the early stages of research, such departures call into question the rigidity of the empirical model. In addition, the exclusion of withdrawal symptoms from the measuring instrument questions the validity of medicalization—as diagnosis and treatment have been predicated on assumptions of physical or emotional superficialities.

Summarily, the APA has successfully renovated outdated substance abuse criterion into a foundation for pathological gambling. While this approach has traditionally been financially and politically advantageous, individual implications remain unclear. In fact, many "experts" are encouraging their colleagues to look elsewhere for the addiction gravy train–warning of a social backlash.

If we continue trying to establish the validity of pathological gambling by claiming it is a disease just like alcoholism, we may find ourselves on a limb destined for pruning. (Rosenthal, 1989, 106–107)

Finally, the medicalization model necessitates a subjective judgment on the part of the treatment provider. Certainly, the determination of control is individually perceived. As such, contemporary definitions must develop standards and criteria independent of traditional definitions–eradicating the structure and rebuilding the foundation.

EMERGING DEFINITIONS

Not all researchers have relied upon assumptions of empiricism and interpretive accuracy. A more sophisticated distinction was introduced that claimed to overcome traditional deficiencies in terminology. Shaffer and Hall (1997, 9) argued that the term *disordered gambling* recognizes that variation in gambling behavior and "transcends each of the existing constructs by recognizing that each of these categories represents at various levels of intensity, a lack of order in one of the major systems of human experience." In addition, this approach was one of the first to suggest that gamblers and their activities were more appropriately situated on a continuum. According to the study, gambling behavior is a tripartite phenomenon. Accordingly, level-one gambling was classified as recreational gambling, in which individual gamblers experienced no adverse consequences. Level-two gambling, which may be classified as *problem, at risk, in transition,* and *potential pathological,* was a pattern of gambling that was associated with subclinical levels of adverse reactions or consequences. And finally, level-three gambling was defined as behavior that satisfied diagnostic criteria and had clinical significance. Unfortunately, no clear distinction between recreational and intemperate gambling was identified.

Summarily, it appears that no concise definition of pathological, problem, compulsive, disordered, and so on, gambling has yet been established within the extant literature. In fact, in their haste to develop clinical classifications and diagnosable conditions, psychiatrists and the like have removed gambling behavior from the vague continuum on which it should reside. Accordingly, definitions of problem/pathological/excessive/disordered/compulsive gambling tend to be study specific, and any estimation of problem behavior lacks even superficial generalizability. As such, discussions of gambling prevalence and characterizations of affected individuals become meaningless outside the confines of contextual description. Thus, readers should proceed with extreme caution as few authors include warning labels regarding their study's generalizability.

SQUARE PEGS IN ROUND HOLES: GAMBLING THEORIES

Although gambling was reported as early as biblical times, it was not until the twentieth century that medicalization of the phenomenon hit its stride. Indeed, early prevention models relied heavily on religious teaching and moral restrictions—as religious leaders were touted as harbingers of morality. However, the increase in religious plurality and the weakening of secular influence signaled the beginning of state-sanctioned morality and medicalization of deviance. As a result, federal and state monies—available through granting agencies—became the preferred audience for treatment providers. Thus, behaviors that were traditionally considered inherently sinful were now explained through individual pathologies or medical diagnoses. In fact, identification and observation of factors external to the individual remained largely unexplored until the 1960s.

Traditional Psychoanalytical Approaches

Definition notwithstanding, the majority of literature that has focused on compulsive gambling has largely concentrated on psychoanalytic theories and suppositions. Traditionally, these psychoanalysts sexualized gambling—equating compulsive gambling with excessive masturbation, perverse incestuous desires, and the like. To these theorists, gambling losses were incurred to satisfy subconscious needs for self-punishment. These losses reaffirmed the wrongness of their behavior and assuaged elevated levels of guilt and self-loathing (e.g., Bergler, 1957). Psychoanalysts have also argued that gambling is most apparent in those individuals with unresolved oral and/or anal fixations. These theorists argued that gambling activity is highly correlated with oral behaviors such as smoking and drinking and anal characteristics such as compulsive neatness and the like (Greeson, 1947). Others have argued that gambling activity may be indicative of homosexual tendencies, as gambling has traditionally been characterized as a male phenomenon, or of masochistic desires, as gambling is inherently self-defeating.

Keeping in mind that these decidedly different explanations originated from the same field of study, it is apparent that there is an academic tendency to classify or categorize phenomena. While promoting such distinctions as academic attempts at clarification, it may be suggested that this practice effectively territorializes the behavior, phenomenon, and more important, the treatment of gambling and problems traditionally associated. This tendency to territorialize permeates the gambling literature, as evidenced by the overabundance of psychological explanations and carte blanche dismissal of rival explanations. For example, Rosenthal's (1989) classification of behavioral models included in the extant literature excludes external or sociological factors, such as race, gender, and socioeconomic status (SES); instead, it appears that gambling behaviors, particularly those that prove deviant, may be attributed primarily to individual psychodynamics (i.e., Freudian) or biology. In the rare case in which external factors are incorporated into cognitive models, only characteristics of the game itself are evaluated (i.e., winning/losing, etc.). These theories of behavioral reinforcement negate the possible influence of traditional sociological explanations or causative factors. While certainly one might agree that psychodynamic/Freudian, behavioral/reinforcement, psychobiological models have theoretical merit, an integration of the models without sociological considerations obviously lacks empiricism.

Indeed, this tendency to overlook work in other disciplines is so apparent that even those individuals who condemn others for discipline-related tunnel vision fail to recognize their own. For example, Shaffer (1989) dismisses sociological explanations as "descriptive (rather) than interpretive," using gamblers' descriptions of their own behavior, whereas psychological models are mainly used by providers of treatment and take an outside, interpretive viewpoint (66). However, this bias is only obvious to those outside the particular area that is affected. Unfortunately, academic theorizing is often directly correlated with subsequent government regulation and policy implementation. Thus, the majority of government funding expended has focused on the personal or individual treatment of pathological gambling.

The Sexualization of Gambling

As stated, certain fields of study have recognized the economic and political advantages of medicalization of deviant activities. Building on addiction models, originally established to address alcohol and substance abuse, psychoanalysts have successfully parlayed theories of gambling into lucrative treatment facilities and personal practices. As a result, two distinctive approaches to explanation and treatment have emerged. The first approach focused on game dynamics, rather than individual compulsion. They suggested that individuals engaging in pathological gambling are actually compelled by the game, which has previously provided them with some sort of gratification (Moran, 1970). This Skinneristic approach suggests that individuals who win early in their gambling career are more likely to develop gambling fixations. However, positive augmentations may not be restricted to pecuniary gain. Rather, emotional gambling behavior is a result of positive reinforcement—whether through feelings of omnipotence, exhilaration of winning, escape from reality, or economic rewards. Indeed, as this reinforcement tends to be random rather than routine, patterned responses are harder to manipulate. (Interestingly, a Pavlovian approach that evaluates conditioned responses has not been undertaken.) In addition, Ainslie (1984) argued that the inability to control one's gambling behavior was attributed to the struggle between two competing motivations—each with its own system of reward and punishment. The victor in an individual's struggle was usually the first event that promised some reward. Larger but delayed rewards proved to be less attractive during an individual's decision-making process. Because the emotional high or the positive feeling experienced by gambling necessarily preceded the outcome of the wager, individuals looking for gratification were predisposed to bet. This suggestion has a variety of implications for treatment programs. Theoretically speaking, practitioners could encourage the manipulation of the time factor—holding it constant, thereby negating its causative nature.

The second approach, largely discredited, suggested that compulsive gambling was actually a manifestation of deep-rooted psychosexual inadequacies (Rosencrance, 1989). Originally proposed by H. Von Hattingberg as early as 1914, these theories of self-gratification created a framework for future psychoanalysts. Individuals such as Georg Simmel argued that gambling was a form of auto-erotic gratification—a behavioral manifestation of one's desire for self-insemination. And while these individuals inevitably failed in their desires, an entire discipline was born—a discipline that grossly lacked empiricism but self-gratified (perhaps psychologically as well as economically) its postdates.

Perhaps the best known of these soothsayers was Sigmund Freud, undisputed father of psychoanalysis. As with other projects, Freud's conclusions were based on a rather limited sample—namely, one individual whom Freud had never even met. Freud's analysis of Dostoyevsky, a Russian novelist, likened gambling to self-gratification or masturbation. Dostoyevsky's gambling resulted from repressed oedipal urgings. Cyclical losses and self-punishment assuaged his guilt and reinforced the wrongness of his desires. Thus, gamblers engaged in self-defeating behaviors that resulted in elevated levels of economic loss but relieved the pressure and pain associated with their incestuous desires. Though deeply rooted in the sexual nature of most psychoanalytic explanations, contemporary theorists have tended to distance themselves from the more blatant use of oedipal metaphors. Instead, many of these individuals have stressed the commonalities of many gamblers, highlighting instances of self-reported fatalism (Kusyszyn and Rubenstein, 1985).

Greeson (1947) and Bergler (1957) argued that gambling is actually a manifestation of infantile behavior consistent with oral fixations—inasmuch as gambling behavior is often punctuated by an increase in smoking, drinking, and eating. In keeping with various other activities traditionally labeled as deviant, Greeson (1947) further posited that gambling ran the gamut of psychoanalytic neuroses, including phallic, aggressive, masturbatory, masochistic, and homosexual disorders. This sexualization of gambling activity, the norm throughout the psychoanalytic literature, has been grounded in suppositions of narcissistic tendencies and self-gratification. However, the field has failed to provide an explanation of the inherent contradictions espoused by the approaches. In fact, it is semantically impossible to equate approaches of narcissism and fatalism—an impossibility that has been naively over-looked or intentionally ignored.

Other Psychological Explanations

While many theorists have focused on the erotic attraction of gambling to some individuals, others have suggested various nonsexual explanations. Many psychologists have suggested that certain individuals possess clinical predispositions to addictive behaviors (Jacobs, 1989). Indeed, it would appear that empirical examination has revealed relationships between alcohol and/or substance abuse and excessive gambling (Gowen, 1997; Ramirez, McCormick, Russo, and Taber, 1984). Others have suggested that individuals exhibiting destructive patterns of gambling are actually "suffering" from a variety of other psychological ailments (e.g., Livingston, 1974). This throw-everything-at-them-and-see-which-one-sticks approach is elementary and has grossly empirical validity. However, some theorists suggest that pathological gamblers exhibit a number of indicators for both narcissistic personality disorder and antisocial personality disorder. They argue that self-involvement or self-grandiosement makes individuals susceptible to the monocular world of the gambler. Narcissistic manifestations include depressed levels of self-esteem, disregard for significant others, impulsivity, decreased satisfaction with interpersonal relationships, and shortsightedness. Interesting, these factors are also displayed by individuals clinically diagnosed as "antisocial." Unfortunately, such overlap fails to reasonably address the issue of causality. In fact, reliance on other theoretical constructs all but negates the possibility of empirical evaluation.

Moran's (1970) delineation of five distinctive personalities of pathological gamblers suggested a variety of psychological explanations for excessive gambling. These included:

1. *Subcultural.* Individuals whose gambling behaviors are manifestations of the social setting involved.
2. *Neurotic.* Those not motivated by economic gain.
3. *Impulsive.* Those who display periods of uncontrollable behavior or who report ambivalence toward the gambling experience.
4. *Psychopathic.* Those for whom gambling is one piece in a larger disturbance.
5. *Symptomatic.* Those for whom gambling is actually symptomatic of a larger mental pathology.

Some individuals who have identified with the medicalization model have delineated factors that may "predispose" someone to gambling disorders. In fact, these predisposing factors mirror some of the factors commonly evaluated under sociological approaches and leave nonclinicians pondering the value of a science that leaves the explanation of a phenomenon to a competing discipline.

1. Emphasis on social status in family.
2. A particularly critical or rejecting parent with whom the gambler identified.
3. Father either a failure or very successful; and competitive.
4. A neglecting or inconsistent mother, or one who clearly preferred a sibling.
5. Family history of alcoholism or compulsive gambling.
6. Physical defect, or some other developmental or medical problem causing shame or humiliation. (Rosenthal, 1989, 119)

Criticisms of the Medical Model

The medicalization of gambling is inherently riddled with subjective judgments. For example, clinical diagnosis is predicated on individual decision-making processes and outcomes. More specifically, two of the criteria focus on resolutions previously stated by self-identified "addicts." While certainly this lack of restraint may call into question an individual's strength of character, these criteria alone or collectively may not be indicative of a clinical disorder. Furthermore, this conclusion necessitates a subjective judgment on the part of the treatment provider. Certainly, the determination of control is individually perceived, regardless of clinical directives.

In addition, clinicians only look as far as previously identified pathologies. Determinant factors may be overlooked if not identified prior to medicalization—a fact recognized by others who suggest that

therapists often unknowingly communicate their expectations for patient performance . . . this sequence of events directly influence the clinical setting and whether patients will consider certain material important enough to be discussed and examined . . . psychoanalysts look for and find unconscious material such as unresolved Oedipal conflicts and drive/affect defenses and ignore reinforcing events that might develop a conditioned response pattern. (Shaffer, 1989, 3)

In addition, the vast majority of these studies are so methodologically flawed as to render their findings meaningless. Like much literature in this field, a number of sources rely solely on case studies for data collection and analysis. Empirical criticisms of such an approach are too numerous to mention in their entirety. However, it is sufficient to say that researcher/subject bias directly affects both internal and external validity and negates reliability. Further, nonrandom samples of self-identified problem gamblers lack robusticity in both their design and their findings. It is all but apparent that individuals seeking treatment whether voluntarily or through external encouragement (i.e., court orders, etc.) have preconceived notions of their "addiction" prior to treatment. Thus, causality and time order are indiscernible. Further, purposive sampling in limited jurisdictions known for the availability of gambling opportunities fails to consider the impact of such accessibility. This oversight, coupled with the lack of other sociological characteristics, severely hampers (if not totally decimates) previous findings. And finally, like much of the research that has been conducted on problem gambling, evaluation of gender effects either are overlooked or are predicated on outdated notions of masculinity. For example, one approach suggests that men and women are attracted to gambling for different reasons. Males, it is argued, are attracted to the active nature of gambling opportunities, drawn to highly competitive, nonmonotonous venues such as cards, dice, and racing. These gamblers are characterized as being overly competitive and fantastical in their expectations. Unlike "escape" (i.e., female) gamblers, these individuals are primarily motivated by cynosural narcissism and power. Escape gamblers, on the other hand, are individuals who are seeking respite—albeit temporarily—from their mundane and tortured existence. For the most part, they are described as lonely, depressed, abused females who involve themselves in more passive, less competitive gambling activities such as slot machines, lottery, and bingo (*Harvard Mental Health Letter*, 1996). Like other literature in the field, no empirical research substantiates these generalities. Rather, "findings" are predicated on gender stereotypes and outdated notions of masculinity. Indeed, the very language and usage of pronouns underline the lack of objectivity. For example, the authors report that

"the escape gambler needs to feel more powerful and cope better with *her* life" while the "action gambler's main need is to stop living in the fantasy world created by *his* addiction, and *he* can tolerate the challenges and confrontations of GA meetings."

Also, this approach incorrectly assumes the passivity of certain gambling activities. The characterization of bingo as a noncompetitive game begs validation for any individual who has ever been to "bingo night" at local churches and seen players hunched protectively over their cards. In addition, this study assumes that female gamblers maintain traditional gender characteristics (i.e., disempowerment, dependence, etc.)—making no attempt to evaluate the validity of such an assumption. Finally, this study, like others in the field, ignores recent research in other areas that indicates a rapidly growing female interest in all areas of gambling, including cards and dice. In fact, a 1997 study focusing on gender differences among gamblers reported no significant difference in incidences of pathological gambling or guilt associated with gambling behavior between genders (Ohtsuka et al., 1997).

Sociological and Economic Explanations

Although the majority of gambling-related literature has surfaced in the realm of psychology, limited sociological research is available. For the most part, these approaches have criticized traditional psychoanalytic rhetoric, condemning it as myopic and self-serving (Oldman, 1978). Oldman's work focuses on traditional notions of social stratification and capitalistic culture. He argues that the accommodating nature of the casinos and the dismissal of traditional status requirements prove especially attractive to those individuals who are less than wealthy. "First-come, first-served" policies enable individuals to create a dual existence—one measured by demeanor, comportment, recognizability, and familiarity. Traditional social barriers to status and power are all but removed, and individuals are self-empowered. However, some self-defeating behaviors may be necessary to attain the level of recognition to which individual aspires. For example, individuals who sporadically increase their wagers may receive additional attention from other players, casino employees, and outsiders. In the long term, this style of wagering may have adverse economic consequences on the individual player. However, his or her desire for center stage has been obtained. This "love of losing," then, may not be an actual quest to disperse of personal resources but, rather, an unconscious desire to attract others' attention. As such, not everyone can become a "regular"; as gambling requires an excessive amount of time and money, only those who have an ample supply of both run the risk of destructive gambling activity. In addition, individual finances must be such that fluctuations in income are sufferable. For the most part, this group would comprise small business owners or nonsalaried employees.

Unfortunately for gamblers, the house advantage guarantees the inevitability of losing. In the event of an economic crisis, individuals with no additional resources have only two resources: crime and further gambling. Thus, the motivation to gamble at this point becomes rational behavior—but necessarily a "rationalization" as many psychoanalysts have suggested. Although the likelihood of recouping a significant amount of money previously lost is very small, it becomes one of only two *rational* alternatives. This argument is pivotal in the sociological literature, as some suggest that the "compelling" or "impulsive" nature of gambling is a manifestation of deviations from social expectations. Forsaking family advancement for the purposes of self-gratification is alien to a society that promotes—albeit superficially—family values and protection of loved ones. Succinctly put, "it is easier to be *compelled* to gamble than to admit that the casino is more fun that [*sic*] one's domestic hearth" (Oldman, 1978, 364).

A conflict approach to the phenomenon would argue that disadvantaged segments of the population are overrepresented because of the deluge of social expectations that are unobtainable. The lack of educational opportunities, career counseling, and positive role models creates an environment where gambling appears to be a viable alternative to social and racial stratification. Since most forms of legal gambling present sensationalized images of instant economic gratification and a lack of discrimination among winners, marginalized individuals are attracted to the "opportunities" within. It would appear that this approach has at least superficial legitimacy, as minority groups and impoverished individuals are disproportionately represented among the afflicted (Volberg and Steadman, 1988).

Economists argue that the actual behavior of gambling does not necessarily reflect muted attacks against economic stratification. Rather, rational economic theory suggests that individuals display varying strategies for attaining self-satisfying economic success. Arguing that individuals are generally rational and predictable in their behavior, theorists opine that routines are more important than attainment of articulate goals, because the mechanisms in place reinforce the rationality of behavioral patterning. This type of reasoning, however, is predicated on assumptions of ignorance. While it may be argued that the process for economic fulfillment supercedes actual attainment, it is illogical to suggest that rational individuals would enter into a behavior that is obviously self-defeating and economically detrimental.

Biological Explanations

Deviating from traditional approaches to problem gambling, recent attempts have included consideration of biological factors. This variation is directly contrary to some assertions that gambling is necessarily distinct from biological illness. Goldstein and Carlton (1988) found evidence which suggested that there is some correlation between certain brain characteristics and pathological gambling. Their study, pioneering in nature, suggested that gamblers might experience elevated levels of difficulty in producing a shift of cerebral laterality in response to environmental demands. In laymen's terms—variations in brain composition may affect cognitive interpretations of changing situations.

Other studies have examined the relationship between variables such as levels of serotonin, monoamine oxidase (MAO) activity, norepinephrine, and the like. However, few of these studies have established significant relationships between biological characteristics or genetic underpinnings and gambling behavior. For example, it was hypothesized that low platelet MAO activity was a biological characteristic that predisposed individuals to elevated levels of impulsivity, which, in turn, predisposed individuals to gamble to excess. This study was predicated on the notion that psychological patterning notwithstanding, pathological gamblers differ from "healthy" individuals in some personality traits. While novel in its approach, no significant relationship was found between platelet MAO activity and psychological measures.

Emerging theories suggest that pathological gamblers may be distinguishable from nongamblers in irregular deficiency levels. Linking dysfunctional gambling behavior with childhood experiences of attention deficit disorder (ADD) suggests that pathological gamblers display abnormal levels of impulsivity. Unlike psychological approaches, these theorists argue that this level of impulsivity is actually common among problem gamblers. Manifestations of problem gambling or an inability to focus suggest particular inhibitory deficits. The lack of such inhibitors may result in any number of dysfunctions, including substance abuse and the like (Carlton and Manowitz, 1988). As such, it has been suggested that the neurochemical agent that is responsible, serotonin, may be manipulated to limit the undesirable behavior. This approach has been successful in other areas of addictive behavior, but its effectiveness with problem gambling remains largely unexplored (McGurrin, 1992).

This relationship between impulsivity, gambling, and biological composition has been the predicate in similar studies. Similar studies have incorporated such assumptions in examinations of pathological gambling and norepinephrine (Green, 1998). In one study, fluvoxamine, an antidepressant, was administered to individuals displaying elevated levels of impulsivity. Although researchers claimed success, they cautioned that these antidepressants were merely treating symptoms of loneliness or feelings of abandonment. They also discounted monocular approaches, suggesting that the increase in legalized gambling may also be associated with the rising numbers of compulsive gamblers (Green, 1998). Summarily, while biological approaches are increasingly common, it appears that no evidence exists that supports notions of biological predispositioning. Indeed, it appears that environmental characteristics consistently surface in discussions of pathological gambling.

TREATMENT MODELS

Since the inception of the medicalization of gambling, a variety of "treatment programs" have been developed. For the most part, these programs may be dichotomized as peer support and professional counseling. Perhaps the best known of the former is Gamblers Anonymous (GA)—a nonprofit, self-help group. Designed to be testimonial in nature, members are encouraged to share personal experiences with others. Group interaction is not encouraged during the meeting period. Rather, interpersonal exchanges are reserved for breaks or recesses. This approach allows members to identify problematic behavior and discuss negative consequences in an environment free from censure and criticism. Modeled after Alcoholics Anonymous (AA), members undertake a 12-step program (see Figure 9.2). Although research on the program's effectiveness is scarce, it does appear that the program experiences at least moderate success (Livingston, 1974). This success may be explained by arguing that the negating of personal responsibility effectively removes any corresponding social stigma that may be attached to activities traditionally considered to be deviant.

BENEFITING FROM PEOPLE'S ADDICTIONS

Although self-help organizations may be credited with some proficiency, professional models of treatment are increasingly popular. Based on the theory that the medicalization of deviance encourages active participation, clinicians have successfully created an enterprise of their own design. Approaches are quite varied and have ranged from shock therapy to meditation. The effectiveness of such programs remains in doubt, as some have claimed success based on a sample as small as one. In addition, competing theorists are quick to criticize nontraditional approaches.

Two approaches that are on opposite sides of the spectrum are aversion therapy and paradoxical intention. Aversion therapy is a practice whereby individuals experience negative consequences during displays of the undesired behavior. These negative consequences may be physical in nature, as in the case of electric shock. Paradoxical intention, on the other hand, is a process whereby individuals are forced to engage in the undesired behavior (i.e., gambling). It is argued that this process removes the emotional rewards (i.e., excitement) from the behavior. While claims have been made to the effectiveness of both approaches, no empirical research substantiates such pronouncements. In fact, critics argue that either program may actually be detrimental to patients seeking treatment. It has been argued, for example, that aversion therapy may create feelings of anger and resentment that may manifest themselves as further dysfunctional behaviors, such as excessive masturbation (Slyvain et al., 1997). These same critics are also critical of paradoxical intention approaches, arguing that the suppression of urges actually creates other undesirable behavior (Slyvain et al., 1997).

Other gambling-specific approaches have included cognitive therapy and imaginal desensitization. Cognitive therapy focuses on educating the individual. It is intended to elevate the individual's understanding of the

Figure 9.2
GA's Twelve-Step Program

---

1. We admitted we were powerless over gambling, that our lives had become unmanageable.

2. We came to believe that a Power greater than ourselves could restore us to normal way of thinking and living.

3. We made a decision to turn our will and our lives over to the care of this Power of our own understanding.

4. We made a searching and fearless moral and financial inventory of ourselves.

5. We admitted to ourselves and to another human being the exact nature of our wrongs.

6. We were entirely ready to have these defects of character removed.

7. We humbly asked God (of our understanding) to remove our shortcomings.

8. We made a list of all persons we had harmed and became willing to make amends to them all.

9. We made direct amends to such people whenever possible, except when to do so would injure them or others.

10. We continued to take personal inventory and when we were wrong, promptly admitted it.

11. We sought through prayer and meditation to improve our conscious contact with God (as we understood Him), praying only for knowledge of His will for us and the power to carry that out.

12. Having made an effort to practice these principles in all our affairs, we tried to carry this message to other compulsive gamblers.

---

reality of gambling to a level where cognitive awareness may be achieved. Informational sessions include topics ranging from the dangers of gambling—economic and otherwise—to the seduction by the gaming community and the illogical nature of superstitions. Imaginal desensitization, on the other hand, focuses on the removal of temptation. This approach forces patients to imagine themselves in a gambling establishment while comfortably ensconced in a sterile (i.e., nongambling) environment. This approach tends to be rather costly, and no firm research supports its effectiveness.

Other approaches have focused on the cognitive process of morality. Implementing Piaget's stages of moral development, theorists have likened gamblers to children who are incapable of the conceptualization of intent. As such, treatment of these individuals may only be accomplished through stage graduation. To individual clinicians, the task is quite simple. By forcing individuals into a stage of disequilibrium in which they are forced to face information contrary to previous knowledge, practitioners can manipulate the development of a greater maturity. This maturity may also be achieved individually by the gambler who is confronted by some sort of crisis (Custer, 1982). The treatment phase, then, is initiated when gamblers confront the realization that the behavior that they had previously considered as self-gratifying is, in actuality, self-defeating. This recognition, and the awareness of their own lack of cognitive capability, is diametrically opposed to the premise of medicalization. In addition, it allows individuals to moderate their behavior rather than abstain.

Approaches that allow such moderation are increasingly common. These programs call for control—reducing an individual's gambling until it is no longer a problem. GA, on the other hand, calls for total abstinence—arguing that gamblers cannot just dip their foot in the water of gambling behavior, as it is literally poisonous. Both strategies are intolerant of the other. Those calling for total abstinence argue that moderates are actually denying their clients' addiction and in that sense are actually enabling or contributing to the negative behavior. Control advocates claim that abstinence programs such as GA are unrealistic and actually discourage individuals seeking help. Although the argument cannot be settled without empirical documentation, it appears that nonprofit organizations such as GA and GAMANON are intended to be service oriented. Other private institutions or corporations epitomize capitalist principles. Declaring themselves harbingers of gambling recovery, these establishments have historically played on fears that they themselves have created. By constructing complex—often inarticulate to the general public—strategies couched in academic rhetoric, they have successfully gained a lifetime of lucrative employment. Keep in mind, few of these "healers" are involved in prohibition movements. Indeed, the same disease that they have declared deadly is the same one on which they feed.

CONCLUSION

Although a considerable amount of research has been conducted in the area of excessive gambling, empirical definitions and theoretical foundations remain elementary at best. Private agendas and political posturing have surely affected the way in which the phenomenon was approached. Traditionally claimed by psychoanalysts as a treatable illness, the introduction of competing theoretical approaches has been relatively lacking. The integration of sociodemographic characteristics has been routinely overlooked or ignored. While certainly there are some similarities between excessive gambling and other compulsive-type behaviors, there exist fundamental differences that, when explored, suggest that this behavior may be more appropriately explained through sociological factors.

Throughout the literature, commonalities among affected individuals abound. Regardless of theoretical approach, social and/or cultural variables have routinely surfaced yet are often treated as insignificant. It has been found, for example, that problem gamblers are notable for their general lack of educational attainment (Volberg and Steadman, 1988). Males have been found to be more likely to gamble than women (Volberg and Steadman, 1988). Lower- and middle-class individuals are disproportionately represented among the affected population (Custer and Milt, 1985; Goodman, 1994; Volberg and Steadman, 1988), as are substance abusers (Gowen, 1997; Ramirez, McCormick, Russo, and Taber, 1984). Unless it is argued that individuals with similar demographic characteristics share psychological patterns, these variables must be evaluated if the establishment of causality is desired. However, the ambiguity of phenomena may serve a purpose.

It may be argued that much research has been conducted by individuals or organizations with political or capitalist agendas. In fact, many "studies" have been generated by organizations and/or individuals with a significant interest in the continuation of gambling institutions. Counselors or psychoanalysts have experienced considerable success in soliciting "problem" gamblers. Politicians, on the other hand, have aggressively developed partnerships with gambling corporations, ostensibly to develop guidelines promoting "responsible" gambling. Even literature that appears on its face to be objective, such as books published by university presses, may have vested interests in the gambling debate. Eugene Christiansen, coauthor of *The Business of Risk* (Abt, Smith, and Christiansen, 1985) is a paid consultant to the gaming industry. Other authors in the field are actively pursuing gambling-related enterprises. In addition, groups that are designed to identify negative consequences and develop treatment programs often benefit from "donations" from the gambling industry itself! Is it naive to think that a vested interest exists for both parties? As long as strategies are developed that successfully "control" negative consequences such as "problem gambling," both sides are content and, perhaps more important, employed. The issue, then, becomes not whether gambling creates untreatable social ills but how society can treat nonpathological ones. But to date, purely theoretical or academic approaches to the phenomenon of excessive gambling are all but nonexistent.

REFERENCES

Abt, Vicki, James F. Smith, and Eugene Christiansen. (1985). *The Business of Risk: Commercial Gambling in Mainstream America*. Lawrence: University Press of Kansas.

Ainslie, G. (1984). "Behavioral Economics II: Motivated Involuntary Behavior." *Social Science Information* 23: 735–779.

"All Eyes on France: World Cup '98." (1997). *The Wager* 3(27).

American Psychiatric Association. (1994). *DSM–IV: Diagnostic and Statistical Manual of Mental Disorders.* 4th ed. Washington, D.C.: American Psychological Association.

Bergler, Edmund. (1957). *The Psychology of Gambling.* New York: Hill and Wang.

Carlton, P. L., and P. Manowitz. (1988). "Physiological Factors as Determinants of Pathological Gambling." *Journal of Gambling Behavior* 3: 274–285.

Crist, Steven. (1998). "All Bets Are Off." *Sports Illustrated,* January 26.

Custer, R., and Harry Milt. (1985). *When Luck Runs Out: Help for Compulsive Gamblers and Their Families.* New York: Facts on File.

Custer, Robert L. (1982). "An Overview of Compulsive Gambling." In P. A. Carone, S. F. Yoles, S. N. Kiefer, and L. Krinsky, eds., *Addictive Disorders Update: Alcoholism, Drug Abuse, Gambling.* New York: Human Sciences Press.

Goffman, Erving. (1967). *Interaction Ritual.* Garden City, N.Y.: Doubleday.

Goldstein, L., and P. L. Carlton. (1988). "Hemispheric EEG Correlates of Compulsive Behavior: The Case of Pathological Gamblers." *Research Communications in Psychology, Psychiatry, and Behavior* 13(1–2): 103–111.

Goodman, Robert. (1994). *Legalized Gambling as a Strategy for Economic Development.* Northampton, Mass.: United States Gambling Study.

Gordon, Britta. (1996). "Gaming on the Internet: The Odds Are on the House, but How Long Will It Last?" *Texas Tech Law School's Cyberjournal.* www.law.ttu.edu/cyberspc/jour9.htm.

Gowen, Darren. (1996). "Pathological Gambling: An Obscurity in Community Corrections?" *Federal Probation* 6(2): 3–7.

Green, William. (1998). "An Antidote to Credit Cards? Drug Therapies for Compulsive Spending, Addictive Gambling and Kleptomania." *Forbes* 161(7): 161.

Greeson, Ralph. (1947). "On Gambling." *American Image* 4: 61–67.

Harvard Mental Health Letter. (1996). Center for Addictive Studies, Harvard Medical School.

Jacobs, D. F. (1989). "Illegal and Undocumented: A Review of Teenage Gambling and the Plight of Children of Problem Gamblers in America." In Howard J. Shaffer, Sharon A. Stein, Blasé Gambino, and Thomas N. Cummings, eds., *Compulsive Gambling: Theory, Research, and Practice* (pp. 249–292). Lexington, Mass.: Lexington Books.

Kusyszyn, Igor, and Lome Rubenstein. (1985). "Locus of Control and Race Track Betting Behaviors: A Preliminary Investigation." *Journal of Gambling Behavior* 1(2): 106–110.

Lesieur, H. R. (1984). *The Chase: Career of the Compulsive Gambler.* Cambridge, Mass.: Schenkman.

Livingston, Jay. (1974). *Compulsive Gamblers: Observations on Action and Abstinence.* New York: Harper and Row.

McGurrin, Martin C. (1992). *Pathological Gambling: Conceptual Diagnostic and Treatment Issues.* Sarasota, Fla.: Professional Resource Press.

Miller, D. C., and J. P. Byrnes. (1997). "The Role of Contextual and Personal Factors in Children's Risk Taking." *Developmental Psychology* 33(5): 814–823.

Moran, E. (1970). "Varieties of Pathological Gambling." *British Journal of Psychiatry* 116(535): 593–597.

Ohtsuka, Keis, Eric Bruton, Louisa DeLuca, and Victoria Borg. (1997). "Sex Differences in Pathological Gambling Using Gaming Machines." *Psychological Reports* 80(3): 1051–1057.

Oldman, David. (1978). "Compulsive Gamblers." *Sociological Review* 26: 369–370.

Ramirez, Luis F., Richard A. McCormick, Angel M. Russo, and Julian I. Taber. (1983). "Patterns of Substance Abuse in Pathological Gamblers Undergoing Treatment." *Addictive Behaviors* 8(4): 425–428.

Rosencrance, J. (1989). "Controlled Gambling: A Promising Future." In Howard J. Shaffer, Sharon A. Stein, Blasé Gambino, and Thomas N. Cummings, eds., *Compulsive Gambling: Theory, Research, and Practice* (pp. 147–160). Lexington, Mass.: Lexington Books.

Rosenthal, Richard J. (1989). "Pathological Gambling and Problem Gambling: Problems of Definition and Diagnosis." In Howard J. Shaffer, Sharon A. Stein, Blasé Gambino, and Thomas N. Cummings, eds., *Compulsive Gambling: Theory, Research, and Practice.* Lexington, Mass.: Lexington Books.

Shaffer, Howard J. (1989). "Conceptual Crises in the Addictions: The Role of Models in the Field of Compulsive Gambling." In Howard J. Shaffer, Sharon A. Stein, Blasé Gambino, and Thomas N. Cummings, eds., *Compulsive Gambling: Theory, Research, and Practice.* Lexington, Mass.: Lexington Books.

Shaffer, Howard J., and Matthew N. Hall. (1997). "Estimating the Prevalence of Adolescent Gambling Disorders: A Quantitative Synthesis and Guide toward Standard Gambling Nomenclature." *Journal of Gambling Studies* 12(2): 193–214.

Sylvain, Caroline, Robert Ladouceur, and Jean-Marie Boisvert. (1997). "Cognitive and Behavioral Treatment of Pathological Gambling: A Controlled Study." *Journal of Consulting and Clinical Psychology* 65(5): 727–733.

Volberg, R. A., and H. J. Steadman. (1988). "Refining Prevalence Estimates of Pathological Gambling." *American Journal of Psychiatry* 145(4): 502–505.

Wexler, Arnold. (1992). www.aswexler.com. Visited 1/31/00.

Chapter 10

Effects on Special Populations

As the increase in availability of gaming venues has skyrocketed, many administrators have become concerned that certain populations may experience adverse side effects. Though these populations vary by jurisdiction, most governments either domestic or foreign have expressed reservations about the impact of specific types of gaming on these populations. For example, studies have indicated that women, adolescents, seniors, and low-income groups are more likely to play video poker or fruit machines (England)—both of which have been found to have disproportionate negative consequences when compared to their table game counterparts. Unfortunately, much of the research in this area has been conducted in areas foreign to the United States. As a result, policy makers and administrators remain ill equipped to identify, much less assist, special populations.

YOUTH GAMBLING

Academic interest in youth gambling can be found as early as 1985, when a sampling of one Atlantic City high school indicated that 64 percent of its students had engaged in casino gambling. As expected, a positive relationship was reported between age and casino gambling, with 42 percent of the 14-year-olds and 88 percent of the 19-year-olds partaking (Arcuri, Lester, and Smith, 1985). More recent studies suggest that gambling is almost expected among adolescents, on par with smoking and drinking (Shaffer, 1993). Others proclaim gambling to be the fastest-growing addiction among young people in the United States—estimating that there are almost twice as many adolescent pathological gamblers as in the adult population (Gold, 1998). However, these findings, suggesting that youth gambling will grow proportionately with availability, have not been supported by research sponsored by the National Gambling Impact Study Commission (NGISC, discussed in Chapter 12). In fact, the study's findings and subsequent recommendations were more vague than conclusive:

[D]epending on which measurement approach one prefers, adolescents can be seen as less at risk of gambling problems than adults, about equally at risk, or at greater risk. (NGISC, 1999)

The *Gambling Impact and Behavior Study* (completed in March 1999) reported that roughly two-thirds of the 16- and 17-year-olds included in their study have gambled in some form. (Although they point out that this is much lower than the proportion of adults, it is important to remember that all such activity is illegal.) Their findings indicate that these young players are more likely than their adult counterparts to engage in unregulated activities like private card games and sports pools. Youths were also more likely to favor instant lottery games as opposed to multistate, daily, or big-jackpot tickets. In addition, the data showed that youths wagered substantially smaller amounts of money. Although reported as significant, such findings may be attributed to the lack of funds available to youths (Gerstein et al., 1999). Such downplaying is clearly contrary to earlier studies conducted on adult populations, which have evidenced gambling behavior prior to physical maturity. Indeed, the majority of research on "problem" or "pathological" gambling has suggested that the vast majority of individuals in treatment for their "disorder" began gambling as youths (Custer, 1982; Lesieur et al., 1991; Livingston, 1974). In fact, youth gambling appears to be increasing across the globe. Sixty-five percent of British adolescents reported playing fruit machines (Griffiths, 1991), a particular favorite of American youths, and 20 percent of children between the ages of 11 and 16 (Fisher, 1995).

The increase of youth gambling has been attributed to a number of factors. American children are presently more likely to be raised with a familiarity with video and computer-type activities, making video gaming less threatening owing to their knowledge of technologically advanced game simulations. In addition, the advent of state-sponsored gambling, unregulated Internet access, and the medicalization of deviance have diminished traditional stigmas associated with gambling behavior (Lesieur et al., 1991). As a result, more underage gamblers are emerging. No wonder, considering that youths are more likely to engage in risk-taking activity than their adult counterparts (Moore and Gullone, 1996). In the absence of informal mechanisms of social control, such as peer disfavor, adolescents are less likely to adhere to formalized punish-

ments that may be sporadically enforced or investigated or simply unclear to adolescents. In addition, parents may actually encourage betting
behavior through indifference (Arcuri, Lester, and Smith, 1985). Other
parents may actually facilitate gambling by introducing their children to
this form of "entertainment" (Smith and Abt, 1984).

In 1989, many Americans were disturbed to hear allegations that football coaches
and game officials in a small, Alabama town had fixed high school football
games. Though disturbing, many representatives said that it was not altogether
surprising. Illegal sports wagering and local bookies are all but expected in such
areas. One local townsperson, familiar with the local betting scene, expressed
regret that the incident might mar the reputation of the fine high school. He
expressed skepticism that the charges were actually valid—suggesting that it was
not a moneymaking proposition for the local bookie that could not lay off action
out of town. Stating that such allegations appeared illogical as local bookies only
established lines for the local schools as a "service to his customers." (Neff, 1989,
11)

   In addition to family characteristics, current legislation regarding gambling sends mixed messages to the younger generation. When governments and educational systems support institutions of chance, traditional
definitions of deviance become blurred. In Louisiana, for example, current legislation has come under fire after it was exposed that educational
institutions were accepting "charitable" donations from neighboring casinos including T-shirts, notebooks, and writing utensils bearing casino
logos and insignias. Although the gaming industry from whence these
"donations" came argued that they were simply addressing community
needs and donated such goods for the benefit of the community at large,
critics argued that such donations actually encourage youth gambling.
In addition, the introduction of coin pushing machines and slot-type
games at children's video arcades may promote patterns of risk-taking
activities inconsistent with childhood naïveté. Family-oriented video arcades and amusement areas along the Jersey Coast offer real slot action,
with the exception that players are paid in some sort of merchandise
credit. Finally, little or no security measures are employed by lottery
retailers, and measures at gaming establishments are far from foolproof.
Indeed, some reports suggest that while nearly 300,000 underage gamblers were turned away from Atlantic City casinos in 1990, over 25,000
were ejected from the casino floor (Chavira, 1991; Levine, 1990). It is
logical to assume that many other minors remain undetected and that
the 25,000 ejections are but a mere fraction of the underage population
gaining entrance. In fact, some argue that some casinos allow underage
gambling to occur if the player is a significant one—a young high roller.
The case of a 15-year-old female in Atlantic City received national atten-

tion when it was reported that her father, a detective for the city, repeatedly sent photographs and descriptions asking that they deny his daughter access. Although these events happened in the early 1990s, their significance can only increase with the increased legitimization of casino-type gambling, the introduction of the Internet, and subsequent availability of gambling. Coupled with findings that suggest that the majority of gambling pathologies are related to adolescent behaviors, such increases will almost certainly result in problem gambling and associated behaviors.

Adolescent gamblers are more likely to display truancy and low educational ratings than their nongambling counterparts (Lesieur and Klein, 1987). In addition, these students are also more likely to engage in other illegitimate behavior such as drinking and substance abuse (Jacobs, 1989). Many of these coexisting behaviors are reinforced by the casino environment. At least 26 percent of one sample of high school children reported requesting or accepting free alcoholic drinks while on the casino floor. At the same time, 13 percent reported falsifying identification documents for entrance purposes (Lesieur and Klein, 1987). Thus, administrators should evaluate the delinquent synergy that may result from the increased availability.

COLLEGE GAMBLING

Although not specifically addressed in the latest reports from the National Gambling Impact Study Commission, gambling on college campuses seems to be increasing. Many academicians even argue that ratios of problem gambling among college students exceed that of the adult population (Lesieur, 1988). As early as 1990, reports suggested that 69 percent of underage college students in Atlantic City gambled in the casinos, of which 75 percent also played the lottery (Frank, 1990). Later reports suggest that as many as 85 percent of college students have gambled in some form, with 23 percent gambling at least once a week (Lesieur et al., 1991). Such behaviors have been found to be correlated with other types of risk-taking behavior such as tobacco usage, alcohol consumption, substance abuse, criminal acts, and illegal parking (Lesieur et al., 1991). For the most part, traditional research suggests that college students are most likely (54 percent) to bet with electronic gaming devices (i.e., video poker, slots, etc.), with playing cards closely following at 51 percent (Lesieur et al., 1991). However, current research and anecdotal media accounts suggest that sports betting is becoming increasingly popular across college campuses.

In 1994, a gambling ring established by a former sportscaster and four Arizona State fraternity brothers was uncovered. Investigators found over 245 accounts, 140 of which belonged to fraternity brothers across the university. In the six-month period between August 1993 and February 1994, an estimated $120,000 per month was wagered through their sports book (Layden, 1995). According to William "B. J." Jahoda, a former Chicago mob bookmaker-turned-government-informant, college campuses are easy money—an epidemic that creates easy pickings for entrepreneurs (Layden, 1995). In fact, gambling rings have been investigated on a variety of college campuses across the country. Such investigations, however, have not been successful in curtailing gambling activity. Insignificant penalties, the thrill of the chase, and the lack of stigma associated with gambling have resulted in an increase in all sorts of gambling activity on campus. Many fraternities or social organizations, for example, now routinely sponsor casino junkets. Some are even courted by gaming interests, paid by the head as an unofficial tour guide.

Like youth gambling, explanations of the increase in college gambling have taken many approaches. One approach suggests the increase on college campuses is actually just a reflection of the increase in adolescent/teen gambling. They credit such prevalence to social learning theory, arguing that gambling behavior is learned through interaction with significant others. They argue that such behaviors are actually encouraged prior to college entrance and are learned in adolescence (Browne and Brown, 1994). Others argue that peer groups within college environments and patterns of risk-taking behavior among cohorts promote gambling activity. Like a social disease, gambling develops a life of its own, infecting a campus one student at a time (Layden, 1995). Still others credit the growth to factors external to the gambling realm but indigenous to college campuses (i.e., easy credit, fast living, liquid intoxicants).

One of the most attractive factors of on-campus sports betting is the extension of credit. Like the drug dealer who offers free samples to new customers, many bookies take wagers prior to deposit. Unlike the off-campus bookie, these individuals may extend credit with little risk of fleeing clients—campuses can be a remarkably small world. (Because on-campus bookies are often students themselves, they make use of "seasonal collection" methods—appearing at the beginning of the semester when students are more likely to have student-aid money.) In addition, many college students have deep pockets—Mom and Dad's. For them, it is often easy to justify an increase in allowance without revealing their betting behavior. Desperation may result in the establishment of other credit relationships (i.e., Visa, MasterCard, Discover). Virtually every creditor in the country is competing for new customers, often sending college students preapproved cards based on the concept that they will one day be wage earners. These factors often lead some students down the road to significant economic problems that may have long-lasting side effects. This negates suggestions made by some that gambling activities may mirror narcotics experimentation—decreasing with age (Lesieur et al., 1991). In fact, the increase in sports betting across the country seems to have taken on a life quite different from other forms of gambling. Indeed, this phenomenon has reached such proportions that even individuals involved in the actual contest have been unable to resist temptation.

Athletes and Gambling

Recent allegations of large-scale corruption of intercollegiate athletic programs have created an increased interest in gambling among athletes. Incidents have occurred at all levels of collegiate competition and have been found across the country. The most recent happenings have affected such notables as Arizona State University, University of Colorado, Fresno State University, Northwestern University, University of Notre Dame, and the ever-present Boston College. Unfortunately, scant academic research exploring the relationship between athletes and gambling exists. The limited data available suggest that as many as 25 percent of Division I football and basketball (male) players have placed wagers on collegiate athletics (Cullen and Latessa, 1996). Other research indicates that this number is much higher. According to Cross and Vollano (1998), as many as 35 percent of the individual athletes included in their sample gambled on sporting events. Their study, one of the first to include female athletes, indicated increased levels among the male population, with as many as 45 percent wagering on competitions. Their findings also indicated that over 5 percent of male student athletes had provided insider information, accepted money for guaranteed poor performances, or actually wagered on a game in which they participated.

While unsettling, such results are not surprising in light of the recent scandals at both college and professional levels. Northwestern University and Boston College University seem to be two of the hardest hit in recent years, with point shaving and game fixing infiltrating both basketball and football programs. In 1998, Northwestern basketball players Dion Lee and Dewey Williams were sentenced to jail terms for a 1995 point-shaving scheme in which Williams admitted taking money (AP, 1998). Days later their football team was placed under scrutiny when four former players were indicted for perjury in a sports gambling case concerning their Cinderella season. Initially denying the allegations, Dennis Lundy, a Wildcat standout, was accused of intentionally fumbling a goal line touchdown to cover his bets (Munson, 1998). Lundy was formally charged with perjury—stemming from statements made during a grand jury investigation of Northwestern gambling. He has recently acknowledged his wrongdoing. Others indicted in the Northwestern scandal included athletes from a variety of Division I programs such as Notre Dame place-kicker Kevin Pendergast. Indictments are continuing. On

April 22, 1999, a former Northwestern player was indicted on perjury charges.

Boston College, another school with a traditional reputation of questionable athletic practices, has also been plagued with gambling scandals in recent years. Individuals accused in a 1996 scandal included Brandon King, the grandson of boxing promoter Don King. Mob biographies over the years have consistently included Boston College in their discussions of point shaving and game fixing. However, these are not the only teams that have been plagued with such scandals, nor are they the worst cases. The first documented (i.e., prosecuted) case of point shaving happened almost five decades ago. A total of 32 players from 7 institutions were implicated in a wide-sweeping gambling scheme involving over 80 games (Cross and Vollano, 1998). Eleven years later, 37 players from 22 institutions were implicated in a similar scheme. In fact, gambling scandals have affected virtually every conference of Division I competition and a variety of smaller arenas. Although many of the participants were not gambling per se, they were involved in the business of luck—not necessarily their own. Explanations for this infestation are not too hard to uncover. The media promotion of and the amount of monies wagered on Division I athletics make it a prime target for criminal manipulation. In addition, many of the players participating are recruited from teams unlikely to participate in postseason play. Thus, athletes may justify their activity by claiming that they didn't betray their team, because they did not have a shot at winning.

The seduction of collegiate athletes is easily accomplished as many of them perceive that they have "insider" information, unavailable to the general public. This arrogance is based on the premise that the average bettor does not know the game or the individuals involved in these sporting contests. Even those athletes who have not wagered on games involving their teams have been encouraged by these false perceptions to gamble on others. Such activity can have significant repercussions on their professional careers. In 1982, Art Schlichter should have been on top of the world. A college standout at Ohio State, Schlichter was making a significant amount of money and playing in the National Football League (even if it was for the Baltimore Colts). In 1983, Schlichter was suspended indefinitely from the League for wagering on at least 10 league games in the preceding year. With gambling debts exceeding $750,000, Schlichter also had cash flow problems. He had tapped out his friends and family and was being threatened by the bookies owed. With little recourse, Schlichter contacted the FBI, who arrested four men in connection with the charges (Looney, 1983). Schlichter had come a long way from the sophomore All-American.

Gambling among athletes is similar to gambling in the general population. Most have admitted to a variety of gambling activities including casino gaming, lotteries, slots, and card games. Though their involvement in intercollegiate or interleague wagering is of significant concern to the NCAA, the NFL, and other regulatory groups interested in the "integrity of the game," there is no evidence to support that their behavior is disproportionate to the population at large. Media hype and public interest have promoted the concept that sports gambling among college athletes is out of control. It must be pointed out that this is no more true for athletes than it is for the general population. It is ironic that many agencies focus on the dangers of gambling to "game integrity" but allow unfair bargaining practices, drug abuse, and felonious assaults outside of the spectator arena.

SENIOR CITIZENS GAMBLING

Although adolescent and college-age gaming have become the focus of many politicians and academicians alike, another age group that appears to be disproportionately represented in irresponsible gambling is that which includes senior citizens. According to the Council on Compulsive Gambling of New Jersey, 10 percent of calls made to their problem gambling hotline were made by individuals over the age of 55. They report that the increase in legitimate gaming venues has resulted in a near explosion of participation among seniors. They suggest that these individuals are more susceptible to irresponsible economic risk taking due to the feelings of worthlessness some experience during retirement. This desire for self-affirmation results in problem gambling. Many feel that the preferential treatment offered by gaming establishments replaces traditional notions of success, recognition, and utility (Council on Compulsive Gambling of New Jersey, 1998).

To the majority of Americans, the desire for personal recognition is often commonplace. American ideals of importance and acclaim, byproducts of an often-faceless society, are often left unsatisfied. In a culture where individuals are often associated with their occupations, feelings of worthlessness may be exacerbated postretirement. Thus, essential elements of self-categorization may be lost. To compensate, many elders may patronize establishments that assuage identification dilemmas. Businesses that recognize such uncertainty may capitalize on such feelings. In fact, many industries have created programs specifically designed to attract elders. These entities appear to glorify or revere senior status, offering packages, discounts, and preferential programming for this increasing population. Indeed, individuals over 55 are highly valuable. Most are law-abiding and unrestricted in their availability, and most important, they have a stream of income not contingent upon their behavior. Although this income may be relatively modest, the nature of its receipt allows individuals the luxury of autonomy. In addition, the expenditure of such funds allows the recipient to recapture a semblance of independence.

Golf packages, casino junkets, and guided tours are but some mechanisms intended to separate older individuals from their maintenance. Savvy entrepreneurs promote such excursions as exclusive—designed to cater to and reward seniors. Gaming establishments, expert in the art of hospitality, have targeted such populations. Subsequently, access to established transportation and security have enabled seniors to venture to remote locations without fear or extensive planning. Some companies have even provided relatively inexpensive housing developments for senior citizens. One such example, the Best of Life apartment complex owned by Donald Trump, was promoted as a community service project—providing retirees with a cheap getaway or retirement villa. In fact, many residents believe that the community was established for their benefit only. Attached to the Taj Mahal in Atlantic City, they suggest that their quality of life has improved with a beachfront apartment and access to a variety of entertainment and dining experiences. Indeed, the residents are often given cash and food vouchers for the casino. Blinded by the glare of the lights and deafened by the sound of the casino, these individuals fail to recognize the profitability of the program. Cynics would argue that the project is actually intended to serve as a steady stream of revenue for the casino and its related enterprises, at the same time providing tax shelters and a humanitarian reputation for its founder.

Though less obvious, other programs have been established by gaming establishments that secure the patronage of senior citizens. "Bingo for Seniors" and other weekly drawings for seniors only promote an image that such establishments prize older customers. For individuals recently widowed or couples experiencing "empty nest" situations, these events provide a source of entertainment and fraternity—a place to socialize, renew acquaintances, or wax nostalgic about past glories. In addition, they provide a sense of familiarity as individuals become recognized by personnel and friends alike. Finally, their accessibility, excitement, and continuous nature relieve feelings of boredom or mundaneness often experienced by individuals who are suddenly alone.

Without a doubt, the senior citizen market has been targeted by casino owners since Bill Harrah's efforts in Reno, Nevada. Several gambling cities, such as Reno and Laughlin, Nevada, have a long history and reputation for soliciting the low-risk, low-stakes, low-rolling senior citizens. "Laughlin, Nevada is to Las Vegas what Wal-Mart is to Macy's," catering to the "senior citizen Winnebago crowd" (Wrobel, 1996, 66–67). Laughlin is characterized by cheap buffets, informal attire, and an unthreatening atmosphere. Furthermore, supporters of legalized gambling efforts, particularly casino gambling, have singled out the senior citizen voting bloc.

Murray Raphel (1989) states that the difference between the first failed referendum and the second referendum's success was targeting "the most powerful voting bloc: senior citizens." Seniors were targeted as potential customers and recipients of the tax revenues. The wording on the ballot stated that all funds would be restricted to be used solely to pay property taxes or rent and utility bills for senior citizens and disabled residents of New Jersey.

Research has indicated that gambling among adolescents, college students, and seniors is increasingly popular. These populations appear to be especially prone to problem or dysfunctional gambling. However, the variety of research in the area has excluded senior citizens from analysis while concentrating on the younger generations. This concern, while certainly valid and worthwhile, often overlooks the senior population that may experience greater levels of negative consequences. Unlike adolescents or college students, many seniors do not have the capability of securing gainful employment to recoup gambling losses. At the same time, many elderly individuals are seeking the social affirmation and the personal recognition—usually associated with occupational success—factors that may or may not be found in younger gamblers. Indeed, these individuals may find confidence replenishment through the overt hospitality and fawning of casino personnel.

Many critics of the gaming industry have argued that such actions, junkets, and/or promotional packages target the most vulnerable of generations. Inasmuch as the gaming industry is a capitalistic endeavor, they are probably right. However, the industry should not be viewed as more Metosopholistic than theaters advertising "Senior Nights" or vacation resorts that promote "Golden Packages." Instead of viewing these practices as corruptive or seductive, they should be viewed as what they are—products of a capitalist society that revolves around economic competition.

WOMEN

An additional population that appears to experience negative consequences from gambling are females. Although the majority of research in the area of problem gambling has focused on males, the increase of economically independent women and the destigmatization of gambling have resulted in a subsequent increase in betting behavior among females. As stated in Chapter 8, early research, based on traditional gender stereotypes, suggested that males were attracted to games characterized by skill and competition (i.e., "action" gamblers—individuals who prefer cards, dice, racing, sports betting, stocks and commodities, and other fast-moving activities). Thus, male gamblers were characterized as being overly competitive and fantastical in their expectations. Unlike female gamblers who were traditionally characterized as "escape" gamblers, these individuals are primarily motivated by power. According to such stereotypes, female gamblers tended to be individuals removed—albeit temporarily—from their mundane and tortured existence (*Harvard Mental Health Letter*, 1996). Such characterizations served to obscure prevalence rates among females, as their behavior was perceived simply as a manifestation of loneliness, depression, and abuse. Further, the recognition of gambling problems associated with slot machines and other "passive" machines was virtually nonexistent until very recently. Thus, inclusion of female gamblers in academic research is minimal. What research does exist suggests that females are increasingly attracted to card and dice games. In addition, a 1997 study focusing on gender differences among gamblers reported no significant difference in incidences of pathological gambling or guilt associated with gambling behavior (Ohtsuka et al., 1997). Other studies have indicated that nearly one-half of all women sampled have gambled (Abbott and Cramer, 1993) and that one-third of compulsive gamblers are women (*Harvard Mental Health Letter*, 1996). In addition, both men and women increasingly support gambling within their communities—although women less so than men (Abbott and Cramer, 1993). Thus, it is unclear as to the actual extent of female gamblers. However, it is clear that problem gambling behavior by females requires closer inspection.

According to some treatment providers, adolescent females are more likely to gamble if they have significant others who gamble, have coexisting behavioral problems (i.e., substance or alcohol abuse, eating disorders, etc.), or have experience with video and computer games. Senior women, on the other hand, are more likely to gamble if they are experiencing health problems, grief, isolation, loss of finances or home, domineering spouse, or mourning the passage of youth (Peardonville House, 1998). (Unfortunately, such characterizations fail to explain why others experiencing the same sorts of situations are not attracted to gambling.) In fact, a typology of female gamblers in general reaffirms traditional notions of gendered behavior, suggesting that females gamble as a means of escape and are more solitary in their behavior. They further suggest that the increase in legitimate venues has removed traditional barriers and that "victims" perceive gambling as harmless and socially acceptable (Peardonville House, 1998).

Like their male counterparts, recognition of self-destructive behavior does not necessarily result in cessation of activity. However, females are more likely to lose their family, job, and occupation. Many attribute these disproportionate consequences to social expectations of gender roles. Females are expected to serve as the cohesive agent within the family structure—forgiving transgressions and committing few. Such socialization mandates compliance, as punishments accompany role deviation. These characteristics coupled with the absence of supportive significant others may also decrease the likelihood that individuals affected will seek treatment. Unfortunately, such claims tend to be largely unsupported as the majority of research is conducted in the very environment that females are assumed to avoid—that is, treatment facilities. Thus, estimation of the prevalence of female gamblers is guesswork at best. Limited research has been conducted on the continuation of gender-role stereotyping. Recent studies indicate that males are perceived as more competitive and more adventuresome in regard to risk taking (King, Miles, and Kniska, 1991). Although not surprising, such findings may explain traditional reluctance expressed by females to participate in table games. It may also suggest that less traditional females may not be as intimidated. Suppositions aside, it appears obvious that the increasing availability of gaming machines and increasing legitimization of gambling venues will likely result in a subsequent increase in female gamblers—both at and around casino tables.

REFERENCES

Abbott, Douglas A., and Sheran L. Cramer. (1993). "Gambling Attitudes and Participation: A Midwestern Survey." *Journal of Gambling Studies* 9(3): 247–263.

Arcuri, A. F., D. Lester, and F. O. Smith. (1985). "Shaping Adolescent Gambling Behavior." *Adolescence* 20: 935–938.

Associated Press (AP). (1998). "Northwestern Athletes Indicted for Gambling: They Lied to Federal Grand Juries Investigating Sports Betting." *MSC Sports*, December 3.

Browne, B. A., and D. J. Brown. (1994). "Predictors of Lottery Gambling among American College Students." *Journal of Social Psychology* 134(3): 339–347.

Chavira, Ricardo. (1991). "The Rise of Teenage Gambling: A Distressing Number of Youths Are Bitten Early by the Betting Bug." *Time* 137(8): 78.

Council on Compulsive Gambling of New Jersey, Inc. (1998). "Gambling Away the Golden Years: Compulsive Gambling and New Jersey's Senior Citizens." www.800gambler.org/gol001.htm. Visited 5/17/99.

Cross, Michael E., and Ann G. Vollano. (1998). *The Extent and Nature of Gambling among College Student Athletes.* Ann Arbor: University of Michigan.

Cullen, F. T., and E. J. Latessa. (1996). *The Extent and Sources of NCAA Rule Infractions: A National Self-Report Study of Student-Athletes.* Kansas City, Mo.: National Collegiate Athletic Association.

Custer, Robert L. (1982). "An Overview of Compulsive Gambling." In P. A. Carone, S. F. Yoles, S. N. Kiefer, and L. Krinsky, eds., *Addictive Disorders Update: Alcoholism, Drug Abuse, Gambling.* New York: Human Sciences Press.

Fisher, Sue, and Mark Griffiths. (1995). "Current Trends in Slot Machine Gambling: Research and Policy Issues." *Journal of Gambling Studies* 11(3): 239–247.

Fisher, Sue E. (1995). "The Amusement Arcade as a Social Space for Adolescents: An Empirical Study." *Journal of Adolescence* 18(1): 71–86.

Frank, M. L. (1990). "Underage Gambling in Atlantic City Casinos." *Psychological Reports*: 907–912.

Gerstein, Dean et al. (1999). *Gambling Impact and Behavior Study: Final Report to the National Gambling Impact Study Commission.* N.p.

Gold, Mattea. (1998). "New Gamblers Find Old Troubles: Going for Broke, Part 1." *Los Angeles Times*, December 13.

Griffiths, M. D. (1991). "Amusement Machine Playing in Childhood and Adolescence: A Comparative Analysis of Video Games and Fruit Machines." *Journal of Adolescence* 14: 53–73.

Harvard Mental Health Letter. (1996). Center for Addictive Studies, Harvard Medical School.

Jacobs, D. F. (1989). "Children of Problem Gamblers." *Journal of Gambling Behavior* 5: 261–268.

King, Wesley C., Edward W. Miles, and Jane Kniska. (1991). "Boys Will Be Boys (and Girls Will Be Girls): The Attribution of Gender Role Stereotypes in a Gaming Situation." *Sex Roles* 28(11–12): 607–623.

Layden, Tim. (1995). "Bettor Education." *Sports Illustrated* 82(13): 68–83.

Lesieur, Henry R. (1988). "Altering the DSM–III Criteria for Pathological Gambling." *Journal of Gambling Behavior* 4: 38–47.

Lesieur, Henry R., John Cross, Michael Frank, Michael Welch, Carolyn M. White, Garry Rubenstien, Karen Moseley, and Marie Mark. (1991). "Gambling and Pathological Gambling among University Students." *Addictive Behaviors* 16: 517–527.

Lesieur, Henry R., and R. Klein. (1987). "Pathological Gambling among High School Students." *Addictive Behaviors* 12: 129–135.

Levine, Art. (1990). "Playing the Adolescent Odds: The Latest Peril for America's Troubled Teenagers Is the Lure of Scoring Big in Lotteries and Casino Halls." *U.S. News & World Report* 108(24): 51.

Livingston, Jay. (1974). *Compulsive Gamblers: Observations on Action and Abstinence.* New York: Harper and Row.

Looney, Douglas S. (1983). "A Big Loss for a Gambling Quarterback (Art Schlichter Suspended from NFL)." *Sports Illustrated* 58: 30–32.

Moore, S. M., and E. Gullone. (1996). "Predicting Adolescent Risk Behavior Using a Personalized Cost-Benefit Analysis." *Journal of Youth and Adolescence* 25: 343–359.

Munson, Lester. (1998). "Gambling at Northwestern." *Sports Illustrated* 89(24): 31.

National Gambling Impact Study Commission (NGISC). (1999). "Gambling Impact and Behavior Study." www.ngisc.gov.

Neff, Craig. (1989). "A High School Fix." *Sports Illustrated* 71(4): 11.

Ohtsuka, Keis, Eric Bruton, Louisa DeLuca, and Victoria Borg. (1997). "Sex Differences in Pathological Gambling Using Gaming Machines." *Psychological Reports* 80(3): 1051–1057.

Peardonville House. (1998). www.cobra-net.com/peardonville.

Pimental, Paul. (1999). "Gambling Problems Hit 'Alarming' Level: Governments Profit, but at What Expense?" *The Ottawa Citizen*, January 4.

Raphel, Murray. (1989). "Double or Nothing." In Kathryn Hashimoto and Sheryl Fried Kline (1996), *Casino Management for the 90's.* Dubuque, Iowa: Kendall/Hunt.

Shaffer, H. J. (1993). "The Emergence of Youthful Addiction: The Prevalence of Underage Lottery Use and the Impact of Gambling." Technical Report 121393-100. Boston: Massachusetts Council on Compulsive Gambling.

Shaffer, Howard J., and Matthew N. Hall. (1996). "Estimating the Prevalence of Adolescent Gambling Disorders: A Quantitative Synthesis and Guide Toward Standard Gambling Nomenclature." *Journal of Gambling Studies* 12(2): 193–214.

Smith, J. F., and V. Abt. (1984). "Gambling as Play." *Annals of the American Academy of Political and Social Sciences* 474: 123–132.

Volberg, Rachel A., Donald C. Reitzes, and Jacqueline Boles. (1997). "Exploring the Links between Gambling, Problem Gambling and Self-Esteem." *Deviant Behavior: An Interdisciplinary Journal* 18: 321–342.

Wrobel, David. (1996). "Don Luughin." In Kathryn Hashimoto and Sheryl Fried Kline (1996), *Casino Management for the 90's.* Dubuque, Iowa: Kendall/Hunt.

Chapter 11

Effects on Communities

Independent research on community impact is all but nonexistent. Buffered by personal interests and economic gain, both advocates and proponents have consistently produced research beneficial to their position. Research that is contrary to their interests has been harshly criticized. This polarization has even quashed government efforts to evaluate long- and short-term consequences. On one side of the table, anti-gambling forces blame the gaming industry for a variety of social ills including, but not limited to, increased suicide rates, elevated patterns of criminal behavior, and the cannibalization of small businesses. Painting the gaming industry as the proverbial horned devil, they assert that gamblers are helpless victims preyed upon voraciously by an institution representing evil incarnate. On the other side of the table, the gaming industry promotes itself as community savior—lifting impoverished areas out of their economic depression. (The economic, political, and social impacts discussed in this chapter involve communities who have introduced non-Indian casino gaming unless otherwise noted. It makes no attempt to explore the impacts of lotteries, Indian gaming, or nonregulated gaming, such as South Carolina's poker industry.) Disavowing any negative intentions or repercussions, they have presented themselves as responsible businessmen concerned with the small minority of individuals displaying destructive gambling tendencies. While both images are clearly embellished to the point of absurdity, a characterization somewhere in between has not yet been established.

Whether positive or negative, it is apparent that the explosion of gambling venues in the past decade has significantly affected community leaders, businesses, and residents. For the most part, little regard has been given to residential concerns. Rather, the lure of increased revenue and decreased taxation has proven irresistible to politicians seeking re-election. Even areas that have traditionally been opposed to legalized gambling have now bowed to economic pressures. Indeed, many states notorious for their anti-gambling, Bible-thumping histories are now poised on the verge of the legalization abyss. Recent elections in Alabama, California, Missouri, South Carolina, and the like, reflect the confidence of the populace that gambling is the wave of the future. As a result, a sudden urgency has replaced traditional caution. Spurred by the fear that neighboring communities will steal the pot of gold, and seduced by the promise of enhanced educational initiatives, communities are plunging headlong into the often uncharted waters of legalized gambling.

St. Croix, hard-hit by several hurricanes, has traditionally resisted gambling. But the decaying economy and the competition for tourist dollars have recently led to the passage of casino gambling. Unlike other jurisdictions, however, St. Croix has a firm economic strategy in place. Requiring potential licensees to build or renovate accompanying hotels, government officials are seeking to recapture the success of pre-Hugo St. Croix with noncruise tourists. This increase in hotel capacity is designed to promote overnight guests—guests who will shop in local stores, eat at local restaurants, and gamble at local casinos. Promises made by incoming casino companies have included significant employment promises to residents. Though the expectations or community revitalization remain high, it is unclear whether the introduction of casino gambling will replenish the prosperity of traditional establishments or replace them.

Having said that, it appears that the greatest danger to community stability results from poor planning and limited supervision.

    Explanations for such abandon are not as mysterious as one might suppose. The shotgun marriage of politics and gaming was originally produced by farsighted entrepreneurs and gullible politicians. Although contemporary politicians are anything but naive, recent marriages still tend to be one-sided. In fact, savvy entrepreneurs have often purchased mail-order brides—expensive but subservient and pliable. Although the methods may be more subtle, casino executives have successfully hedged their bets contributing greatly to the political campaigns of individuals amenable to gaming initiatives in their jurisdiction. For example, Mr. Las Vegas himself, Steve Wynn, has successfully courted national figures such as Bob Dole and Senate Majority Leader Trent Lott and local politicians. In some jurisdictions, he has even retained the very same law firm representing city interests, that is, Biloxi, Mississippi (Pulley, 1998). Other approaches have marketed casino gambling as a revenue producer for educational initiatives—especially popular in southeastern areas notorious for substandard educational programs. Although such practices are not reserved for the gaming industry, some find it ironic that the increase in criminalization of vices such as tobacco and alcohol has been paralleled by a decriminalization of gambling. In fact, many are concerned that governments that are passing laws to eliminate seductive marketing campaigns in private business (i.e., Joe Camel) are actively developing strategies to increase state coffers with gaming revenue.

Gambling appears to transcend even the most fundamental of differences. Take the example of the Oasis casino, owned and operated by Yasser Arafat and the Palestinian National Authority. Opening weekend, coinciding with one of the holiest of Jewish holidays, saw Jews flocking to the casinos openly abandoning their religious obligations. As Palestinians are forbidden from partaking, the majority of dollars are spent by Israelis—seemingly oblivious to the irony that their dollars may fuel their own persecution.

Needless to say, legalized gambling has become a hotly debated topic. Unfortunately, much of the debate occurs postimplementation. Both sides have created publication machines that market information most favorable to their position. The American Gaming Association, for example, has argued that it is only interested in responsible gamblers. Indeed, the creation of the National Center for Responsible Gaming was ostensibly to produce academic research on the root cause of problem gambling. Noticeably absent from such research are findings negative to the gaming industry. On the other hand, various grassroots movements have sprouted across the nation preaching the danger of legalized gambling. Although not as common as their pro-gambling counterparts, these movements have been predicated on hyperbole, which through repetition has been accepted as fact. Citing a variety of tragic examples, this movement has likened the gaming industry to a metisopholistic juggernaut—seducing innocents and spewing tragedy in its wake. Thus, two different versions of reality emerge.

HE SAYS: THE AMERICAN GAMING ASSOCIATION

The American Gaming Association is a political lobbying group in Washington, D.C. Chaired by the former head of the Republican National Committee, Frank Farenkopf, they have successfully cultivated an image of professionalism and political power. They have consistently denied the majority of allegations leveled at them by anti-gambling activists—claiming casinos actually stimulate economic development and restore dwindling revenue for community projects. In fact, their revitalization argument—coupled with the lack of empirical evidence presented by their opponents—has resulted in an increasing acceptance of gaming venues in numerous jurisdictions.

Community Revitalization

While certainly not true for all new casino communities, many small communities have benefited from the onslaught of legalized wagering. Decaying communities such as East St. Louis, Illinois, and other Midwest cities experienced an immediate increase in nonresident expenditures, employment opportunities, and new construction. Once considered the poorest city in the poorest county in the richest nation, the landscape of Tunic, Mississippi, has changed dramatically since the introduction of casino gambling. As of 1992, Tunic had only 16 hotel rooms in the entire city; today there are more than 6,000. In addition, the city that traditionally collected less than $4 million in taxes is reaping increased revenues of $35 million (Brown, 1998). At the same time, unemployment is below the national average, and public projects such as roadways and tourist attractions are on the rise. In fact, many sparsely populated areas like Tunic are experiencing an unprecedented level of competition for qualified workers. Consequently, individuals along the Gulf Coast are experiencing increased wages and elevated benefits. Mirage's new Beau Rivage casino/hotel in Biloxi, for example, is nullifying traditional incubation periods for health insurance to attract workers from other casinos. The recipients of such incentives are potential workers. Other casinos, attempting to maintain the consistency of their job force, are scurrying to develop competitive packages (Palermo, 1998). Communities that require proportional employment of residents are particularly rewarded. However, other communities that have haphazardly entered the playing field without the proper equipment have been particularly devastated in the absence of legally binding commitments with successful casino applicants.

It must be noted that some of the benefits reaped initially by new casino jurisdictions have been negated when more lucrative partnerships became available. One such example involved The Diamond Lady in Bettendorf, Iowa, who pulled up anchor shortly after no-limit betting was approved in neighboring Illinois. This relocation was certainly costly to Bettendorf's local economy that had become increasingly dependent on riverboat revenue and employment. Although their move to Biloxi was certainly beneficial to the company (now known as Casino America or the Isle of Capri), little regard was given to the community left in the wake of their departure. However, the failure should be given to the administrators who exposed their community without proper precautions—not the gaming industry that is in the business of making money.

Replenishing Government Coffers and Educational Improvements

Many gaming entrepreneurs gain entrance into guarded communities with promises of educational improvements. Particularly attractive in rural areas and southeastern jurisdictions—notorious for the substandard educational institutions—casinos have long been regarded as the proverbial cash cow for communities struggling with increased costs and decreased revenue. While it must be noted that the majority of new casino jurisdictions have not made significant improvements in their educational systems (Tunica test scores still rank among the worst in the country, whereas their dropout rate continues to exceed 50 percent), the blame must again be credited to local administrators who have diverted funds into pet projects. In addition, these same administrators often fail to obtain assurances from state governments. Revenue sharing and jurisdictional obligations aside, many administrators have allowed states to siphon money earmarked for community revitalization. Such shortsightedness has resulted in an apparent failure to local school boards and community leaders. However, with proper planning and supervision, community administrators may secure adequate revenue for educational incentives and beautification initiatives.

SHE SAYS: ANTI-GAMBLING ACTIVISTS

While the gaming industry extols the merits of casino construction, anti-gambling activists argue that the introduction of such an industry is tantamount to giving Satan a key to the city. They argue that due to the nature of this productless industry, community mainstays and traditional morality are destined for disaster. They argue that the social costs associated with legalization are far greater than the revenues created through regulation. In fact, they argue that the introduction of casino gaming increases the numbers of bankruptcies, suicides, alcoholics, divorces, and all sorts of dysfunctional behavior (Figure 11.1 lists common arguments against legalization). However, much of their research is predicated on suppositions and unsubstantiated stereotypes.

Social Costs of Compulsive Gambling

There appears to be no argument that an increase in legitimate gambling venues directly affects the number of compulsive or problem gamblers within a community. Some reports suggest that gambling disorders have increased by 55 percent in the last two decades. Iowa, for example, has experienced an increase of 1.3 percent since the introduction of casino gambling ("When the Wheels Won't Stop," 1997). In fact, many

Figure 11.1
Arguments Commonly Used by Anti-gambling Activists

---

1. Gambling increases the costs of governmental programs, welfare, and counseling.
2. Gambling encourages deviant behavior.
3. Gambling is regressive—disproportionately affecting the lower class.
4. Gambling tends to be a disincentive to industrialization or commerce.
5. Gambling cannibalizes other industries.
6. Gambling creates unrealistic hopes, aspirations, and consequently apathy.
7. Gambling is reliant upon uncontrollable economic forces such as consumer interest, jurisdictional competition, and market saturation.
8. Gambling creates a false sense of security about frozen taxation, merely delaying the inevitable.
9. Casinos prey on their own communities.
10. Casinos are associated with organized crime.
11. Casinos decrease the quality of life experienced by lower economic families.
12. Casinos destroy local economies while state government reaps the profits.
13. Casino gaming creates economic dependence.

---

jurisdictions introduced gambling with strict betting limits and credit restrictions. Many of these safeguards, however, have been removed as the market becomes increasingly saturated and communities fight for customers. The resulting increase in problem gambling has also increased the social costs associated with applicable treatment. According to Kindt (1997), an anti-gambling advocate, gambling abuse outweighs drug abuse by a margin of $70 million to $80 million. Other research has also claimed that the increase in economic revenues generated by the introduction of casino gambling is far outweighed by the social costs of treating compulsive gambling (Thompson, Gazel, and Rickman, 1996). While such claims are common in politicized studies, no empirical research has actually calculated the economic costs associated with compulsive gambling. In fact, research has consistently failed to consider alternative explanations for such increases, such as the greater availability of treatment providers and a decrease in the social stigmatization that has traditionally been associated with such behavior. Similarly, arguments that claim that gambling actually encourages other forms of deviant behavior lack merit in the absence of academic empiricism.

Other arguments that claim that gambling tends to act as a regressive tax on the lower class do appear to have some merit. Some methodologically sound studies have indicated that individuals from lower economic classes disproportionately spend their earnings on gambling activities. Even in Las Vegas, which traditionally had the highest proportion of nonresident gaming traffic, investment payoffs were significantly shorter on casinos in impoverished neighborhoods. However, there is indication that low educational status and low economic class may be directly related to the method of preferred gambling. These individuals are more likely to play games that heavily favor the house, such as video poker and slot machines. Their counterparts occupying higher economic positions and educational levels are more likely to play games that have a greater likelihood of payoffs, such as blackjack and baccarat. This characteristic has not been considered in academic research and should be included in future studies. Superficially at least, it appears that individuals playing lower percentage games are more likely to collect an individual's money faster, encouraging them to spend more, whereas individuals playing higher percentage games have the luxury of playing longer on the same amount of money.

Other allegations, though common among anti-gambling activists, also lack empirical support. The much-cited notion that gambling creates unrealistic hopes and aspirations, and decreases the traditional work ethic, has not been methodologically evaluated. To the contrary, the prosperity and low unemployment rates that have often followed the introduction of casino gambling appear to negate this argument. However, casino advertisements adorn city transit vehicles—most commonly found in economically depressed areas—like designer jeans. In addition, many initiatives to limit the impact on economically disadvantaged populations have met with considerable resistance. A bill proposed before the Illinois legislature that prohibited cashing of welfare checks at gambling establishments was defeated (Simon, 1995). Again, the failure of community administrators is more than apparent.

Arguments have also included allegations that the presence of casino gambling acts as a disincentive to industrialization or commerce. In fact, some communities have experienced a decrease in industrial-type employment. Eastern Iowa, for example, saw the closing of Case tractors, I.H., and Cat, whereas John Deere laid off thousands (Cooper, 1996). However, anti-gambling activists rarely account for environmental factors such as a decaying farm industry, rural depression, and the like. In the light of such conditions, correlations between casino gambling and deindustrialization remain unclear. Some advocates even claim that potential investors are discouraged by the presence of casino gaming. However, many of the jurisdictions claiming to be adversely affected by such an introduction were probably not considered prime markets prior to introduction.

Community Cannibalization

One of the most common allegations levied by anti-gambling advocates is that casinos are inherently cannibalistic—gobbling up traditional businesses and transforming community culture. This argument does appear to have some merit. Many local communities have experienced a significant decrease in the number of nongaming businesses. Unable to pay taxes as land valuation skyrockets and unable to compete with the low prices found in casino restaurants and entertainment venues, many local businesses have been forced to close up shop. A prime example appears to be Atlantic City. Prior to legalized gambling in Atlantic City, there were over 240 independent restaurants; 10 years and gambling legislation later, there were under 150 in 1995 (Goodman, 1995). In addition, outlying communities appear to be suffering.

While the casinos of Tunica and the Gulf Coast of Mississippi appear to be successful, surrounding communities such as Memphis, Tennessee, have expressed reservations concerning their positive impact. In fact, outlying communities that have temporarily experienced a honeymoon boom following introductions of casinos are now experiencing unprecedented competition for entertainment and services due to market saturation. For example, tourist destinations such as Memphis, Tennessee, are now complaining that they can no longer compete with casinos that offer cut-rate performances of national celebrities. In an attempt to attract local consumers and middle-class tourists, many new casinos offer headlining entertainment at minimal prices—recouping their fees through dollars spent on the carpet. Local venues, however, have suffered due to the necessity of demanding higher ticket prices to pay for such luminaries. In fact, outlying communities that once embraced surrounding casinos have now recognized the damage to their local markets. In 1997,the Memphis Convention and Visitors Bureau expelled several Tunica casinos, arguing that the $25,000 gained in membership fees was far outweighed by drains on the local economy. Industry officials, on the other hand, say that such sentiment is misleading and that their success simply reflects the prosperity of local tourist communities. Increasing competition for gambling dollars has certainly increased the quality of life for those individuals attaining employment within the industry. It would appear that anti-gambling forces should recognize that claims of "'employee pirating" are actually detrimental to their cause. Indeed, the competition for employees is indicative of a low unemployment rate, and it only increases benefits and salaries for community residents.

It is apparent, then, that gambling does appear to damage existing business. Unfortunately for anti-gambling activists, this argument fails to hold much water, as it is utterly alien to a capitalist society to criticize one business for being too successful. Capitalist markets are inherently unfair and skewed to those businesses that supply that which is needed or desired in society. Indeed, the generation of such desire fuels an entirely different industry—advertising. While we can certainly argue that mom-and-pop establishments add local color and flavor to the community, we cannot condemn the casino industry for overlooking (or even overstepping) them. Furthermore, due regard for such market displacement has traditionally been absent. In fact, no such industry has created such a desire to protect American mainstays. When multiplexes replaced drive-in movies, little furor was created. Indeed, many individuals were pleased that their communities were so progressive.

Crime

One of the most comprehensive and compelling diatribes against casino gambling was entered into government proceedings by prosecuting attorney Jeffrey Bloomberg of Deadwood, South Dakota. In brief, he argued that the promises of lower taxation, economic stimulation, and increased employment opportunities made by gaming lobbyists were not fulfilled. He discussed the repercussions for non-casino-related businesses, arguing that the casinos flourished at the expense of community mainstays. He stated that property and personal taxes had risen every year and that jobs that were created were mostly low paying and non-skilled. But most important, Bloomberg discussed the quality-of-life issue of utmost concern in most communities—rising crime rates and child abuse. He outlined various criminal activities that had escalated in pace with casino construction, and he identified patterns of child neglect. Many of the tragedies he detailed are similar to ones included in local papers. In fact, many anecdotal stories that detail specific tragic consequences of problem gamblers are often offered as evidence of increasing crime rates in casino communities. The nation watched with great interest as the trial of the individual charged with the rape and murder of a small child playing in a video arcade unfolded. Other accounts of individuals turning to street crime to finance their gambling habits are also common in the media.

Although such anecdotal accounts suggest that increased criminal behavior is directly proportional to the proximity of gambling venues, empirical research does not support such allegations. Beginning with the seminal work of Albanese (1985), several studies have been conducted that suggest that the introduction of casino gambling has had no significant impact on street crime. In fact, some studies have found that crime rates have actually decreased (Chang, 1996; Illinois Criminal Justice Information Authority, 1992; Southern Indiana Chamber of Commerce, 1993).

Like other areas of research in the realm of gambling, many academic studies that evaluate the relationship between crime and casinos appear to be rather biased or methodologically flawed. For example, many studies that have found increases in criminal activity have failed to control for the increase in daily population (Giacopassi and Stitt, 1993; Hakim and Buck, 1989; Ryan, Connor, and Speyrer, 1990). Albanese (1985) was the first to realize that the probability of victimization is proportional to the increase in transient population. Thus, if a community traditionally experienced a 1 in 100 risk of victimization, the ratio of risk would remain constant regardless of population increase. This recognition, however, has often been intentionally overlooked in later studies. Albanese also suggested that community demographics, such as police presence, increase in multifamily dwellings, and variations in numbers of hotels, apartments, and businesses should be included in any attempts at statistical analyses. Replication of his work has affirmed the conclusion that the introduction of casino gambling has little, if any, significant negative impacts on local crime rates. Curran and Scarpitti (1991) actually found a decrease in street crimes committed outside the boundaries of the casinos themselves. They argued that the rate of measured crime in Atlantic City has been falsely inflated by the inclusion of criminal activity committed on casino property (i.e., incidents not directly affecting community residents). Intuitively, it would appear that consideration of these inflationary characteristics should be discussed separate from traditional street crime ratios. Unfortunately, current research, highly politicized in nature, has omitted such considerations—strictly using any source of straight-line data consistent with their positions.

Other theorists have developed complicated prediction models that purportedly indicated that casinos, in and of themselves, are crime machines—entities that create crime by their very existence. One such model even predicted an exact numerical increase in crimes that would be caused by casino gambling. Implementing a model including race, employment, and most important, a "gambling dummy variable," Ryan, Connor, and Speyrer (1990) predicted an increase of 132 crimes per 1,000 residents in the city of New Orleans (Margolis, 1997, 53). However, such projections lose forecastability in light of contradictory statistical evidence that is readily available to interested parties. Evaluation of the Uniform Crime Reports indicates that index crimes in Atlantic City have remained consistent or slightly decreased over the past 15 years—a period of wide-scale casino expansion. In fact, experiences and crime rates in casino communities are remarkably similar to nongaming communities—an overall decrease in predatory crime often attributed to innovative police practices and the onslaught of community policing.

The impact of casino gaming on rates of white-collar crime remains largely unexplored. Although Goodman (1995) reported that 40 percent of white-collar crime could be traced to gambling, the study that established this "fact" has never been located. In fact, the American Insurance Institute (AII) appears to be a fabrication of anti-gambling forces as far back as the 1960s. (Not that Goodman is alone is propagation of such misinformation. Rather, the "findings" of the "'AII study'" appear in virtually any work created by gambling antagonists.

It is apparent that statements attributing increased crime rates to casino introduction are not only misleading but also overwhelmingly lacking in empirical support. The single-most important omission in such "studies" appears to be the calculation of increased transient or nonresident population. In fact, studies that have compared casino communities to tourist jurisdictions with similar visitor ratios have actually found that some casino venues have less predatory crime than comparable tourist areas (Chiricos, 1994; Margolis, 1997). Indeed, crime rates within casino communities tend to experience the same fluctuations experienced by nongaming communities based largely on sociodemographic characteristics (Margolis, 1997).

A review of the extant literature overwhelmingly negates the notion of significant increases in criminal activity when transient population is controlled for. This is not to suggest, however, that communities considering the introduction of casino gambling should ignore the possibility of increased demand for law enforcement services. Studies have indicated that many communities have experienced an increase in traffic-related incidents (Margolis, 1997; Southern Indiana Chamber of Commerce, 1993). These incidents include vehicular accidents, congestion, parking violations, and the like. As such, city administrators should be prepared for an increase in traffic enforcement personnel.

Organized Crime and Legalized Gambling

One of the most commonly cited reasons for community objections to the introduction of casino gaming appears to be the fear of organized crime infiltration. Beginning with Siegel's Flamingo and continuing through public hearings initiated by individuals such as Kefauver, Las Vegas and other gambling venues have tried for decades to shed their image as a haven for wise guys. While casino towns such as Vegas and Atlantic City certainly have had their share of organized crime scandals, the introduction of strong regulatory agencies and the involvement in publicly traded companies have radically changed the face of casino gambling in the United States. While certainly casino lore is rich with examples of wise guys and mob bosses, recent requirements by state gaming commissions and the Securities and Exchange Commission have radically changed the personality of organized gaming. In fact, the gaming industry itself appears to be the biggest supporter of regulatory supervision.

In Nevada and New Jersey in particular, the power and authority of the state gaming regulators are absolute. Individuals or entities found wanting may be denied access to or removed from the industry with the stroke of a pen. State courts have upheld the constitutionality of such powers and routinely deny procedural appeals. Newcomers to the industry have followed suit. A review of license processing in several states indicates that high priority is given to comprehensive background investigations, including employment histories, family connections, and full financial disclosures, for all key players. This is not to suggest—as Janet Reno has proclaimed—that any and all vestiges of organized crime have been removed from the carpeted world of casino ownership and management. But it has certainly decreased the likelihood of large-scale mob infiltration. In addition, as we stated earlier, requirements set forth by the SEC act as a further barrier to criminal organizations.

Publicly traded companies are required to submit to microscopic examination and publication of findings. Criminal violations, financial records, and employment histories are mandated for all major stockholders, officers, and trustees. These documents are available not only to government regulatory agencies but to individual investors as well. Not a comfortable setting for underworld figures who thrive on their very obscurity. Indeed, easier pickings and far less scrutiny are relatively easy to find.

Suicide

Anecdotal evidence by journalists from jurisdictions contemplating the legalization of gambling have found that bylines in prominent places are assured with tragic examples of gambling's power (see Figure 11.2). According to critics, suicide rates in casino jurisdictions are "four times" higher than in noncasino communities. Lesieur and Anderson (1995) report that 63 percent of the compulsive gamblers in their study had contemplated suicide and 79 percent stated their desire to die. And others (Gold, 1998) suggest that one in five compulsive gamblers attempts suicide. While such allegations seem logical, statistics do not support such allegations. In fact, one of the few empirical studies in the extant literature found "no evidence to support the proposition that residents or visitors of gaming areas . . . faced heightened risks of suicide because of the presence of gaming" (McCleary and Chew, 1998, 12). Evaluation of an array of traditional and nontraditional gaming jurisdictions and surrounding communities revealed that while casino towns appear to have an elevated number of visitor suicides, suicide *rates* among visitors

Figure 11.2
Ranking of Visitor Suicides per Million Visitors

1. Hamilton, OH	32. Stockton, CA	64. Corpus Christi, TX
2. Gary, IN	33. South Bend, IN	65. San Francisco, CA
3. Wilmington, DE	34. St. Louis, MO	66. Dayton, OH
4. Jersey City, NJ	35. Louisville, KY	67. Sarasota, FL
5. Lakeland, FL	36. Eugene, OR	68. Minneapolis, MN
6. Trenton, NJ	37. Reno, NV	69. Oklahoma City, OK
7. Portland, OR	38. Madison, WI	70. Charleston, WV
8. Toledo, OH	39. El Paso, TX	71. Nassau-Suffolk, NY
9. Daytona Beach, FL	40. Pittsburgh, PA	72. W. Palm Beach, NY
10. Chattanooga, TN	41. Tucson, AZ	73. Oakland, CA
11. Memphis, TN	42. Canton, OH	74. Los Angeles, CA
12. Colorado Springs, CO	43. Riverside, CA	75. Bergen, NJ
13. Jacksonville, FL	44. Tampa, FL	76. San Diego, CA
14. Washington, DC	45. Cleveland, OH	77. Ft. Worth, TX
15. Ft. Lauderdale, FL	46. Grand Rapids, MI	78. Flint, MI
16. Omaha, NE	47. Kansas City, MO	79. Dallas, TX
17. Honolulu, HI	48. Dutchess County, NY	80. Providence, RI
18. Vallejo, CA	49. San Jose, CA	81. Detroit, MI
19. Greensboro, NC	50. Norfolk, VA	82. Bakersfield, CA
20. Columbia, SC	51. Allentown, PA	83. Salinas, CA
21. Melbourne, FL	52. Lancaster, PA	84. Houston, TX
22. Provo, UT	53. Philadelphia, PA	85. Sacramento, CA
23. Wichita, KS	54. Spokane, WA	86. Milwaukee, WI
24. Middlesex-Somerset, NJ	55. Albany, NY	87. Atlantic City, NJ
25. Phoenix, AZ	56. Erie, PA	88. Columbus, OH
26. Las Vegas, NV	57. Greenville, SC	89. San Antonio, TX
27. Baltimore, MD	58. Miami, FL	90. Orlando, FL
28. Cincinnati, OH	59. Buffalo, NY	91. Newark, NJ
29. New Orleans, LA	60. Appleton, WI	
30. Charleston, SC	61. Denver, CO	
31. Salt Lake City, UT	62. Chicago, IL	

Source: McCleary and Chew, 1998.

were similar to noncasino communities. Statistically speaking of course, these numbers lose all significance when increases in daily population and the like are controlled for. However, as is the case in much of the gambling literature, intervening variables are seldom discussed in this highly politicized arena. Indeed, there seems to be little evidence to support arguments that the introduction of gaming increases mortality rates—natural, accidental, self-inflicted, or otherwise.

Divorce and Bankruptcies

In addition to allegations of high crime rates, anti-gambling forces have traditionally argued that legalization adversely affects divorce rates and personal bankruptcies. They blame the increase in divorce on several factors including: (1) the solitary nature of the gambling lifestyle, (2) the preoccupation that often accompanies gambling, (3) debts incurred, and (4) a pattern of lying inconsistent with levels of honesty expected by marital partners. Anti-gambling activists estimate that 22 percent of compulsive gamblers divorce because of their gambling (Simon, 1995). While this certainly appears to be a significant concern, studies have not evaluated national averages nor provided comparisons between rates of casino versus noncasino jurisdictions. In addition, such "research" has failed to address changing norms within society.

Some anti-gambling advocates have argued that divorce rates are simply a reflection of dysfunctional consequences of casino gaming. They argue that bankruptcies are also symptomatic of such pathology. In a 1997 study, Yacik reported that bankruptcy rates in counties with gambling were 18 percent higher than their counterparts. Additionally, he reported that the rate rose to 23 percent in counties with five or more casinos. Other research has consistently focused on disproportionate bankruptcy rates in Atlantic City, which some have reported are 71 percent higher than any other county in New Jersey. Others have suggested that gambling is the fastest-growing cause of personal bankruptcy ("When the Wheels Won't Stop," 1997). Unfortunately, methodological flaws in each study have all but negated the impact of their findings. Without exception, these studies have failed to include factors such as national averages, unemployment ratios, relaxed bankruptcy laws, and aggressive solicitation of credit card customers. In addition, these studies have overwhelmingly concentrated on Atlantic City—a jurisdiction that tends to suffer disproportionate maladies in relation to other casino jurisdictions. Empirically, such rates lack reliability in the absence of control groups.

Incestuous Relationships and Public Corruption

Many crusaders have argued that the marriage between politics and gaming is inherently destructive as it leads to political corruption and disproportionate regulation. They argue that gambling communities have become so reliant on casino revenues that the regulations that were created to reduce negative consequences are all but ignored. This argument appears to have considerable merit and would seem to be the crux of their position. Many gaming jurisdictions included provisions in their original plans that were designed to safeguard communities against anticipated negative consequences, such as increases in compulsive gambling and casino foreclosure. Limitations on the number of slot and video poker machines—often called the "crack cocaine of gambling"—restricted wagering, and strict boundaries on credit allowances were created to reduce the likelihood of economic devastation. However, the majority of jurisdictions have reduced or lifted such restrictions as the market has become increasingly competitive. As such, governments have displayed vested interests in the deregulation that is resulting. These same governments that have traditionally been empowered to regulate avenues of commerce that may pose a threat to community residents, property values, and moral order are increasingly promoting gaming interests and selling out community ones. In fact, many state and local governments have increasingly solicited gaming entrepreneurs and promoted their endeavors to the community. Initially arguing that legalization was necessary for economic revitalization and community protection, government interests—and loyalty—have shifted. As such, many are involved in aggressive marketing strategies and have lessened the scrutiny of operational practices. Many have even been convicted of political payoffs and other illegal practices (Figure 11.3).

The individual exchange of monies and promises is but one of the methods of corruption involved in the political process, according to anti-gambling activists. They argue that the dependent relationship has resulted in disproportionate enforcement. Obviously, governments that stand to lose in the hundreds of thousands of dollars for temporary casino closures for "'minor" violations, such as alcohol restrictions, are more than reluctant to impose standard penalties for their partners, while at the same time they are hesitant to remove these restrictions from existing codes. Thus, disproportionate justice appears—those involved in the casino industry are protected, whereas local businesses, having far less to offer to their elected officials, bear the brunt of civil and criminal prosecutions. One notable example, Foxwoods Casino in Ledyard, Connecticut, racked up over 200 violations for underage drinking, yet did not receive even one license suspension. Skeptics may claim that this type of deferential treatment may be a result of the tens of millions of dollars the establishment has poured into government coffers over the years or the $500,000 the government would lose in taxation if a one-day suspension occurred. Thus, disproportionate enforcement is the norm.

CONCLUSION

While it may intuitively appear that the introduction of gambling increases all sorts of social ills, empirical research does not support the majority of such presumptions. Indeed, it appears that the only negative consequences of casino gaming are an increase in the number of problem

Figure 11.3
Political Corruption and the Appearance of Impropriety

Indiana

Former House Ways and Means Chairman Sam Turpin indicted on felony bribery and perjury charges for his involvement with a riverboat casino contractor.

Louisiana

Former Governor Edwin Edwards also faces trial in an alleged scheme to extort millions of dollars from riverboat casino applicants (also implicated is Eddie DeBartolo, Jr., sports mogul and owner of the San Francisco 49ers).

Louisiana granted only 15 licenses, which ostensibly limited any negative consequences resulting from oversaturation of gaming markets. Unfortunately, this practice may have actually increased political corruption due to the lucrative nature of awarding a limited amount of valuable commodities. A case in point involved the final license granted in the state. The recipient, Edward DeBartolo, Jr., owner of the San Francisco 49ers, allegedly engaged in nefarious business practices with then Governor Edwin Edwards. This license is currently in limbo amid allegations that Governor Edwards extorted $400k from DeBartolo and others.

Missouri

Then House Speaker Bob Griffin was accused of demanding that a casino firm "donate" $16 million to his friends and clients to secure a riverboat license. Griffin, indicted on unrelated charges stemming from a wide-ranging federal investigation, is now in prison for bribery and mail fraud.

Missouri

The government allowed the Flamingo Casino to remain open, after Hilton paid a fine of $655,000 amid allegations that Hilton executives offered more than $1 million in bribes to Kansas City officials.

South Carolina

Traditionally known for its Religious Right posturing, the State of South Carolina recently unseated incumbent Governor David Beasley for pro-gambling candidate Jim Hodges. As South Carolinians could testify, video poker mogul Fred Collins had a direct impact on the election—paying dearly for signs proclaiming Beasley's ineptitude and failure to South Carolina's educational system. Marketing the idea that taxes on video poker and a statewide lottery would benefit the state's flagging academic standards, Collins and his counterparts handed Hodges a victory. As political promises go, the assurance that gambling taxes would benefit public schools remains to be seen. Meanwhile, former Governor David Beasley has characterized video poker as the "crack cocaine of gambling."

gamblers within a community and the foreclosure of traditional businesses. Although often cited as reasons to avoid such relationships, neither is very compelling. Indeed, the number of dysfunctional gamblers displayed within a community may represent only a very small number of its residents. In addition, free markets and capitalism demand that the pursuit of commerce not become stagnated by an overabundance of regulation. On the other hand, taxes and levies against casinos have significantly fattened government coffers. Although these increased funds are often misappropriated, the fact remains that casinos increase community and state revenues.

Problems and Suggestions

Now that we have explored the impact of casino gaming on communities, it appears that proper planning may eliminate some of the problems experienced in new casino jurisdictions. It appears that once casinos are entrenched, communities are powerless to expel them—irrespective of economic impact or negative consequences. Much like the unwanted house guest, casinos build a nest and flourish. Thus, administrators must establish legal boundaries with an eye toward longevity. For the most part, the issues expressed most often by community residents concerned quality-of-life issues and, as such, are relatively easy to address *if* a strategic plan is developed prior to casino opening. These issues may be categorized as environmental, social, and economic.

Environmental Problems

Without exception, perceptual studies of community satisfaction suggest that residents are most dissatisfied by the decrease in parking availability and the increase in traffic-related congestion. These quality-of-life issues are not unique to casino communities. Any jurisdiction heavy in tourism experiences parking, traffic, and congestion problems. In fact, many areas that have long relied on dollars from the tourist industry for survival are still adversely affected by increased traffic flow. To suggest that casino communities are unique in this respect is a disservice. These inconveniences, however, may be alleviated if proper planning is undertaken prior to grand openings. Limited parking and traffic congestion, in particular, appear to be problems that can be easily prevented. Remote parking areas for all casino employees and supplemental workers should be located in sparsely populated areas. Tram systems for casino players should be considered. Routine deliveries to and from the casino should be scheduled for late-night or nonpeak hours for both aesthetic and congestion purposes. In addition, docking increments of riverboats should be planned to coincide with low-level traffic ebbs. Fi-

nally, increases in police personnel should be considered. Casino operators in Gulfport have financed hirings within their local departments to
enhance existing patrol and traffic control during peak hours. Jurisdictions unwilling to shoulder the expense of additional sworn officers may
also consider utilization of civilian personnel. And finally, parking ga-
rages should be included in all casino plans and should provide spaces
equal to at least 75 percent of the occupancy rate of casino/hotels and
100 percent of the expected daily attendance of casinos.

As much as possible, communities should separate casino traffic from
residential traffic. While initially expensive, additional roadways, by-
passes, and the like would benefit both casino and noncasino businesses.
Traditional businesses, fearful of loss of patronage, would be appeased
if traffic levels, both vehicular and pedestrian, remain constant. Casinos
that theoretically attract nonresidential patronage would be served by
straight-line access. While some communities may balk at this suggestion—arguing that increased traffic enhances the visibility of their
establishments—this process should circumvent hostile relations or
accusations of cannibalization.

Social Solutions

Although much of the literature on gambling lacks empiricism, the
relationship between accessibility and problem gambling appears a fore-
gone conclusion on which all sides agree. In fact, research conducted by
both anti-gambling forces and the gaming industry indicate that the introduction of casino gambling increases the number of compulsive /
pathological /problem/ disordered (or whatever term is in vogue at the
time) gamblers. While anti-gambling crusaders argue that social and economic costs inherently outweigh any community revenues generated
by the presence of casinos, empirical substantiation is lacking. However,
the American Gaming Association and numerous independent casino
operators have supported hotlines and research while promoting self-
help groups and treatment centers. Motivations not withstanding, the
gaming industry has done more to address issues of dysfunctional behavior than the alcohol, tobacco, and smut industries combined.

Prior to casino licensing, individual communities must determine their
individual tolerance of such behavior—that is, decide whether the legalization issue is to be morally or economically guided. While this is
not to suggest that gambling is or is not moral, it is intended to encourage administrators to employ logical strategies in the development of
casino-community relations. For example, communities who decide that
the morality question is irrelevant according to the constitutional sepa-
ration of church and state could simply require casinos to contribute to
the development of treatment centers, so that the economic burden to

municipal government is negated and the economic advantages are maintained. In addition, such administrators could require postings of hotlines and the like. And finally, if casino operators and state legislators are genuinely concerned about possible negative consequences, some commonsense barriers may be implemented to limit the impulsivity common to previously identified "compulsive gamblers." For example, the elimination of ATM machines and a curtailing of the availability of credit would provide individuals with the opportunity to make more rational decisions outside the confines of the fantasy world in which casinos thrive. While society does not expect that from, say, the liquor industry, it may decrease anti-gambling sentiment while protecting casinos (and their host municipalities) from litigious responsibility. In other words, although government has not found a way to protect people from themselves, they can at least say they are trying.

Economic Solutions

Perhaps one of the most commonly cited arguments against casino gambling is the destruction or cannibalization of existing businesses and community mainstays. While this argument appears to contradict American values of market competition and capitalism, many local businesses have successfully petitioned community leaders on such platforms. However, it appears that communities voicing such concerns can limit the negative impact of casino gambling on existing establishments through careful planning and strategic zoning.

To limit the impact of increased taxation on real estate, communities may proportionately limit tax increases and appreciation scales. By restricting levies on existing businesses, communities may stimulate economic growth by making these establishments more competitive with incoming businesses. Further, the additional taxes collected from newcomers may be gathered as a buffer against economic depression in years to come—safeguarding communities from market depreciation or collapse. Revenue stockpiling coupled with increased competition would inherently benefit community consumers and may even stimulate nonresident spending. However, city planners must not be overzealous in application of protective measures. These measures are simply intended to maintain the competitiveness of traditional establishments while stimulating community growth. Realistically, overimplementation may actually stagnate economic development if incumbents are so insulated from market demands, competitive pricing, and other free market conditions that socialism or the impossibility of failure supplants capitalism. In essence, the most that any jurisdictional government can offer to proprietors, new or old, is a *chance* to succeed, not a certainty.

This is not to suggest that government take an Orwellian approach—

identifying favorite siblings and controlling commercial destiny. Rather, it is simply intended to protect community interests—residential and commercial. In order to determine an appropriate or healthy level of casino development, city administrators must recognize structural characteristics and systemic faults. Variables such as target population, market saturation, and environmental landscaping must be evaluated by communities as they are individually determined. As such, the number of licenses to be granted will vary across jurisdiction—the import of careful licensing will not.

Two of the most effective ways to protect community interests is the application and distribution of licensing and zoning—both of which should be considered prior to legalization. The number of licenses should be directly proportional to the expected influx of nonresident patronage—keeping in mind that underestimation is preferred. This shelters the community—and the industry—from oversaturation that inevitably harms all parties. Underestimation also pillows economic blows that may result from legislative and market conditions in neighboring communities. Overestimation, on the other hand, may lead to cannibalization—which anti-gambling forces foretell—as decreasing gaming and hotel revenues demand comparable increases in nongaming revenue. Finally, careful control of limited licensing will place the community permanently in the driver's seat—as limited supply inevitably increases demand. Competition for such a commodity will enable communities to select proposals most beneficial to themselves. As such, communities can secure both long- and short-term commitments from the successful applicant. This in no way suggests, however, that casinos will be victimized from overzealous community leaders. Indeed, the same bargaining chip used by city administrators will become the successful applicant's greatest strength as a limited amount of competition inevitably enhances the lucrativeness of such enterprise, whereas careful zoning will protect nongaming businesses.

Administrators must maintain this level of circumspection while regulating zoning in their changing community. As mentioned previously, land appreciation may accompany casino construction. Superficially at least, such occurrences are usually a cause of célèbre. Indeed, to some residents, such appreciation serves as a windfall, as some newly made millionaires in Atlantic City may attest. However, many incumbent businesses and/or residents are all but forced to relocate due to the comparable increase in taxation—a choice that is not easy for many. While absolute protection for residential communities may not be possible, community administrators may eliminate much of the damage through careful zoning. Administrators may wish to consider, for example, limitations on the amount of residential areas that may be purchased by casinos or forbid it altogether (though this would probably be impossible in most jurisdictions). Planners may also wish to consider a voting proposal in which neighborhood groups articulate their feelings and have the opportunity to address their concerns. Finally, communities must protect the interests of those individuals on government assistance who are traditionally overlooked in such decision making. Comparable housing with equivalent accessibility to employment and public transportation should be provided for those affected. If none exists, revenue from sale of such property should fund its creation.

In sum, the introduction of casino gambling into communities has been accompanied by both positive and negative consequences—not dissimilar to the inauguration of any large industry. While certainly some individuals have been adversely affected, allegations of wide-scale community destruction have not been substantiated. Anecdotal stories of individual pathology or tragedy, while heartrending, should not pass for empirical proof. At the same time, due regard must be given to the minority of individuals who exhibit self-defeating inclinations exacerbated by the accessibility of legitimate gambling venues. The creation and promotion of self-help or professional alternatives must continue and must be the responsibility of *all* community residents.

Prior to relationship building, community leaders should recognize that the Metastopholic stereotype attributed to the gaming industry by anti-gambling forces is as inaccurate as the angelic one promoted by the AGA. The gaming industry is just that—an industry. One that creates a product that is much in demand. The argument that they create the demand is probably not too far off the mark. Self-promotion has traditionally been considered an acceptable—even highly desirable—goal in the entirely capitalist society that is America; it should not be different in the gaming community. As such, city planners, public officials, and community residents alike should carefully consider the fit of such an industry within their boundaries, while recognizing its self-serving nature. Administrators must recognize that profit margins and the consistency of community worth are closely related. As such, they should avoid the trap that other communities have not—false expectations. Anticipations of community salvation are not only naive but absurd. Greedy administrators have no part in the development of casino-community relations. Revenues generated by the introduction of casinos whether through taxation or other means should be earmarked for community projects that benefit all members. Increasing the number of civil servants, enhancing educational initiatives, beautification projects, and so forth, should be improvements easily accomplished in the absence of self-serving administrators. If determined to be advantageous, a relationship founded on realistic expectations coupled with statutory limitations and community oversight should be developed. With such foundations, a pairing that proves to be equally beneficial may be established.

REFERENCES

Albanese, Jay. (1985). "The Effect of Casino Gambling on Crime." *Federal Probation* 48: 39–44.

Brennan, Richard. (1998). "Canada Urged to Recriminalize Gambling." *Ottawa Citizen*, December 5.

Brokaw, Chet. (1999). "Video Study Survey Show Lawmakers Doubtful about Chances of Repealing Video Lottery." *BC-SD*.

Brown, Joseph H. (1998). "Tunica Finds No Gold in Gambling." *Tampa Tribune*, December 6.

Chang, Semoon. (1996). "Impact of Casinos on Crime: The Case of Biloxi, Mississippi." *Journal of Criminal Justice* 5: 431–436.

Chiricos, Ted. (1994). *Casinos and Crime: An Assessment of the Evidence*. Washington, D.C.: American Gaming Association.

Cooper, Marc C. (1996). "America's House of Cards." *The Nation*, February 19.

Curran, D., and F. Scarpitti. (1991). "Crime in Atlantic City: Do Casinos Make a Difference?" *Deviant Behavior* 12: 431–449.

Drinkard, Jim, and William M. Welch. (1999). "Gambling Industry Ups the Ante in Politics." *USA Today*, January 8.

Ferrell, David, and Matea Gold. (1998). "Casino Industry Fights an Emerging Backlash." *Los Angeles Times*, December 14.

Giacopassi, David, and Grant Stitt. (1993). "Assessing the Impact of Casino Gambling on Crime in Mississippi." *American Journal of Criminal Justice* 18(l): 117–132.

Gold, Mattea. (1998). "New Gamblers Find Old Troubles: Going for Broke, Part 1." *Los Angeles Times*, December 13.

Goodman, Robert. (1995). "Chasing after Bad Bets." *Christian Science Monitor*, October 31.

Hakim, Simon, and Andrew Buck. (1989). "Do Casinos Enhance Crime?" *Journal of Criminal Justice* 17(5): 409–425.

Illinois Criminal Justice Information Authority. (1992). "Casino Gambling and Crime in Chicago: The Impact of the Proposed Casino Complex on Chicago, Cook County and Selected State and Federal Criminal Justice Agencies."

Kindt, John Warren. (1998). "Follow the Money: Gambling, Ethics, and Subpoenas." *The Annals of the American Academy of Political and Social Science* 556: 85–98.

Lesieur, Henry, and Christopher Anderson. (1995). "Results of a 1995 Survey of Gamblers Anonymous Members in Illinois." Illinois Council on Problem and Compulsive Gambling, June 14.

Margolis, Jeremy. (1997). *Casinos and Crime: An Analysis of the Evidence*. Washington, D.C.: American Gaming Association.

McCleary, Richard, and Kenneth Chew. (1998). "Suicide and Gambling: An Analysis of Suicide Rates in U.S. Counties and Metropolitan Areas." *Report to the American Gaming Association*, September 24.

Palermo, Dave. (1998). "Employees Reaping Benefits of Casino Boom." *Sun Herald*, December 6.

Pulley, Brett. (1998). "Betting on Politics: A Special Report—A Gambling Impresario Leaves Little to Chance." *New York Times*, December 6.

Ryan, Timothy, Patricia Connor, and Janet Speyrer. (1990). *The Impact of Casino Gambling in New Orleans*. New Orleans: Division of Business and Economic Research, University of New Orleans.

Simon, Paul. (1995). "The Explosive Growth of Gambling in the United States." U.S. Senate, July 31. Congressional Record for the 104th Congress.

Southern Indiana Chamber of Commerce. (1993). "Indiana Gambling Task Force Report."

Thompson, W. N., R. Gazel, and D. Rickman. (1996). "The Social Costs of Gambling in Wisconsin." *Wisconsin Policy Research Institute Report* 9(6): 1–44.

Welch, William M., and Jim Drinkard. (1999). "Simple Pinball Machine Evolved into Huge Industry." *USA Today*, January 8.

"When the Wheels Won't Stop: Statistics Show that Compulsive Gambling Is Becoming a Problem for a Growing Number of Americans." (1997). *The Economist* (December 13): 22.

Chapter 12

Enter the Federal Commission

Pro and anti-gaming forces fired opening rounds against each other today, as the National Gambling Impact Study Commission [meeting in Chicago May 20–21, 1998] continued its year-long tour of the country. A small group of clergy and followers, carrying signs that read "gambling hurts," conducted a prayer meeting outside the downtown James R. Thompson Center before the nine-member gambling commission began its hearing. One minister prayed for help in protesting the "wickedness that has come into our city."

Inside the main lobby of the Thompson Center, representatives from surrounding cities with riverboat casinos set up booths touting the positive economic impact of gambling.

—Citizen Link: Focus on the Family (n.d.)

INTRODUCTION

Pro-gambling forces stress the 3Rs of legalized gaming—recreation, revenue, and revitalization—whereas the anti-gambling forces stress the ABCs of gambling—addiction, bankruptcy, and crime and corruption. The battle between these two groups and the phenomenal growth of legalized gambling in the United States led to the creation of the National Gambling Impact Study Commission in 1996.

The last federal commission to study the social and economic consequences of gambling was the 1976 Commission on the Review of the National Policy towards Gambling. This commission worked for four years on the study of gambling. At the time, gambling was largely illegal; casino gambling was legal in one state—Nevada. Thirteen states had lotteries. There were no such things as Indian casinos, and Internet gambling was not even a dream. It was estimated that only $17 billion was wagered yearly on all forms of legal gambling. However, at the close of the commission, several states outside of Nevada were considering legalized gambling. Taking this into account, the 1976 Commission did provide a caution against the spread of legalized gambling, particularly casino gambling: "The Commission does not believe that any clear benefits would derive from passage of legislation in the various states to establish casinos.... The likely effects of casino gambling outweigh purely economic considerations" (Commission on the Review, 1976, 102). The commission was especially critical of the location of casinos in urban areas. It concluded that the location of casinos in urban areas would result in increased social problems that would offset any economic advantages (102).

The 1976 Commission cautioned against the location of slot machines in commercial nongaming establishments and predicted that the widespread availability of legal gambling would increase compulsive gambling. It concluded that the expenditures on legalized gambling at that time were regressive, adversely affecting the lower classes more than upper-income groups (102). The commission was especially critical of lottery advertisements and the states actively encouraging the public to play. All of these issues, and some new ones not foreseen by the 1976 commission (e.g., Indian and Internet gambling), would be revisited by the 1996 NGISC.

1996 NATIONAL GAMBLING IMPACT STUDY COMMISSION

The House bill (H.R. 497), which was to become Public Law 104–169, was first introduced in 1996 in the House of Representatives by Congressman Frank Wolf, an evangelical Christian from Virginia. The bill set off a spirited debate between pro- and anti-gambling groups. The gambling industry attempted to kill the legislation. Unable to kill the bill, the gambling industry pushed for representatives from the industry on the commission.

In creating the National Gambling Impact Study Commission Act, Congress based their decision on the following findings:

The Congress finds that—

1. the most recent Federal study of gambling in the United States was completed in 1976;
2. legalization of gambling has increased substantially over the past 20 years, and State, local and Native American tribal governments have established gambling as a source of jobs and additional revenue;

3. the growth of various forms of gambling, including electronic gambling and gambling over the Internet, could affect interstate and international matters under the jurisdiction of the Federal Government;

4. questions have been raised regarding the social and economic impacts of gambling, and Federal, State, local, and Native American tribal governments lack recent, comprehensive information regarding those impacts; and

5. a Federal commission should be established to conduct a comprehensive study of the social and economic impacts of gambling in the United States. (Public Law 104–169, 104th Congress)

Congress provided that the membership would be composed of nine members with three members appointed by the president, the Speaker of the House of Representatives, and the Majority Leader of the Senate. The president, the Speaker of the House of Representatives, and the Senate Majority Leader were to designate one commissioner as chairman. Those appointed as commissioners were to be public or private individuals with knowledge or experience in the areas to be examined by the commission. The nine commissioners chosen were:

Kay Coles James (chair); dean of the Robertson School of Government, Regent University

William A. Bible, chairman of the Nevada State Gaming Control Board

James C. Dobson, Ph.D., founder and president of Focus on the Family

J. Terrence Lanni, chairman of the board and CEO of MGM Grand, Inc.

Richard C. Leone, president of the Twentieth Century Fund

Robert W. Loescher, president and CEO of Sealaski Corporation and a Native American

Leo T. McCarthy, former lieutenant governor of California

Paul Harold Moore, M.D., founding member and president of Singing River Radiology Group

John W. Wilhelm, general secretary-treasurer for the Hotel Employees & Restaurant Employees International Union

The commission's daunting two-year duties began with a meager $4 million budget. A constant complaint for the life of the commission was the lack of money to do the needed research. The commission had six mandated topics of inquiry:

A review of existing federal, state, local, and Native American tribal government policies and practices with respect to the legalization or prohibition of gambling, including a review of the costs of such policies and practices;

An assessment of the relationship between gambling and levels of crime, and of existing enforcement and regulatory practices that are intended to address any such relationship;

An assessment of pathological or problem gambling, including its impact on individuals, families, businesses, social institutions, and the economy;

An assessment of the impact on individuals, families, businesses, social institutions, and the economy generally, including the role of advertising in promoting gambling and the impact of gambling in depressed economic areas;

An assessment of the extent to which gambling provides revenues to state, local, and Native American tribal governments, and the extent to which possible alternative revenue sources may exist for such governments; and

An assessment of the interstate and international effects of gambling by electronic means, including the use of interactive technologies and the Internet. (Public Law 104–169, 104th Congress)

The two-year study began on June 20, 1997. It ended on June 18, 1999, with a report to the president, Congress, governors, and tribal leaders.

Meetings

At the first organizational meeting (Washington, D.C., June 20, 1997), Chairperson James attempted to set the tone for the meetings to follow. The first issue she dealt with was the moral implications of gambling.

[W]e will limit our work to what the legislation calls for—a legal and factual study of the social and economic implications of gambling. . . . We have not been tasked by Congress to examine the moral implications of gambling. (NGISC, June 20, 1997, 2)

Notwithstanding the chair's statement on the moral implications of gambling, the sponsor of the legislation, Congressman Frank Wolf, made his view very clear.

Let me say at the outset, I strongly oppose gambling. I think it is anti-family. I think it is anti-business and does more harm than good. I certainly don't want it in my community or in my state, and I would fight and will fight it from coming to my area with all of my energy. (17)

Congressman Wolf also stated that his examination of this "dubious enterprise" (gambling) convinced him it "led to crime, to corruption, the cannibalization of existing businesses, and it certainly caused social ills" (22).

Senator Richard Bryan, a two-term senator from Nevada and a former governor of that state, made his views clear at the August meeting of the commission.

The drive for this Commission did not come out of a desire for legitimate study of the business of gambling. It came from a desire to portray gambling as evil in all its many forms and in such disreputable light that the gaming industry would either find itself banned outright or loaded with such restrictions and cost that it would have no ability to operate. (NGISC, August 19, 1997, 18)

The moral implications of gambling would be debated by pro- and anti-gambling forces at every meeting of the commission.

The commission made six on-site visits to conduct public hearings. The first on-site meeting was held at the Atlantic City Convention Center, Atlantic City, New Jersey, on January 21 and 22, 1998. The purpose of their visit, according to Chair James, was to "learn first hand about the impact of legalized gambling upon this community and surrounding areas" (NGISC, January 21, 1998, 8).

The Atlantic City public hearings elicited comments from politicians (federal, state, and local), community residents, casino employees, disgruntled casino employees, clergy, self-admitted compulsive gamblers (members of Gamblers Anonymous), treatment professionals, and union members. The public hearings were marked by advocacy and hyperbole, a common thread that would run through the public hearings at all on-site meetings. There were also panels of experts that included a number of well-known researchers, describing what was known and not known in the gambling area. The researchers' comments to the commission generally asked for more scientifically valid research on the social and economic implications of gambling, a common thread that would run through most expert testimony. However, some of the so-called panel experts also engaged in advocacy and outlandish hyperbole, a practice that became more common in later on-site meetings. One treatment expert stated, "The chances of winning the state lottery are just as good if you got [sic] or you don't have a ticket" (NGISC, January 22, 1998, 169).

The second on-site visit took place in Boston, Massachusetts, on March 16 and 17, 1998. The meeting examined state lotteries. Boston was chosen because "this region has a number of very aggressive and some would argue successful lottery games" (NGISC, March 16, 1998, 6). The chair stated that the commission would consider the following questions: In this era of downsizing and right sizing, can continued government in a function like lotteries be justified? Is government regulation, of itself, even possible? Is government competition with other forms of gambling fair? Are funds raised by the lotteries used as they were promised? Are marketing limitations appropriate? Should lotteries run as businesses or as public sector venues/ventures? What contribution does the lottery make to the problem of compulsive gambling? The commission also began its study of Native American gambling issues, including a trip to the Pequot Indians' Foxwoods Casino in Connecticut.

In her opening remarks, Chairperson James complained about the lack of research on lotteries and "the overall lack of research in general about the impact of gambling" (NGISC, March 16, 1998, 11–12). The expert panels included a number of state lottery directors and the state attorney general. The consensus among the experts was that the public supports lotteries and that virtually every state lottery has passed a public referendum. The public hearings were composed of the same groups as the first on-site meeting, including pro- and anti-gambling supporters and the liberal use of hyperbole and anecdotal horror or success stories.

Chicago, Illinois, was the location for the commission's third on-site visit on May 20–21, 1998. Riverboat gambling and gambling on the Internet were the focuses of this meeting. A number of Midwest state and local officials testified to the positive economic impact of riverboat gambling on their communities. They saw gambling as a positive economic development tool for their communities, but not for all communities. Their remarks were vigorously countered by anti-gambling advocates. One professor in his written testimony compared the costs of legalizing gambling to the costs of legalizing cocaine, without any benefits. He also testified that all pathological gamblers commit crimes. Citing a "reformed" organized crime member as the source, he wrote that politicians supporting legalized gambling are either "ignorant" or "on the take."

In the second day of their Chicago meeting, the commission stepped into the abyss of Internet gambling. The panel experts testifying before the commission raised more questions than answers. Comments from the commissioners demonstrated a real concern for the problems associated with in-home gambling, particularly underage and problem gambling. Strict regulation by the states or federal prohibition appeared to be the only answers to Internet gambling. However, either option raised other issues.

The West Coast was the location of the commission's fourth on-site visit. The first day, July 29, 1998, was spent in San Diego, California. The meeting's focus was twofold. The commission began their examination of the parimutuel betting industry (horse racing, greyhound racing, and jai alai) and continued its examination of Native American gambling. During the staff briefing, the commission's Director of Policy argued that "the most contentious issue facing horse racing [and greyhound racing] are proposals to introduce slot machines and other casino-type games at the racetracks" (NGISC, July 29, 1999, 13). That observation was borne out by the panel experts that followed. (The chairman and CEO of the Thoroughbred Horseman's Association, the president of Churchill Downs, and the administrator of the Iowa Racing Commission appeared on one panel.)

The afternoon session on Native American gambling was at times contentious. With the California vote on Proposition 5 four months down the road, a number of the Native American representatives made impassioned pleas in support of Indian gambling and their firm stand to protect their "sovereign nation" status. One tribal chairman argued, "The Issue of gaming is more than betting, regulation and taxes. It is finally allowing Native Americans a place of respect and equal opportunity in America's economic picture" (NGISC, July 29, 1998, 117).

The second day (July 30, 1998) of the fourth on-site visit was spent in Tempe, Arizona. The entire day's hearings were spent on Native American gambling. The chairman of the Hopi Tribe reported that the Hopi people rejected, by a referendum, gaming as a means of economic development because the "potential risk to the cultural integrity of the Hopi society seemed to outweigh the potential benefits to engaging in a tribal gaming enterprise" (NGISC, July 30, 1998). However, he added that the Hopis would respect the rights of other tribes to choose differently. Several other tribal representatives extolled the beneficial economic impact on their tribes.

Commissioner Wilhelm (general secretary-treasurer for the Hotel Employees & Restaurant Employees International Union) asked the tribal leaders pointed questions concerning employees' rights at tribal gaming facilities, particularly the right to organize a union and bargain collectively. The National Labor Relations Act does not apply to Indian lands.

Commissioner Bible (chairman of the Nevada State Gaming Control Board) asked the deputy general counsel of the Indian Gaming Commission, "[W]hy did it take [the Indian Gaming Commission] ten years to just adopt minimum control standards[?] That's sort of the fundamental to the business. That's what you do first before you start operating" (NGISC, July 30, 1998, 151). Her answer was evasive and shed little light on the subject. During the public panels, numerous self-confessed compulsive gamblers and members of Gamblers Anonymous testified that they became compulsive gamblers at Indian casinos or that their gambling "addiction" became worse gambling on Indian lands.

The commission traveled south to Biloxi, Mississippi, on September 10, 1998, and New Orleans, Louisiana, on September 11, 1998, for their fifth on-site visit. The chair said that the commission had come to Biloxi to understand the social and economic impact of legalized gambling. In New Orleans, the commission would "consider the issue [sic] of pathological gambling, state regulation of the gaming industry and [hear] further testimony on gambling and crime" (NGISC, September 10, 1998, 7). Again, the chair mentioned the "void in the available literature" and expressed the hope that the panel experts would attempt to fill in that void.

Jason Adler, senior managing director of Bear, Stearns and Company, testified that there had been a dramatic change in investor confidence in the last few years because of market saturation (NGISC, September 10, 1998, 13). He pointed out that Las Vegas was one area where "supply appears to be outpacing demand." Adler stressed that "gaming markets are extremely vulnerable to increased competition. One new competitor in a market can severely impact margins for other operators in that market" (NGISC, September 10, 1998, 17). However, he pointed out that Wall Street views the Gulf Coast as one of the most promising areas for growth. However, competition is increasing on the Gulf Coast with the recently completed Beau Rivage Hotel and Casino in Biloxi and the Harrah's Casino under construction in New Orleans.

The local politicians testified to the economic "Mississippi Miracle" resulting from the legalization of casino gambling. This was countered by the anecdotal horror stories provided by anti-gambling forces, particularly compulsive gamblers and their families. These public hearings followed the themes set at the outset of the commission's first hearing with the pro-gambling forces stressing the economic benefits of legalized gambling and the anti-gambling forces stressing the social costs—pathological gambling and crime.

The most interesting testimony at the Biloxi meeting was provided by a "reformed" criminal. The 15-year veteran of Chicago's Organized Crime Syndicate testified that organized gambling in the United States was controlled by three cartels: "number one, organized crime; number two, corporate gambling interests; number three, state governments who promote gambling" (NGISC, September 10, 1998, 219). His testimony was colorful, philosophical at times, potentially libelous on occasion, and largely unbelievable.

From Biloxi the commission moved on to the second day's meeting in New Orleans. The staff member briefing the commission on pathological gambling warned that "this topic [pathological gambling] is relatively new and underresearched [sic]; thus, please note that my presentation will neither be comprehensive nor final, but simply an introduction to the topic" (NGISC, September 11, 1998, 8). The panel of experts that followed the staff briefing was also "neither comprehensive nor final." However, one expert in answering the question, Why do people gamble? testified that the first reason was entertainment, fun, pleasure, excitement, or avoidance of conflict. The second reason was to win money.

During the regulation panel, the deputy general counsel for litigation to Texas Governor Bush brought up the problem of illegal eight-liners or "Cherry Masters" gambling machines in his state. These machines, sometimes called "gray machines," are a problem nationwide. Located primarily in truck stops and veteran, fraternal, and civic clubs, they carry the signs for "Amusement Only." However, they pay off in cash if the player is known by the operators.

The political corruption problems connected to legalized gambling were thoroughly discussed in the hearings, often by Louisiana politicians. The New Orleans meeting was suspended after the regulation panel because of heavy rain and flooding in the hotel. Hurricane Georges was forming in the Caribbean.

For their last on-site visit the commission traveled to the "Gambling Capital of the World," Las Vegas. The first day's meeting (November 10, 1998) examined three areas: sports wagering, neighborhood gambling and casinos focused on local clientele, and gambling and employment. Neighborhood gambling—slot machines in grocery stores, convenience markets, and so on—elicited strong comments of caution from the panel members and the commissioners. A researcher from South Carolina testified that the state of South Carolina currently has only convenience gambling (NGISC, November 10, 1998, 96). He pointed out that in addition to convenience stores, South Carolina has video poker machines in tanning salons, laundromats (sic), and one real estate office.

The local and state politicians, not surprisingly, were in agreement that decisions concerning legal gambling should be made at the local or state level, except for Internet and Indian gambling. They were also in agreement that no additional federal regulations or taxes should be imposed on the gambling industry. There were numerous union and nonunion casino employees testifying before the commission. Many of their complaints concerning nonunion casinos were similar to those expressed by the employees of nonunion Native American casinos.

The second day of the meeting (November 11, 1998) was devoted to the following topics: youth and adolescent gambling; marketing, advertising, and promotions; problem gambling; industry credit practices; and regulatory models. The conclusion of those addressing the casino regulation was that there were two basic regulatory models: the New Jersey model and the Nevada model. The regulatory models in the other states are based on these models. New Jersey has the largest and most expensive casino regulation system in the world.

COMMISSION RECOMMENDATIONS

The commission made 76 formal recommendations (see Appendix B). They recommended, as did the 1976 Commission, that the regulation and taxation of gambling remain at the state level. The commission did not recommend a federal tax on gambling, allaying the fears of the gambling industry. In an ironic twist to the report, several days after the report was made public, Representative Frank Wolf, the sponsor of the bill creating the commission, proposed a 1 percent tax on gross gambling revenues to treat problem and pathological gamblers, even though the NGISC's report does not support this. His action and the vigorous reaction by gambling industry spokespersons signaled that legalized gambling and its effects will be an issue in the 2000 elections.

The most controversial recommendation of the commission was a pause or moratorium on the expansion of legalized gambling until more was known about its costs and benefits. The commission recommended that the spread of convenience/neighborhood gambling should be halted and the states should consider rollbacks. Their recommended ban on wagering on collegiate athletic events, even where it is currently legal, created a vociferous outcry among the gambling industry, particularly in Nevada.

A total prohibition of Internet gambling at the federal level was recommended. One of their recommendations, if adopted, might put a stop to, or seriously curtail, Internet gambling. They recommended that legislation be passed stating "that credit card debts incurred while gambling on the Internet are unrecoverable."

ATMs should be banned from gambling areas. This recommendation is already in place in several states, with others examining the issue. The recommendation that states and tribal governments should dedicate a portion of casino revenues for problem gambling research, prevention, and education is also being followed by many of these entities and the gambling industry. The commission found that the largest source of funding for problem and pathological gambling was the commercial casino industry.

The recommendation that all states and tribal governments institute a minimum gambling age of 21 was supported by pro- and anti-forces. The two gambling areas that drew the most attention from the commission during their public hearings were underage and problem and pathological gambling.

Future research had 20 separate recommendations. The NGISC recommended two comprehensive research agendas. The first agenda would be a federal general research strategy "to build a knowledge base of gambling behavior and its consequences on individuals and communities." The second recommended research strategy is at the state level. This recommended research strategy would allow the states "to make decisions as to whether gambling should be initiated, expanded, limited, or terminated."

CONCLUSION

The massive scope of the duties and the meager budget to accomplish its task severely limited the impact the commission might have on the study of "social and economic impacts of gambling in the United States." Many of the matters to be studied—particularly Native American gambling; pathological or problem gambling; and the impacts of gambling on individuals, families, businesses, social institutions, and the economy generally—require two-year multimillion-dollar studies by themselves.

The topical areas, as pointed out by the commission, are plagued by a lack of valid scientific research. Repetition of findings, however biased, in these areas passes for evidence. Information, including "research studies," once cited tends to be recited without examining the original source/s. In the area of pathological gambling, speculation and anecdote pass for empirical evidence based on gamblers in treatment, not observations or surveys of gamblers. Often the findings of "research studies" cannot be trusted. Different and contradictory conclusions are often drawn by researchers examining the same data: Crime is up, crime is down, or gambling has no effect on crime. In testimony before the National Gambling Impact Study Commission, one researcher testified that the bias in current gambling studies was unintentional:

Half the reasons for the bias [in gambling research] is unintentional, it's having limited resources, limited models, limited data, applying the models too mechanistically so one could say that there being done by amateurs or not the best people. And the other half are the tendency to leave out major factors or to exaggerate one factor. (Adam Rose, NGISC, September 11, 1998, 183)

Another issue contributing to the lack of gambling research is the lack of interest in the field by academia. One commissioner commented that the lack of interest by academicians was due to two reasons: (1) There is little money available for it and (2) there is no interest in it (NGISC, April 8, 1999, 88).

REFERENCES

Citizen Link: Focus on the Family. (n.d.). www.family.org/cforum/hotissues.
Commission on the Review of the National Policy towards Gambling. (1976). *Gambling in the United States*. Washington, D.C.: GPO.
National Gambling Impact Study Commission. (1996–1999). Proceedings transcripts. http://www.ngisc.gov/index.html.

Chapter 13

Enough Is Enough

INTRODUCTION

Legal gambling has been in an unprecedented growth period in the United States. However, there is evidence that this growth is slowing down and may soon come to a halt. Rosecrance (1988) stated that the legitimation of gambling would continue until it was taken for granted. The United States is at that point today. As we have stated, gambling is no longer considered deviant behavior by most scholars and the public. Legal gambling is a new form of entertainment, engaged in by a majority of Americans. Gambling is a leisure activity engaged in by most players with disposable income. However, gambling is a problematic behavior with good and bad effects. Unfortunately, we know more about the good than the bad.

MARKET SATURATION

The U.S. gambling industry is mammoth and glutted. Anyone in this country who desires to play the lottery, a gambling machine (slot, video, or VLT), visit a casino, or engage in some other form of gambling can do so easily and legally. As stated earlier, before 1988, the trip to Atlantic City or Las Vegas required a plane trip and time, not to mention money. Today a visit to a casino—land-based, riverboat, dockside, Indian, or day cruise—is within driving distance for all Americans. Day-trippers are the mainstay for many casinos. Convenience/neighborhood gambling has spread to convenience stores, restaurants, bars/taverns, and truck stops. Lottery tickets can be bought in supermarkets and from vending machines. Parimutuel betting, including racinos, exists in 43 states.

The existing lotteries, competing for their own and other states' players, are aggressively advertising and introducing new games to stimulate play in a saturated market. Multimillion-dollar lottery jackpots, created from multistate associations, are hot topics on national and local news, stimulating feverish buying among in-state and out-of-state players. These same state lotteries, in addition to generating revenues, have created new state bureaucracies loaded with career-minded bureaucrats interested in job survival.

One end result of this market saturation is fierce competition among the states and the gambling industries. "Growing the market" of potential gamblers is a popular phrase in the gambling industry.

COMPETITION

In 1993, gambling expert I. Nelson Rose predicted that competition is the most obvious threat to legal gambling.

For Nevada and Atlantic City casinos, like a death by a thousand pinpricks, the market is getting nibbled away at its fringes, particularly by state lotteries, quasi-casinos, and real casinos on Indian land, riverboats, and in mountain towns. (Rose, 1993, 40)

The casino gaming industry is a highly competitive industry that has begun feeding on itself. This has affected vendors and casinos. According to Randy Adams, director of marketing and game development at Anchor Gaming, "There's just too many casinos and too many slot machines and just not enough players anymore" (*National Gaming Summary*, 1998j, 6). Several casinos and casino operators have gone bankrupt in the last two years in the big three gaming markets: Las Vegas, Biloxi, Mississippi, and Atlantic City.

The Northeast

The Northeast is crowded with gaming opportunities and growing. In the future, it is highly likely that casino gambling, in addition to the two Indian casinos, will become legal in New York. Atlantic City's gaming monopoly is already being challenged by casino enterprises in Connecticut (two huge Indian casinos), central New York (Oneida Indian casino), and Niagra Falls, Ontario (Conner, 1998, 22). The Pequot Indians' Foxwoods Casino in Ledyard, Connecticut, has a round-trip ferry service linking New London and Martha's Vineyard, Massachusetts, with Jersey City, New Jersey. The installation of slot machines at racetracks in Delaware, Rhode Island, and West Virginia has impacted Atlantic City (22). Gamblers in the 300-mile radius (north, Manchester, New Hampshire;

west, Pittsburgh, Pennsylvania; south, Raleigh, North Carolina) from which Atlantic City draws it players have other gambling options available.

Atlantic City met this challenge with new construction intended to grow the market. Speaking on new construction, Richard D. Bronson, president, New City Development Corp., The Atlantic City Development Division of Mirage Resorts, said the following:

Growing the Atlantic City Market

We're not going to build something that appeals only to people who already come to Atlantic City. We're going to build something that will make someone who has no desire to come to Atlantic City to want to come here. (*National Gaming Summary*, 1998h, 2)

The new construction is not met with enthusiasm by all. Paul Henderson, president, Atlantic City Hilton Casino Hotel, stated that unless the Las Vegas–style theme resorts grow the market significantly, some current casinos will go out of business. He added that Atlantic City needed more than regional interest. Henderson stated Atlantic City would soon have to start drawing from east of the Mississippi (*National Gaming Summary*, 1998l). That is not likely to happen, given the expansion in the South, particularly along the Gulf Coast.

The South

The growth of legal gambling in Mississippi has been truly phenomenal. It has been a "Mississippi Miracle." The Mississippi gaming industry progressed from small boats moving in as fast as possible after legalization to barge-based dockside casinos. The barges are still there, but the boats, such as the Biloxi Bell Casino, have gone bankrupt and left. Now the Mississippi gaming industry is moving to the Las Vegas–style themed resorts. However, the new casino operations are going to have to aggressively grow the market. Beverly Martin, the executive director of the Mississippi Casino Operators Association, states that the new Mirage's Beau Rivage casino in Biloxi will "grow the market and bring in additional tourists, additional revenue and hopefully additional airlines" (*National Gaming Summary*, 1998a, 2). She also believes that larger gaming companies will come into the area and take over the smaller gaming companies. That is in progress now.

A spokesperson from the Mississippi Gaming Association says that the Vicksburg, Mississippi gaming market is already saturated (*National Gaming Summary*, 1998g, 2). He opined that no casino company could come in and grow the market right now. Tunica's gaming market is satiated, and the casinos are growing the market in the neighboring states of Arkansas, Alabama, Georgia, and Tennessee.

Louisiana, where it has been said that politics corrupted gambling and not the other way around, has more legalized forms of gambling than any state in the United States. The Louisiana gambling market was already satiated before the land-based casino was planned for New Orleans. The Harrah's Jazz New Orleans land-based casino is expected to operate in the red for its first two years. The prospect of the casino ever turning a profit is in doubt. It will have to grow a market from the tourists who visit New Orleans for other reasons. The competition from the Louisiana riverboats and the nearby Mississippi casinos will also impact the Jazz's future. The first stock trade after the casino came out from under bankruptcy had to be halted after four hours when there were no buyers at $8.25 per share. Trading resumed later at $3.25 per share (*National Gaming Summary*, 1998l). We believe it will go back into bankruptcy in the next three to five years. The Harrah's Jazz had its gala opening on October 28, 1999. More than 5,000 VIP guests attended a private party, where Harrah's CEO Paul Satre predicted monthly revenues of $20 to $30 million (*National Gaming Summary*, 1999g). The first two weeks the new casino registered just over $12 million in winnings. This was a win of $35.29 for each visitor, a win figure lower than that from the nearby three riverboat casinos (*National Gaming Summary*, 1999h, 6). However, the first month's revenues was a disappointing $16.3 million, more than 23 percent below the breakeven level of $21–23 million (*National Gaming Summary*, 1999i). Trading of Harrah's Entertainment shares was stopped temporarily after the release of this report. The December revenues have also failed to reach projections.

Nevada

Several Las Vegas casinos have bankrupted recently: Debbie Reynolds Hotel and Casino, Stratosphere Resort, Arizona Charlie's Neighborhood Casino and Hotel, and the Continental Hotel and Casino. The stocks in Las Vegas casinos dropped almost 41 percent ($18 billion) in two years (*National Gaming Summary*, 1998f, 6). Some of this loss was due to the overall fall in stock prices during that period; however, there is concern on Wall Street about the continued expansion in Las Vegas. Bill Bible, the former chairman of the Nevada Gaming Control Board and member of the National Gambling Impact Study Commission, is worried about some of the present casinos surviving in the expanding Las Vegas (*National Gaming Summary*, 1998i, 2). Terrence Lanni, chairman, MGM Grand, Inc. and also a member of the National Gambling Impact Study Commission, is quoted as suggesting a Las Vegas growth moratorium (*National Gaming Summary*, 1999b). Under his suggestion, new room construction would only be approved if an equal number of old rooms were demolished first.

Las Vegas Harrah's and Rio Hotel and Casino invested in a new airline, National Airlines, in July 1998. The new airline's service to the East Coast "was designed to tap into a feeder market seen as a key to the continued growth of Las Vegas" (*National Gaming Summary*, 1998g, 3). Las Vegas and Atlantic City are both trying to expand or grow the market in the same large metropolitan areas.

Although there are plans for the construction of large destination resorts, MGM Grand, Inc. has terminated its plans to build a 1,500-room hotel at its Las Vegas location. Stratosphere Corp. and Harvey's Casino Resorts have also delayed their plans to build or expand Las Vegas properties. The three companies cited the saturated market as the reason for the change of plans (*National Gaming Summary*, 1999e, 10).

The Parimutuel Industry

The nation's parimutuel industry (horse and dog racing, jai alai) has been particularly hard-hit by competition. Five jai alai frontons in Florida have closed in the last several years. The competition from the Florida lottery in the 1990s hurt the entire state's parimutuel industry, especially jai alai (*National Gaming Summary*, 1998c, 5). Competition from cruises to nowhere and Indian high-stakes bingo also contributed to the woes of the Florida parimutuel industry.

Illinois's Arlington International Racecourse has been voluntarily closed since 1998 (*National Gaming Summary*, 1998d, 4). Citing competition from riverboat gambling, the track's owner wanted tax cuts or permission to install slot machines before reopening.

The nation's racetracks are dying, victims of competition and other forms of gambling growing the market from their patrons. According to Stuart Linde, gaming analyst, Lehman Brothers, their only hope is slot machines turning them into racinos (*National Gaming Summary*, 1998k, 2). However, some states (Alabama, New Hampshire, Kansas, Maryland in 1999) are not willing to grow the racetrack gambling market by installing slots or video at their troubled racetracks. The lawmakers and public in these states, and others, have looked beyond the dubious claims of racetrack owners and seen their arguments for what they are—a smokescreen to grow the market and increase profits.

Racinos—Slots at the Tracks

It becomes obvious to everyone except those who would benefit financially that slot machines can't be realistically linked with horse racing. Horse racing isn't a year-round sport. However, slots operate 24 hours a day, 365 days a year. . . .

What comes out of all of this is the conclusion that while promoters talk about race tracks with slots on the side, lawmakers and the general populace know it's really slots with a race track on the side. From an editorial in the Lake Charles, La. American Press. (*National Gaming Summary*, 1998e, 9)

GAMBLING-LOTTERIES

What Rosecrance (1988) called the lotterizing of America will continue for a short time. Gambling-lotteries are the best examples of the domino effect of legalized gambling. One state legalizes a lottery and adjoining states legalize it, using as one of the reasons "Keep the money at home." Alabama, with strong backing from the governor, entered the race for a lottery in 1999. The pro-lottery forces played their jokers in the form of increased revenues for education based on the Georgia Hope Scholarship model and keeping gambling money from flowing into Georgia (lottery) and Mississippi (casinos). The anti-lottery forces trumped with the religious wild cards and visions of gambling money in the hands of the good'ol boy political network in Montgomery. In a surprisingly high voter turnout, the lottery was turned down by 10 percentage points. South Carolina is expected to vote on a lottery in 2000, but it is not expected to pass. The religious anti-lottery groups, buoyed by the defeat in Alabama, are gearing up for a fight.

We do not expect the lottery to increase beyond the present number of states. We also see serious attempts at reform. We expect more pressure on the states to curb deceptive advertising practices and those targeted at lower-income populations. There will be tighter control on, or elimination of, vending machine sales of lottery tickets to prevent the sale to underage buyers.

CONVENIENCE/NEIGHBORHOOD GAMBLING

The spread of convenience/neighborhood gambling (stand-alone slot machines and other video gambling machines) will slow down soon. South Carolina has already made plans to call for a video poker referendum, cap the number of machines, and impose higher taxes. Many expired licenses have not been renewed.

A 1996 vote in Louisiana gave parishes the option to repeal already established casinos and video poker. Casinos stayed, but six parishes voted out video poker. The repeal was to go into effect July 1, 1998 (*National Gaming Summary*, 1998b). Court challenges delayed its implementation. However, the 1996 vote made video poker illegal in 33 of the 64 Louisiana parishes. Nevada is also taking a serious look at the proliferation of casinos in neighborhoods and slot machines in areas not associated with casinos (stores, service stations, etc.).

FURTHER SIGNS OF TROUBLE

Repeal Efforts

The Mississippi Gaming Association is taking the grassroots initiative to outlaw gaming in Mississippi very seriously. Although three previous attempts to call for a statewide vote failed, the Mississippi gaming industry should take the repeal movement seriously. Even though no state in this century has made a gambling game illegal after it has been legalized (Rose, 1993), a statewide ban has a chance of passing in the Southern Baptist–dominated Bible Belt state of Mississippi. There has never been a statewide vote on gambling in Mississippi. Presently, riverboat/dockside gambling is approved in any Mississippi county by default, unless a petition, signed by 20 percent or 1,500 of the county's registered voters, is produced in opposition within 30 days (Mississippi Casino Gaming Act of 1991, Code Sections 75–76–77).

There is also a strong possibility of casino repeal legislation being introduced in the Louisiana legislature within the next two years. Louisiana Representative Tony Perkins was quoted in the trade journal *International Gaming & Wagering Business* ("Louisiana," 1998, 6) as saying, "There's a growing number of legislatures who think gambling has been the wrong thing for this state." In fact, the newly elected governor of Louisiana, Mike Foster, is expected to spearhead legislation to repeal gambling statewide (*National Gaming Summary*, 1999a).

Iowa state lawmakers plan to reintroduce a gaming moratorium that was vetoed by the governor in 1998 (*National Gaming Summary*, 1999d). The proposed bill would impose a five-year moratorium on issuing new gaming licenses.

No Expansion

The expansion of gambling, particularly casino-style gaming, has been beaten back in several states in 1999. The Pennsylvania State Senate declared a proposed gambling bill unconstitutional. The bill would have authorized a statewide referendum on riverboats, slots at tracks, and video poker in bars and restaurants (*National Gaming Summary*, 1999d, 1). Jason Adler, senior managing editor director of Bear Stearns, is concerned about a virtual halt in the opening of new gaming jurisdictions in the United States (*National Gaming Summary*, 1999c, 3). He is also concerned about the longtime effects of Proposition 5, which could bring large-scale casino gaming to California. North Carolina has banned "cruises to nowhere." The *National Gaming Summary* opines "that gaming will endure yet another year [1999] with no major expansion" (1999f, 1). They cite as evidence the rejection of slots/video poker at racetracks in

New Hampshire, Kansas, and Maryland; the defeated gaming bill in Pennsylvania; and the lack of interest in New York and Massachusetts.

Problem/Pathological Gambling

Any attempts at expansion or efforts to grow the market will have to face the question, Is gambling recreation or a social problem? As stated earlier, for most patrons legal gambling appears to be recreation; however, for some there is no denying that gambling is a problem for them, their families, and society. Although there is no accurate accounting of the number of problem/pathological gamblers, there is renewed interest in the subject. Bill Bible states, "The combination of flattening markets and the spotlight being focused on them [problem and pathological gamblers] are major factors the industry will face in the coming year" (*National Gaming Summary*, 1998i, 2).

CONCLUSION

Even though the National Gambling Impact Study Commission concluded that [e]very prediction that the gambling market was becoming saturated has proven to be premature" (1999, 1–1), we believe this to be the case. Many states that have legalized forms of gambling, particularly lotteries, and rely on gambling monies as the economic "silver bullet" for revenue shortfalls will find themselves "chasing the devil" in the new millennium. *Chasing the devil* is a gambler's term for throwing good money after bad in hopes of reversing a losing streak. And every gambler knows that you can't win playing with scared money. Playing to not lose is very different from playing to win. The gambling industry and the states that have legalized gambling will soon find themselves playing with scared money in the new millennium in order to stimulate a satiated market and reverse a movement toward prohibition and criminalization of some forms of gambling. There will never be a total ban on all forms of gambling. That is an unrealistic and unworkable expectation, although some still argue that prohibition is the absolute prevention for sin and vices: no drugs—no addiction; no alcohol—no addiction; no tobacco—no addiction; no gambling—no addiction. This strategy only works when there is no opportunity and no demand. Any attempt for total prohibition would push gambling into the hands of criminals and organized crime again.

Furthermore, the specter of the unknown social and economic effects of problem/pathological gambling on individuals, families, and communities looms over the glitz, glamour, and action. More research on this topic is needed. Unfortunately, the study of legal gambling has not been an identified area of research for many social and behavioral scientists. As the NGISC concluded, much of the research that has been conducted has been biased or based on selective samples. Others who have "researched" or written on this topic have had a definite financial interest in seeing gambling (legal or illegal) as harmful. This is going to change in the new millennium.

The study of legal gambling raises interesting questions—the questions that are the subjects of theses, dissertations, and academic research. For example; How does behavior (gambling) once defined as deviant become accepted and legal in such a short period of time? What are the various types of gamblers? How does one move (if they do) from one type to the other? What is the role of the state in promoting potentially harmful behavior among its citizens? What are the social and economic effects of legal gambling on individuals, special populations (women, underage gamblers, athletes, and senior citizens), and communities? How did gambling become such a large part of the leisure activities of this society? This is a suggestive—not an exhaustive—list of researchable questions. The role of organized crime in illegal gambling—particularly sports betting—and the manufacture and distribution of "gray machines" in bars, truck stops, and civic/fraternal clubs need additional research.

As stated earlier, the National Gambling Impact Study Commission in a contentious 5–4 vote recommended a moratorium on new gambling expansions until further research is conducted. While it is an excellent idea, it will not be followed by the states and the Indian tribes. The commission's recommendations are not binding on these sovereign entities. Nevertheless, legal gambling has reached the point in the United States where enough is enough. Market forces and the increased study of the benefits and problems will soon bring its expansion to a halt. The third wave of legalized gambling is over.

REFERENCES

Conner, Matt. (1998). "A Question of Loyalty: In the New Competitive Landscape, Keeping Players True to a Casino Can Be an Uphill Battle." *International Gaming and Wagering Business (IGWB)* (June).

"Louisiana: Harrah's Jazz Still Stuck in Limbo." (1998). *IGWB* (May).

National Gambling Impact Study Commission. (1999). Final Report (June). Washington, D.C.: GPO.

National Gaming Summary. (1998a). June 22.

National Gaming Summary. (1998b). July 13.

National Gaming Summary. (1998c). July 27.

National Gaming Summary. (1998d). August 10.

National Gaming Summary. (1998e). August 24.

National Gaming Summary. (1998f). August 31.

National Gaming Summary. (1998g). September 7.

National Gaming Summary. (1998h). September 14.
National Gaming Summary. (1998i). September 21.
National Gaming Summary. (1998j). October 5.
National Gaming Summary. (1998k). November 16.
National Gaming Summary. (1998l). December 14.
National Gaming Summary. (1999a). January 4.
National Gaming Summary. (1999b). January 18.
National Gaming Summary. (1999c). March 8.
National Gaming Summary. (1999d). March 15.
National Gaming Summary. (1999e). March 28.
National Gaming Summary. (1999f). April 12.
National Gaming Summary. (1999g). November 1.
National Gaming Summary. (1999h). November 29.
National Gaming Summary. (1999i). December 20–27.
Rose, I. Nelson. (1993). "Gambling and the Law—Update 1993." In Kathryn Hashimoto and Sheryl Fried Kline (1996), *Casino Management for the 90's.* Dubuque, Iowa: Kendall/Hunt.
Rosecrance, John. (1988). *Gambling without Guilt: The Legitimation of an American Pastime.* Pacific Grove, Calif.: Brooks/Cole.

Appendix A

Nature of the Industry

Our literature review revealed that as of December 1998 the following 34 states had casino gambling (land-based, riverboat/dockside, Indian, and offshore cruises commonly known as "cruises to nowhere") or gambling machines (*American Casino Guide*, 1998; Thompson, 1997).

Arizona. In 1993, the governor signed a compact with the state's Indian nations allowing them to offer slot machines on 13 Indian reservations. All Arizona Indian casinos have slots, video poker, and video keno. Optional games include video blackjack, video craps, poker, keno, bingo, and simulcast races.

California. At the current time, the Indian casinos are involved in a legal dispute with the governor concerning the kinds of gambling machines allowed. As of late 1998, the 32 Indian casinos offered video poker, slots, keno, and video pull-tabs. Optional games include blackjack, poker, Caribbean stud, Let It Ride, bingo, and simulcast racing.

Colorado. Colorado turned to legalized casino gambling in 1990 to boost the economy in devastated mining towns. They followed the lead of Deadwood, South Dakota, another failing mining town. There is "limited gaming" in 49 casinos in the mountain towns of Black Hawk, Central City, Cripple Creek, and two Indian casinos. The two limitations for casino games are: (1) Only electronic games (poker, blackjack, and keno) and the table games of poker, blackjack, and three-card poker are allowed; and (2) a single wager cannot exceed $5.

Connecticut. The Mashantucket Pequot Indian Foxwoods Casino, owned and operated by Native Americans, is the largest casino in the world. The mammoth casino has 314,000 square feet of gambling space, 5,750 slot machines, and 370 table games. The Indian Temple of Chance is strategically located two and a half hours from New York City and one and a half hours from Boston. It is the most profitable casino in the United States, and maybe the world. The *American Casino*

Guide (1998) reports that the Foxwoods Casino's slot machines bring in $1.5 million a day in gross profit. A second Indian casino, Mohegan Sun Casino, with 150,000 square feet of gambling space, 3,000 slot machines, and 180 table games, opened in October 1996. It is the fourth largest casino in the country. The Mohegan Sun is a joint venture between the Mohegan tribe and the South African casino conglomerate Sun International. These two casinos offer a full range of casino games, including $100 slot machines.

Delaware. Delaware does not have any casinos; however, the state's three parimutuel racetracks (racinos) have VLTs (poker, keno, and blackjack).

Florida. The Sunshine State, where voters have turned down casinos twice in recent years, has four Indian casinos offering high-stakes bingo, video pull-tabs, and low-limits poker. In addition, cruise lines on the East Coast sail three miles into the Atlantic Ocean for gambling. On the West Coast, cruise ships sail nine miles out of the Gulf of Mexico for on-ship casino gambling. These trips are made daily from Fort Lauderdale, Fort Myers, Fort Pierce, Jacksonville, Key Largo, Key West, Marco Island, Miami, Palm Beach, Panama City, Port Canaveral, Port Manatee, Port Richey, Riviera Beach, St. Augustine, St. Petersburg, Tarpon Springs, and Venice.

Georgia. Two gambling cruise lines make daily trips from Tybee Island and Brunswick three miles out into international waters where casino gambling is permitted. Georgia has recently introduced "quick-draw" keno (VLT) into selected lottery locations. The fast-moving game, called "video crack" by many, can be played every five minutes for up to $100.

Idaho. Five Indian casinos, with high-stakes bingo and electronic pull-tab machines, operate in Idaho.

Illinois. Illinois, the second state to legalize riverboat gambling, has issued 10 licenses for riverboats. Each licensee is allowed two boats. However, there were only nine boats operating as of January 1999. They brought in $1.1 billion in 1998 (*National Gaming Summary*, 1999b, 4)—their best year ever. The *Grand Victoria* riverboat, located 40 miles from Chicago on the Fox River, is elegant and crowded; players wait two hours to board. The state has a graduated tax system ranging from 15 to 35 percent.

Indiana. Seven gambling riverboats operate in Indiana at this time. Two more are scheduled to open in the near future. Indiana taxes gambling revenues at a rate of 20 percent. In addition, the state levies a $3 tax for each patron's cruise. Twenty-five percent of this admission's tax must be spent on gambling addictions through the Department of Mental Health.

Iowa. Iowa was the first state to legalize riverboat gambling, setting off a legalization rush in neighboring states. Currently, Iowa has 11 riverboats and three Indian casinos. Slot machines are located at the Prairie Meadows Racetrack. The 1997 slot revenue for the track was $128 million, $38 per visitor (*National Gaming Summary*, 1998e). A measure to remove ATM machines was defeated. Iowa taxes gambling revenues at 20 percent. Sixty percent of the revenues go to the general fund. The rest is used to repair deteriorating state buildings.

Kansas. Kansas has three Indian casinos, offering blackjack, craps, roulette, slots, video poker, and high-stakes bingo.

Louisiana. Louisiana has 13 riverboat casinos operating in 12 different locations. In addition, there are three land-based Indian casinos. A financially troubled land-based casino, Harrah's Jazz, opened in New Orleans on October 28, 1999. Video poker is permitted at truck stops, racetracks/OTBs, and bars/taverns. Truck stops are limited to 50 machines; bars/taverns are permitted only 3 machines. There are no limitations on the number of gambling machines allowed at racetracks and offtrack betting locations. VLTs are also permitted in Louisiana (Thompson, 1997, 165).

Maryland. There are no legal casinos in Maryland; however, the *IGWB* (1998) reports the 1997 handle for Maryland gambling devices was $188 million. Since 1987, Maryland has charitable slot machines in eight counties on the Eastern Shore (*Grand Rapids Press*, 1994). These machines are located in fraternal, veterans, and social clubs.

Massachusetts. A casino ship complete with slot machines and other gambling devices sails twice daily out of Gloucester for gambling in international waters (*National Gaming Summary*, 1998b).

Michigan. At this time, Michigan has fourteen—mostly small—Indian casinos; however, three land-based casinos opened in Detroit in 1999. The three casinos— Greektown Casino, MGM Grand Detroit Casino, and MotorCity Casino—are operating as temporary casinos with permanent ones opening in four years.

Minnesota. There are 16 Indian casinos located in Minnesota.

Mississippi. Mississippi's 29 riverboat casinos are boats and floating barges, appearing to be land-based casinos rather than riverboats. Biloxi has more casinos and casino gambling space than Atlantic City, New Jersey. A land-based Indian casino is located in Philadelphia, Mississippi. Mississippi, in a move to encourage more resort-style development, now requires new casinos to make dollar-for-dollar investments in land-based facilities (*National Gaming Summary*, 1999a, 6). The investments must be hotel or nongambling amenities such as theme parks, golf courses, marinas, tennis complexes, or entertainment facilities. The tax on gambling revenues in Mississippi is 10 percent and produced tax revenues of $250.3 million in 1998.

Missouri. The 15 dockside riverboat casinos in Missouri have a $500 loss limit on each two-hour gambling session. The "Show Me" state levies an 18 percent tax on gambling revenues. All state gambling revenues (riverboat, lottery, and bingo) are earmarked for K–12 and higher education.

Montana. Montana has five Indian casinos and allows bars and taverns to have up to 20 video gambling machines. In addition, the state lottery has VLTs in selected locations.

Nevada. Nevada, including Las Vegas, the "gambling capital of the world," has 187 casinos. Boulder City is the only Nevada municipality that prohibits gambling. Nevada has one of the lowest taxes on gambling revenues of any state— 6.25 percent. Bally's Las Vegas has a special $1,000 slot machine. A single thousand-dollar token pays off a jackpot of $400,000. The maximum two-token jackpot is $1 million.

New Jersey. All of New Jersey's 12 casinos are located in Atlantic City. The New

Jersey lottery also operates VLTs. The tax on gambling revenues for Atlantic City casinos is 8 percent.

New Mexico. New Mexico has 11 Indian casinos. A 1997 law allows veterans organizations, fraternal clubs, and racetracks to have slot machines. Clubs are limited to 15 machines. Racetracks can have up to 300 slot machines (*National Gaming Summary*, 1998d).

New York. There is one Indian casino in New York and two casino ships sailing daily out of New York City into international waters. The latest legalized casino gambling effort failed in the New York legislature, making a ballot referendum not possible until 2001 (*National Gaming Summary*, 1998a).

North Carolina. The Eastern Band of Cherokee Indians operates a casino in Cherokee, North Carolina. According to the compact, the tribe can offer video poker, video craps, and video blackjack with jackpots up to $25,000.

North Dakota. According to the *American Casino Guide* (1998), North Dakota has over 800 sites offering blackjack for the benefit of charities. The maximum bet is $5. In addition, North Dakota has six Indian casinos.

Oregon. By law, Oregon's bars and taverns are allowed up to five different versions of video gambling machines. Oregon has five Indian casinos and VLTs.

Rhode Island. The two parimutuel facilities in Rhode Island have video lottery terminals programmed to play blackjack, keno, slots, and three versions of poker.

South Carolina. South Carolina has over 30,000 video poker machines located in 200 video poker parlors, bars, and taverns. South Carolina is the best example of what has become to be known as convenience/neighborhood gambling (gambling in close proximity and readily available). The video machines had a profit of more than $23,000 per machine in 1997 (*National Gaming Summary*, 1998c). On November 13, 1998, a "cruise to nowhere" casino made its maiden voyage from Little River near the North Carolina border (*National Gaming Summary*, 1998c).

South Dakota. South Dakota bars and taverns can have up to 10 VLTs offering poker, keno, blackjack, and bingo. There is a state-run casino in Deadwood and eight Indian casinos with slot machines, poker, and blackjack. A $5 maximum bet limit is imposed in all casinos.

Texas. Texas has two Indian casinos that offer poker, pull-tabs, and blackjack. Blackjack players pay a 50-cent commission to the house for each hand. However, a Washington federal court (June 1998) ruled that the games were illegal. The matter is under appeal.

Washington. Twelve Indian casinos, operating with a state compact, offer only table games. Six other Indian casinos, operating without a state compact because of a legal dispute, offer table games and slot machines. In addition, the state has seven non-Indian casinos offering house-banked table games.

West Virginia. The four parimutuel facilities in West Virginia have VLTs that play slots, blackjack, and poker. In 1990, West Virginia was the first state on the East Coast to install VLTs in racetracks.

Wisconsin. Wisconsin has 16 Indian casinos.

REFERENCES

American Casino Guide. (1998). Dania, Fla.: Casino Vacations.

Grand Rapids Press. (1994). December 24.

National Gaming Summary. (1998a). June 28.

National Gaming Summary. (1998b). September 28.

National Gaming Summary. (1998c). November 23.

National Gaming Summary. (1998d). November 30.

National Gaming Summary. (1998e). December 7.

National Gaming Summary. (1999a). February 1.

National Gaming Summary. (1999b). February 8.

Thompson, William N. (1997). *Legalized Gambling: A Reference Handbook.* 2nd ed. Santa Barbara, Calif.: ABC-CLIO.

International Gaming & Wagering Business. (1998). "The United States Gross Annual Wager—1997" (August). Special supplement.

Appendix B

Recommendations of the National Gambling Impact Study Commission

NGISC REPORT RECOMMENDATIONS
June 18, 1999

Chapter 3. Gambling Regulation

3–1 The Commission recommends to state governments and the federal government that states are best equipped to regulate gambling within their own borders with two exceptions—tribal and Internet gambling. (See separate recommendations on tribal and Internet gambling in their respective sections.)

3–2 The Commission recommends that all legal gambling should be restricted to those who are at least 21 years of age and that those who are under 21 years of age should not be allowed to loiter in areas where gambling activity occurs.

3–3 The Commission recommends that gambling "cruises to nowhere" should be prohibited unless the state from which the cruise originates adopts legislation specifically legalizing such cruises consistent with existing law.

3–4 The Commission recommends that warnings regarding the dangers and risks of gambling, as well as the odds where feasible, should be posted in prominent locations in all gambling facilities.

3–5 The Commission recognizes the difficulty of campaign finance reform in general and an industry-specific contribution restriction in particular. Nonetheless, the Commission believes that there are sound reasons to recommend that states adopt tight restrictions on contributions to state and local campaigns by entities—corporate, private, or tribal—that have applied for or have been granted the privilege of operating gambling facilities.

3–6   The Commission received testimony that convenience gambling, such as electronic devices in neighborhood outlets, provides fewer economic benefits and creates potentially greater social costs by making gambling more available and accessible. Therefore, the Commission recommends that states should not authorize any further convenience gambling operations and should cease and roll back existing operations.

3–7   The Commission recommends that betting on collegiate and amateur athletic events that is currently legal be banned altogether.

3–8   The Commission recommends that in states where there is little regulatory oversight for organizations contracted to help manage or supply the lottery, states should put all individuals, entities, and organizations involved with managing or supplying the lottery through a rigorous background check and licensing process.

3–9   The Commission recommends to states with lotteries that the states should publicly develop and review model regulations for their lottery in the form of "best practices," designed to be adopted legislatively.

3–10 The Commission urges states with lotteries to not allow instant games that are simulations of live card and other casino-type games. Generally, the outcome of an instant game is determined at the point of sale by the lottery terminal that issues the ticket.

3–11 The Commission recommends that all relevant governmental gambling regulatory agencies should ban aggressive advertising strategies, especially those that target people in impoverished neighborhoods or youth anywhere.

3–12 The Commission recommends that states should refuse to allow the introduction of casino-gambling into pari-mutuel facilities for the primary purpose of saving a pari-mutuel facility that the market has determined no longer serves the community or for the purpose of competing with other forms of gambling.

3–13 The Commission recommends to state and tribal governments, the NCAA, and other youth, school, and collegiate athletic organizations that because sports gambling is popular among adolescents and may act as a gateway to other forms of gambling, such organizations and governments should fund educational and prevention programs to help the public recognize that almost all sports gambling is illegal and can have serious consequences. The Commission recommends that this effort should include public service announcements, especially during tournament and bowl game coverage. The Commission recommends that the NCAA and other amateur sports governing bodies adopt mandatory codes of conduct regarding sports gambling education and prevention. The Commission also calls upon the NCAA to organize America's research universities to apply their resources to develop scientific research on adolescent gambling, sports gambling, and related research.

3–14 The Commission recommends that each gambling operation, state lottery, tribal government, and associations of gambling organizations voluntarily adopt and then follow enforceable advertising guidelines. These guidelines should avoid explicit or implicit appeals to vulnerable populations, including youth and low-income neighborhoods. Enforcement should include a mechanism for recognizing and addressing any citizen complaints that might arise regarding advertisements. Additionally, the Commission recommends that Congress amend the federal truth-in-advertising laws to include Native American gambling and state-sponsored lotteries.

3–15 The Commission recommends that Congress should delegate to the appropriate federal agency the task of annually gathering data concerning lottery operations in the United States, including volume of purchase; demographics of lottery players and patterns of play by demographics; nature, content, accuracy, and type of advertising spending regarding problem and pathological gamblers; spending on regulation; and other relevant matters.

3–16 The Commission recommends that states and tribal governments should conduct periodic reassessments of the various forms of gambling permitted within their borders for the purpose of determining whether the public interest would be better served by limiting, eliminating, or expanding one or more of those forms.

3–17 The Commission recommends that federal, state, and tribal gambling regulators should be subject to a cooling-off period that prevents them from working for any gambling operation subject to their jurisdiction for a period of 1 year. Federal, state, or tribal lottery employees should be subject to a cooling-off period that prevents them from working for any supplier of lottery services for a period of 1 year.

3–18 The Commission recommends that jurisdictions considering the introduction of new forms of gambling or the significant expansion of existing gambling operations should sponsor comprehensive Gambling Impacts statements. Such analyses should be conducted by qualified independent research organizations and should encompass, insofar as possible, the economic, social, and regional effects of the proposed action.

3–19 The Commission recommends that states with lotteries reduce their sales dependence on low-income neighborhoods and heavy players in a variety of ways, including limiting advertising and number of sales outlets in low-income areas.

3–20 The Commission recommends that states with lotteries create a private citizen oversight board. The board would make data-based policy decisions on types of games to offer, marketing strategies to follow, etc.

3–21 The Commission recognized that lotteries and convenience gambling may play a significant role in the development of youth gamblers. Further, with respect to all forms of legal and illegal gambling, the Commission recommends that all relevant governmental gambling regulatory agencies enact and enforce harsh penalties for abuse in this area involving underage gamblers. Penalties and enforcement efforts regarding underage gambling should be greatly increased.

3-22 Heavy governmental promotion of lotteries, largely located in neighborhoods, may contribute disproportionately to the culture of casual gambling
in the United States. The Commission, therefore, recommends that states
curtail the growth of new lottery games, reduce lottery advertising, and
limit locations for lottery machines.

Chapter 4. Problem and Pathological Gambling

The Commission respectfully recommends that all governments take every
step necessary to implement all relevant components of the recommendations
listed here before lotteries or any other form of legalized gambling is allowed to
operate or to continue to operate. Such requirements should be specifically item-
ized in a state statute as applicable to a state-run lottery. Similarly, such requirements should also be specified and made applicable for inclusion in tribal
government law and tribal-state compacts.

4-1 The Commission respectfully recommends that all relevant governmental
gambling regulatory agencies require, as a condition of any gambling facility's license to operate, that each applicant adhere to the following:

—Adopt a clear mission statement as to applicant's policy on problem and
pathological gambling.

—Appoint an executive of high rank to execute and provide ongoing oversight of the corporate mission statement on problem and pathological gambling.

—Contract with a state-recognized gambling treatment professional to
train management and staff to develop strategies for recognizing and addressing customers whose gambling behavior may strongly suggest they
may be experiencing serious to severe difficulties.

—Under a state "hold harmless" statute, refuse service to any customer
whose gambling behavior convincingly exhibits indications of a gambling
disorder.

—Under a state "hold harmless" statute, respectfully and confidentially
provide the customer (as described above) with written information that
includes a state-approved list of professional gambling treatment programs
and state-recognized self-help groups.

—Provide insurance that makes available medical treatment for problem
and for pathological gambling facility employees.

4-2 The Commission recommends that each state and tribal government enact,
if it has not already done so, a gambling privilege tax, assessment, or other
contribution on all gambling operations within its boundaries, based upon
the gambling revenues of each operation. A sufficient portion of such monies shall be used to create a dedicated fund for the development and ongoing support of problem gambling-specific research, prevention,
education, and treatment programs. The funding dedicated for these purposes shall be sufficient to implement the following goals:

—Undertake biennial research by a nonpartisan firm experienced in problem-gambling research to estimate the prevalence of problem and pathological gambling among the general adult population. Specific focus on major subpopulations including youth, women, elderly, and minority group gamblers should also be included. An estimate of prevalence among patrons at gambling facilities or outlets in each form of gambling should also be included.

—Initiate public awareness, education, and prevention programs aimed at vulnerable populations. One such purpose of such programs will be to intercept the progression of many problem gamblers to pathological states.

—Identify and maintain a list of gambling treatment services available from licensed or state-recognized professional providers, as well as the presence of state-recognized self-help groups.

—Establish a demographic profile for treatment recipients and services provided, as state and federal laws permit. Develop a treatment outcome mechanism that will compile data on the efficacy of varying treatment methods and services offered, and determine whether sufficient professional treatment is available to meet the demands of persons in need.

—When private funding is not available, subsidize the costs of approved treatment by licensed or state-recognized gambling treatment professionals for problem and pathological gamblers as well as adversely affected persons. Additionally, such funds shall ensure that persons in need of treatment can receive necessary support based upon financial need. Treatment cost reimbursement levels and protocols will be established by each state.

4-3   Despite the fact that pathological gambling is a recognized medical disorder, most insurance companies and managed care providers do not reimburse for treatment. The Commission recommends to states that they mandate that private and public insurers and managed care providers identify successful treatment programs, educate participants about pathological gambling and treatment options, and cover the appropriate programs under their plans.

4-4   The Commission recommends that each gambling facility must implement procedures to allow for voluntary self-exclusion, enabling gamblers to ban themselves from a gambling establishment for a specified period of time.

4-5   The Commission recommends encouraging private volunteerism of groups and associations working across America to solve problem gambling, especially those involving practitioners who are trying to help people who are problem gamblers. This should include strategically pooling resources and networking, drawing on the lists of recommendations these organizations have presented to the Commission, and working to develop uniform methods of diagnosis.

4–6   The Commission recommends each state-run or approved gambling operation be required to conspicuously post and disseminate the telephone numbers of at least two state-approved providers of problem-gambling information, treatment, and referral support services.

Chapter 5. Internet Gambling

5–1   The Commission recommends to the President, Congress, and the Department of Justice (DOJ) that the federal government should prohibit, without allowing new exemptions or the expansion of existing federal exemptions to other jurisdictions, Internet gambling not already authorized within the United States or among parties in the United States and any foreign jurisdiction. Further, the Commission recommends that the President and Congress direct the DOJ to develop enforcement strategies that include, but are not limited to, Internet service providers, credit card providers, money transfer agencies, makers of wireless communications systems, and others who intentionally or unintentionally facilitate Internet gambling transactions. Because it crosses state lines, it is difficult for states to adequately monitor and regulate such gambling.

5–2   The Commission recommends to the President, Congress, and state governments the passage of legislation prohibiting wire transfers to known Internet gambling sites or the banks who represent them. Furthermore, the Commission recommends the passage of legislation stating that any credit card debts incurred while gambling on the Internet are unrecoverable.

5–3   The Commission recognizes that current technology is available that makes it possible for gambling to take place in the home or the office without the participant physically going to a place to gamble. Because of the lack of sound research on the effects of these forms of gambling on the population and the difficulty of policing and regulating to prevent such things as participation by minors, the Commission recommends that states not permit the expansion of gambling into homes through technology and the expansion of account wagering.

5–4   The Commission recommends to the President and Congress that because Internet gambling is expanding most rapidly through offshore operators, the federal government should take steps to encourage or enable foreign governments not to harbor Internet gambling organizations that prey on U.S. citizens.

Chapter 6. Native American Tribal Gambling

6–1   The Commission acknowledges the central role of the NIGC as the lead federal regulator of tribal governmental gambling. The Commission encourages Congress to assure adequate NIGC funding for proper regulatory oversight to ensure integrity and fiscal accountability. The Commission supports the NIGC's new Minimum Internal Control Standards [MICS], developed with the help of the National Tribal Gaming Commissioners and Regulators, as an important step to assure such fiscal accountability. The Commission recommends that all tribal gaming commissions work to ensure that the tribal gambling operations they regulate meet or exceed these minimum standards and the NIGC focus special attention on tribal gambling operations struggling to comply with these and other regulatory requirements.

6–2   The Commission recommends that IGRA's classes of gambling must be clearly defined so that there is no confusion as to what forms of gambling constitute Class II and Class III gambling activities. Further, the Commission recommends that Class III gambling activities should not include any activities that are not available to other citizens, entities, or organizations in a state, regardless of technological similarities. Indian gambling should not be inconsistent with the state's overall gambling policy.

6–3   The Commission recommends that labor organizations, tribal governments, and states should voluntarily work together to ensure the enforceable right of free association—including the right to organize and bargain collectively—for employees of tribal casinos. Further, the Commission recommends that Congress should enact legislation establishing such worker rights only if there is not substantial voluntary progress toward this goal over a reasonable period of time.

6–4   The Commission recommends that tribal governments, states and, where appropriate, labor organizations should work voluntarily together to extend to employees of tribal casinos the same or equivalent (or superior) protections that are applicable to comparable state or private-sector employees through federal and state employment laws. If state employee protections are adopted as the standard for a particular tribal casino, then they should be those of the state in which that tribal casino is located. Further, the Commission recommends that Congress should enact legislation providing such protections only if there is not substantial voluntary progress toward this goal over a reasonable period of time.

6–5   The Commission recognizes that under IGRA, Indian tribes must annually report certain proprietary and nonproprietary tribal governmental gambling financial information to the NIGC through certified, independently audited financial statements. The Commission recommends that certain aggregated financial Indian gambling data from reporting tribal governments, comparable by class, to the aggregated financial data mandatorily collected from commercial casinos and published by such states as Nevada and New Jersey should be published by the NIGC annually. Further, the Commission recommends that the independent auditors should also review and comment on each tribal gambling operation's compliance with the Minimum Internal Control Standards promulgated by the NIGC.

6–6   The Commission recommends that upon written request, a reporting Indian tribe should make immediately available to any enrolled tribal member the annual certified independently audited financial statements and compliance review of the MICS submitted to the National Indian Gaming Commission. A tribal member should be able to inspect such financial statements and compliance reviews at the tribal headquarters or request that they be mailed.

6–7   The Commission recommends that tribal and state sovereignty should be recognized, protected, and preserved.

6–8   The Commission recommends that all relevant governmental gambling regulatory agencies should take the rapid growth of commercial gambling, state lotteries, charitable gambling, and Indian gambling into account as they formulate policies, laws, and regulations pertaining to legalized gambling in their jurisdictions. Further, the Commission recommends that all relevant governmental gambling regulatory agencies should recognize the long overdue economic development Indian gambling can generate.

6–9   The Commission has heard substantial testimony from tribal and state officials that uncompacted tribal gambling has resulted in substantial litigation. Federal enforcement has, until lately, been mixed. The Commission recommends that the federal government fully and consistently enforce all provisions of the Indian Gaming Regulatory Act.

6–10 The Commission recommends that tribes, states, and local governments should continue to work together to resolve issues of mutual concern rather than relying on federal law to solve problems for them.

6–11 The Commission recommends that gambling tribes, states, and local governments should recognize the mutual benefits that may flow to communities from Indian gambling. Further, the Commission recommends that tribes should enter into reciprocal agreements with state and local governments to mitigate the negative effects of the activities that may occur in other communities and to balance the rights of tribal, state, and local governments; tribal members; and other citizens.

6–12 IGRA allows tribes and states to negotiate any issues related to gambling. Nothing precludes voluntary agreements to deal with issues unrelated to gambling either within or without compacts. Many tribes and states have agreements for any number of issues (e.g., taxes, zoning, environmental issues, natural resources management, hunting and fishing). The Commission recommends that the federal government should leave these issues to the states and tribes for resolution.

6–13 The Commission recommends that Congress should specify a constitutionally sound means of resolving disputes between states and tribes regarding Class III gambling. Further, the Commission recommends that all parties to Class III negotiations should be subject to an independent, impartial decisionmaker who is empowered to approve compacts in the event a state refuses to enter into a Class III compact, but only if the decisionmaker does not permit any Class III games that are not available to other citizens of the state and only if an effective regulatory structure is created.

6–14 The Commission recommends that Congress should adopt no law altering the right of tribes to use existing telephone technology to link bingo games between Indian reservations when such forms of technology are used in conjunction with the playing of Class II games as defined under the Indian Gaming Regulatory Act.

6–15 The Commission recommends that tribal governments should be encouraged to use some of the net revenues derived from Indian gambling as "seed money" to further diversify tribal economies and to reduce their dependence on gambling.

Chapter 7. Gambling's Impact on People and Places

7–1 Because the easy availability of automated teller machines and credit machines encourages some gamblers to wager more than they intended, the Commission recommends that states, tribal governments, and parimutuel facilities ban credit card cash advance machines and other devices activated by debit or credit cards from the immediate area where gambling takes place.

7–2 While the Commission recognizes that the responsibility for children and minors lies first and foremost with parents, it recommends that gambling establishments implement policies to help ensure the safety of children on their premises and to prevent underage gambling. Policies that could be implemented include the following:

—Post local curfews and laws in public areas and inform guests traveling with minors of these laws.

—Train employees working in appropriate areas to handle situations involving unattended children, underage gambling, and alcohol and tobacco consumption or purchase.

7–3 The Commission recommends to state, local, and tribal governments that (when considering the legalization of gambling or the repeal of gambling that is already legal) they should recognize that especially in economically depressed communities, casino gambling has demonstrated the ability to generate economic development through the creation of quality jobs.

7–4 The Commission recommends to state, local, and tribal governments that (when considering the legalization of gambling or the repeal of gambling that is already legal) they should recognize that lotteries, Internet gambling, and non-casino EGDs do not create a concentration of good quality jobs and do not generate significant economic development.

7–5 The Commission recommends to state, local, and tribal governments that (when they are considering the legalization of casino gambling) casino development should be targeted for locations where the attendant jobs and economic development will benefit communities with high levels of unemployment and underemployment and a scarcity of jobs for which the residents of such communities are qualified.

7–6 The Commission recommends to state, local, and tribal governments that studies of gambling's economic impact and studies contemplating the legalization of gambling or the repeal of gambling that is already legal should include an analysis of gambling industry job quality—specifically income, medical benefits, and retirement benefits—relative to the quality of other jobs available in comparable industries within the labor market.

7–7   The Commission recommends to state, local, and tribal governments that when planning for gambling-related economic development, communities with legal gambling or that are considering the legalization of gambling should recognize that destination resorts create more and better quality jobs than casinos catering to a local clientele.

7–8   The Commission recommends to state, local, and tribal governments that communities with legal gambling or that are considering the legalization of gambling should look to cooperation between labor unions and management as a means for protecting job quality.

7–9   The Commission recommends that students should be warned of the dangers of gambling, beginning at the elementary level and continuing through college.

Chapter 8. Future Research Recommendations

8–1   The Commission recommends that Congress encourage the appropriate institutes within the National Institutes of Health (NIH) to convene a multidisciplinary advisory panel that will help to establish a broad framework for research on problem and pathological gambling issues within its range of expertise.

8–2   The Commission recommends that Congress direct the Substance Abuse and Mental Health Services Administration (SAMHSA) or other appropriate agency to add gambling components to the National Household Survey on Drug Abuse. To understand the expanding dimensions of problem and pathological gambling nationwide, gambling prevalence studies need to be of sufficient volume and with annual updates to record changes brought about by expanding legalization, greater accessibility, technological advances, and increasingly sophisticated games. This survey would examine not only the general population but also sizable subgroups like youth, women, elderly, and minority gamblers if no other more appropriate longitudinal studies focusing on each of these groups are available.

In any event, no data gathering pursuant to these recommendations should violate any person's right to medical privacy in seeking treatment for problem or pathological gambling.

8–3   The Commission recommends that Congress direct all federal agencies conducting or supporting longitudinal research panels to consider the feasibility of adding a gambling component to such surveys and, where appropriate, entertain applications to add such components that are determined to be of high scientific merit through scientific peer review. In addition to addressing gambling behavior, these components should include questions about treatment-seeking behavior in order to begin to address the issue of the unmet need for treatment, which is currently unknown.

8–4   The Commission recommends that Congress encourage NIH to issue a revision of the special research program announcement for research applications on pathological gambling to foster research designed to identify the age of initiation of gambling, influence of family and correlates with other youth high-risk behavior such as tobacco, alcohol, and other drug use, early sexual activity, and criminal activity evaluated separately for illegal forms of gambling.

8–5   The Commission recommends that Congress direct the appropriate institutes of NIH to invite, where appropriate, applications for supplemental funds to add legal and illegal gambling components of high scientific merit to appropriate and relevant existing surveys and to issue a revision of the special program announcement for research applications on pathological gambling to include the following areas:

—Effects on family members, such as divorce, spousal and/or child abuse, severe financial instability, and suicide.

—Analysis of public awareness education and prevention programs offered at federal, tribal, state, or corporate levels.

—Analysis of the development of gambling difficulties associated with electronic gambling machines and the risk factors that accompany this evolution for customers most likely drawn to this form of gambling.

—Effects on the workplace, such as economic losses arising from unemployment, loss of productivity, and workplace accidents.

—A study that would establish reliable instruments to measure nonmonetary costs associated with legal gambling, including, without limitation, divorce, domestic violence, child abuse and chronic neglect, suicide, and the secondary effects of bankruptcy and gambling-related crimes, and other outcomes of a similar character.

8–6   The Commission recommends that Congress direct the appropriate institutes of NIH to invite, where appropriate, applications for supplemental funds to issue a revision of the special program announcement for research applications to commence a study of American adult problem gamblers below the pathological gambler threshold (APA DSM-IV). The gambling behavior of those in this large group of 11 million adults and juveniles reveals warning signs that require thorough analysis. The gamblers in this group could go either way—that is, toward diminishing risks or toward pathological status.

8–7   The Commission recommends that Congress direct SAMHSA or other appropriate agency to add specific gambling questions to its annual surveys of mental health providers, which are conducted by the Center for Mental Health Services. The survey should map the availability of both privately and publicly funded treatment services for gamblers. This should include a count of treatment slots for gambling; how many, in a given period, are in treatment for gambling problems alone or for multiple disorders that include problem gambling; a demographic profile of those receiving treatment; an assessment of the level of the gambling disorder; and a description of the services they are receiving. It would identify barriers to treatment, such as a lack of insurance coverage, exclusion of treatment for pathological gambling from HMO [health maintenance organization] and other private insurance policies, stigmatization, or the lack of availability of treatment (including a lack of qualified treatment providers).

8–8   SAMHSA or another appropriate agency should initiate treatment outcome studies conducted by scientists in the treatment research field. Such studies should include formal treatment, self-help groups (Gamblers Anonymous), and natural recovery processes. These studies should encompass the general treatment population and should specifically include youth, women, elderly, and minority gamblers.

8–9   The Commission recommends Congress request the National Science Foundation to establish a multidisciplinary research program that will estimate the benefits and costs of illegal and separately each form of legal gambling allowed under federal, tribal and/or state law, particularly lottery, casino, pari-mutuel, and convenience gambling. Further, the research program should include estimates of the costs and benefits of legal and illegal Internet gambling, assuming Congress prohibits this form of gambling with certain exemptions. Such a program, at a minimum, should address the following factors:

—Benefits associated with different kinds of legal and illegal gambling, including increased income, creation of net new jobs and businesses, improvement in average wages and benefits, increased tax revenues, enhanced tourism and rising property values, and reductions in unemployment, if any.

—Costs associated with different kinds of legal and illegal gambling, including problem and pathological gambling; increased crime, suicide, debts, and bankruptcies; displacement of native inhabitants; traffic congestion; demand for more public infrastructure; and demand for more public services from the courts (criminal, bankruptcy, divorce) and from schools, police, and fire departments.

—The study should include benefits derived or costs incurred not only in "host" communities or states in which gambling facilities are located, but also in so-called feeder communities or states in which a significant number of the gamblers live and work who patronize facilities in the host communities.

8–10 The Commission recommends that Congress direct NIJ [National Institute of Justice] or other appropriate agency to research what effect legal and illegal gambling have on property and/or violent crime rates. Such research should also examine whether gambling-related criminal activity is increased in neighboring jurisdictions where the arrest/gambler lives and/or works but does not gamble.

8–11 The Commission recommends that Congress direct NIJ, the Bureau of Justice Statistics (BJS), or other appropriate agencies to add gambling components to ongoing studies of federal prison inmates, parolees, and probationers who manifest disorders that frequently coexist with pathological gambling.

8–12 The Commission recommends that Congress direct NIJ or other appropriate agency to investigate and study the extent of adolescent participation in illegal gambling and all forms of legal gambling separately. Further, that NIJ focus on sports betting in the nation; work cooperatively with school authorities at high school and college levels; and recommend what effective steps should be taken by federal, state, and school authorities to avoid the corruption of collegiate and amateur sports and reverse steady increases in adolescent gambling.

8–13 The Commission recommends that Congress direct the Department of Labor or other appropriate agency to research job quality in the gambling industry as measured by income levels, health insurance coverage and affordability, pension benefits, job security, and other similar indicators. The research should include a comparison between gambling jobs in a variety of communities and regions of the country. It should also compare job quality and availability in the gambling industry versus other comparable industries within those labor markets. Finally, it should also compare job quality at casinos with distinguishing characteristics, such as those that derive a significant part of their revenues from non-gambling components—like hotels, food, and beverage service and shopping and entertainment (often referred to as destination resorts).

8–14 The Commission recommends that if Congress acts to prohibit Internet gambling that it also require NIJ or other appropriate agency 12 months after the effective date of the enabling statute to measure its effectiveness for a period of 1 year. An estimate should be made of how much illegal Internet betting continues despite the statutory prohibition. The factors contributing to successful evasion of the prohibition should be described in detail. Recommendations to Congress as to methods of closing the channels used to evade the prohibition should be made.

8–15 The Commission recommends that Congress direct the appropriate institutes within NIH to invite, where appropriate, applications for supplemental funds to issue a revision of the special program announcement for research applications to commence a study of prevalence of problem and pathological gambling among gambling industry employees in all forms of legal gambling, including, without limitation, pari-mutuel, lottery, casino and, where feasible, convenience-stop employees.

8–16 The Commission recommends that the appropriate institutes conduct research to determine if an analysis of available gambling patron data derived from banks and other credit agencies can assist in the identification of problem and pathological gamblers.

8–17 The Commission respectfully recommends to state and tribal governments that they should authorize and fund every 2 years an objective study of the prevalence of problem and pathological gamblers among their state's residents by a nonpartisan research firm whose work meets peer review standards. Specific focus on major subpopulations including youth, women, elderly, and minority group gamblers should also be included. An estimate of prevalence among patrons at gambling facilities or outlets in each form of gambling should also be included.

8-18 The Commission recommends to state and tribal governments that they should authorize and fund research programs for those who are or are likely to become problem or pathological gamblers in their resident population.

8-19 The Commission recommends to state and tribal governments that they should require, as a condition of the granting of a license to operate a gambling facility or to sell goods or services in a gambling facility, full cooperation in any research undertaken by the state needed to fulfill the legislative intent of the federal and state statutory policy.

8-20 The Commission recommends that state and tribal governments consider authorizing research to collect and analyze data that would assess the following gambling-related effects on customers and their families resident in their jurisdictions:

—The extent to which gambling-related debt is a contributing factor to personal bankruptcies.

—The extent to which gambling problems contribute to divorce, domestic violence, and child abuse and neglect.

—The extent to which gambling problems contribute to incidents of suicide (or suicidal behaviors).

—The number, types, and average monetary values of gambling-related crimes perpetrated for the primary purpose of gaining funds to continue gambling or to pay gambling debts.

—The extent to which practices of some gambling facilities to provide free alcohol to customers while gambling, the placement of cash advance credit machines close to the gambling area, and the offer of similar inducements are likely to be significant factors in magnifying or exacerbating a gambling disorder.

Report Significance

The members of the Commission agree that there is a need for a "pause" in the growth of gambling. The purpose of the pause is not to wait for definitive answers to the subjects of dispute, because those may never come. Instead the purpose of this recommended pause is to encourage governments to do what, to date, few, if any, have done: to survey the results of their decisions and to determine if they have chosen wisely; to ask if their decisions are in accord with the public good, if harmful effects could be remedied, if benefits are being unnecessarily passed up. Because the search for answers takes time, some policymakers may wish to impose an explicit moratorium on gambling expansion while awaiting further research and assessment.

Source: The National Gambling Impact Study Commission, Final Report, June 1999. Washington, D.C.: U.S. Government Printing Office.

Index

About the Authors

THOMAS BARKER is Professor of Criminal Justice and Police Studies at Eastern Kentucky University. He has been a participant and researcher of gambling for over 30 years. He is the author of six books on criminal justice topics and 25 articles.

MARJIE BRITZ is Associate Professor of Criminal Justice at the Citadel. She has authored or coauthored several books and articles on topics ranging from police pursuit to theories of gambling behavior.